Francois Rabelais

Works of Francois Rabelais translated by Sir Thomas Urquhart and Peter Motteux

With the notes of Duchat, Ozell, and others; introd. and revision by Alfred Wallis.

Book IV

Francois Rabelais

Works of Francois Rabelais translated by Sir Thomas Urquhart and Peter Motteux
With the notes of Duchat, Ozell, and others; introd. and revision by Alfred Wallis. Book IV

ISBN/EAN: 9783337731526

Printed in Europe, USA, Canada, Australia, Japan

Cover: Foto ©ninafisch / pixelio.de

More available books at **www.hansebooks.com**

THE WORKS OF FRANÇOIS RABELAIS

TRANSLATED BY SIR THOMAS URQUHART
AND PETER MOTTEUX, WITH THE
NOTES OF DUCHAT, OZELL, AND
OTHERS; INTRODUCTION
AND REVISION BY
ALFRED WALLIS

BOOK IV.

Interview with the Hermit.

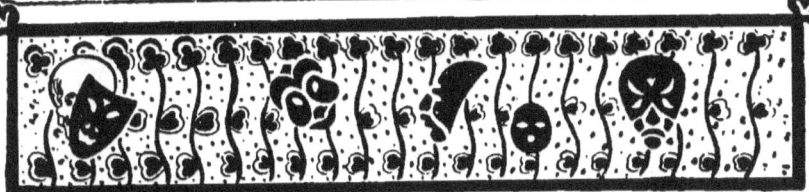

The Fourth Book of
The Heroic Deeds and Sayings
of the
Good Pantagruel
His Voyages and Wonders

Composed by
M. Fran. Rabelais
Doctor in Medicine

London
Gibbings and Company Limited
MDCCCXCVII

CONTENTS

BOOK IV

OF THE HEROIC DEEDS AND SAYINGS OF THE GOOD
PANTAGRUEL

	PAGE
The Translator's Preface,	1
The Author's Epistle Dedicatory,	9
The Author's Prologue,	15

CHAP.
I. How Pantagruel went to sea to visit the oracle of Bacbuc, alias the Holy Bottle, . . 36
II. How Pantagruel bought many rarities in the island of Medamothy, ... 42
III. How Pantagruel received a letter from his father Gargantua, and of the strange way to have speedy news from far distant places, . . 46
IV. How Pantagruel writ to his father Gargantua, and sent him several curiosities, . . . 49
V. How Pantagruel met a ship with passengers returning from Lanternland, ... 53
VI. How the fray being over, Panurge cheapened one of Dingdong's sheep, ... 56
VII. Which if you read, you will find how Panurge bargained with Dingdong, . . . 59
VIII. How Panurge caused Dingdong and his sheep to be drowned in the sea, ... 64

Contents [Book iv.

CHAP.		PAGE
IX.	How Pantagruel arrived at the island of Ennasin, and of the strange ways of being akin in that country,	67
X.	How Pantagruel went ashore at the island of Chely, where he saw King St Panigon,	73
XI.	Why monks love to be in kitchens,	76
XII.	How Pantagruel passed through the land of Pettifogging, and of the strange way of living among the Catchpoles,	80
XIII.	How, like Master Francis Villon, the Lord of Basché commended his servants,	85
XIV.	A further account of Catchpoles who were drubbed at Basché's house,	89
XV.	How the ancient custom at nuptials is renewed by the Catchpole,	92
XVI.	How Friar John made trial of the nature of the Catchpoles,	96
XVII.	How Pantagruel came to the islands of Tohu and Bohu; and of the strange death of Widenostrils, the swallower of Wind-mills,	101
XVIII.	How Pantagruel met with a great storm at sea,	107
XIX.	What countenances Panurge and Friar John kept during the storm,	111
XX.	How the Pilots were forsaking their ships in the greatest stress of weather,	114
XXI.	A continuation of the storm, with a short discourse on the subject of making testaments at sea,	118
XXII.	An end of the storm,	121
XXIII.	How Panurge played the good fellow when the storm was over,	125
XXIV.	How Panurge was said to have been afraid without reason during the storm,	128

Contents

CHAP.		PAGE
XXV.	How, after the storm, Pantagruel went on shore in the island of the Macreons,	132
XXVI.	How the good Macrobius gave us an account of the Mansion and Decease of the Heroes,	135
XXVII.	Pantagruel's discourse of the decease of heroic souls; and of the dreadful prodigies that happened before the death of the late Lord de Langey,	138
XXVIII.	How Pantagruel related a very sad story of the death of the Heroes,	142
XXIX.	How Pantagruel sailed by the Sneaking Island, where Shrovetide reigned,	145
XXX.	How Shrovetide is anatomised and described by Xenomanes,	149
XXXI.	Shrovetide's outward parts anatomised,	151
XXXII.	A continuation of Shrovetide's countenance, postures, and way of behaving,	152
XXXIII.	How Pantagruel discovered a monstrous physeter, or whirlpool, near the Wild Island,	159
XXXIV.	How the monstrous physeter was slain by Pantagruel,	161
XXXV.	How Pantagruel went on shore in the Wild Island, the ancient abode of the Chitterlings,	165
XXXVI.	How the wild Chitterlings laid an ambuscade for Pantagruel,	168
XXXVII.	How Pantagruel sent for Colonel Maulchitterling, and Colonel Cut-pudding; with a discourse well worth your hearing, about the names of places and persons,	171
XXXVIII.	How Chitterlings are not to be slighted by men,	176

Contents [Book iv.

CHAP.		PAGE
XXXIX.	How Friar John joined with the cooks to fight the Chitterlings,	178
XL.	How Friar John fitted up the sow; and of the valiant cooks that went into it,	180
XLI.	How Pantagruel broke the Chitterlings at the knees,	183
XLII.	How Pantagruel held a treaty with Niphleseth, Queen of the Chitterlings,	188
XLIII.	How Pantagruel went into the island of Ruach,	190
XLIV.	How small rain lays a high wind.	194
XLV.	How Pantagruel went ashore in the island of Pope-figland,	198
XLVI.	How a junior devil was fooled by a husbandman of Pope-figland,	203
XLVII.	How the Devil was deceived by an old woman of Pope-Figland,	209
XLVIII.	How Pantagruel went ashore at the island of Papimany,	212
XLIX.	How Homenas, Bishop of Papimany, showed us the Uranopet decretals,	216
L.	How Homenas showed us the Arch-type, or representation of a Pope,	220
LI.	Table-talk in praise of the decretals,	223
LII.	A continuation of the miracles caused by the decretals,	227
LIII.	How by the virtue of the decretals, gold is subtilely drawn out of France to Rome,	234
LIV.	How Homenas gave Pantagruel some bon-Christian pears,	241
LV.	How Pantagruel, being at sea, heard various unfrozen words,	243
LVI.	How among the frozen words Pantagruel found some odd ones,	246

Contents

CHAP.	PAGE
LVII. How Pantagruel went ashore at the dwelling of Gaster, the first master of arts in the world,	250
LVIII. How, at the court of the Master of Ingenuity, Pantagruel detested the Engastrimythes and the Gastrolaters,	254
LIX. Of the ridiculous statue Manduce; and how, and what the Gastrolaters sacrifice to their ventripotent god,	257
LX. What the Gastrolaters sacrificed to their god on interlarded fish-days,	261
LXI. How Gaster invented means to get and preserve corn,	264
LXII. How Gaster invented an art to avoid being hurt or touched by cannon-balls,	267
LXIII. How Pantagruel fell asleep near the Island of Chaneph, and of the problems proposed to be solved when he waked,	272
LXIV. How Pantagruel gave no answer to the problems,	275
LXV. How Pantagruel passed the time with his servants,	281
LXVI. How, by Pantagruel's order, the Muses were saluted near the Island of Ganabim,	284
LXVII. How Panurge bewrayed himself for fear; and of the huge cat Rodilardus, which he took for a puny devil,	288

LIST OF PLATES

INTERVIEW WITH THE HERMIT, . . *Frontispiece*

PAGE
PANTAGRUEL KILLS THE PHYSETER, . . . 162

BOOK IV

TREATING OF THE HEROIC DEEDS AND SAYINGS
OF THE GOOD PANTAGRUEL:

THE TRANSLATOR'S PREFACE

READER,—I don't know what kind of a preface I must write to find thee courteous, an epithet too often bestowed without a cause. The author of this work has been as sparing of what we call good nature, as most readers are nowadays. So I am afraid his translator and commentator is not to expect much more than has been showed them. What's worse, there are but two sorts of taking prefaces, as there are but two kinds of prologues to plays; for Mr Bayes was doubtless in the right, when he said, that if thunder and lightning could not fright an audience into complaisance, the sight of the poet with a rope about his neck might work them into pity. Some, indeed, have bullied many of you into applause, and railed at your faults, that you might think them without any; and others, more safely, have spoken kindly of you, that you might think, or at least speak, as favourably of them, and be flattered into patience. Now, I fancy, there's nothing less difficult to attempt than the first method : for, in this blessed age, 'tis as easy to find a bully without courage, as a whore without beauty, or a writer without wit; though those qualifications are so necessary in their respective professions. The mischief is, that you seldom allow any to rail besides yourselves, and cannot bear a pride which shocks your own. As for wheedling you into a liking of a work, I must confess it seems the safest way : but though flattery pleases you well when it is particular, you hate it, as little concerning you, when it is general. Then we knights of the quill are a stiff-necked generation, who as seldom care to seem to doubt the worth of our writings, and their being liked, as we love to flatter more than one at a time; and had rather draw our pens, and stand up for the beauty of our works (as some arrant fools used to do for that of their mistresses) to the last drop of our ink. And truly this submission, which sometimes wheedles you into pity, as seldom decoys you into love, as the awkward cringing of an antiquated fop, as moneyless as he is ugly, affects an experienced fair one. Now we as little value your pity, as a lover his mistress's, well satisfied that it is only a less uncivil way of dismissing us. But what if neither of these two ways will work upon you, of which doleful truth some of our playwrights stand so many living monuments ? Why, then truly I think on no other way at present, but blending the two into one ; and, from this marriage of huffing and cringing, there will result a new kind of careless medley, which, perhaps, will work upon both sorts of readers, those who are to be hectored, and those whom we must creep to. At least, it is like to please by its novelty ; and it will not be the first monster that has pleased you, when regular nature could not do it.

Preface]   # The Translator's Preface

If uncommon worth, lively wit, and deep learning, wove into wholesome satire, a bold, good, and vast design admirably pursued, truth set out in its true light, and a method how to arrive to its oracle, can recommend a work, I am sure this has enough to please any reasonable man. The three books published some time since, which are in a manner an entire work, were kindly received: yet, in the French, they come far short of these two, which are also entire pieces; for the satire is all general here, much more obvious, and consequently more entertaining. Even my long explanatory preface was not thought improper. Though I was so far from being allowed time to make it methodical, that at first only a few pages were intended; yet as fast as they were printed I wrote on, till it proved at last like one of those towns built little at first, then enlarged, where you see promiscuously an odd variety of all sorts of irregular buildings. I hope the remarks I give now will not please less: for, as I have translated the work which they explain, I had more time to make them, though as little to write them. It would be needless to give here a large account of my performance: for, after all, you readers care no more for this or that apology, or pretence of Mr Translator, if the version does not please you, than we do for a blundering cook's excuse, after he has spoiled a good dish in the dressing. Nor can the first pretend to much praise, besides that of giving his author's sense in its full extent, and copying his style, if it is to be copied; since he has no share in the invention or disposition of what he translates. Yet there was no small difficulty in doing Rabelais justice in that double respect: the obsolete words and turns of phrase, and dark subjects, often as darkly treated, make the sense hard to be understood even by a

Frenchman, and it cannot be easy to give it the free easy air of an original : for even what seems most common talk in one language, is what is often the most difficult to be made so in another ; and Horace's thoughts of comedy may be well applied to this :

> 'Creditur, ex medio quia res arcessit, habere
> Sudoris minimum ; sed habet commœdia tantum
> Plus oneris, quantò veniæ minus.'

Far be it from me, for all this, to value myself upon hitting the words of cant in which my drolling author is so luxuriant ; for though such words have stood me in good stead, I scarce can forbear thinking myself unhappy in having insensibly hoarded up so much gibberish and Billingsgate trash in my memory ; nor could I forbear asking of myself, as an Italian cardinal said on another account, *D'onde hai tu pigliato tante coglionerie?* Where the devil didst thou rake up all these fripperies ?[1]

It was not less difficult to come up to the author's sublime expressions. Nor would I have attempted such a task, but that I was ambitious of giving a view of the most valuable work of the greatest genius of his age to the Mæcenas and best genius of this. For I am not over fond of so ungrateful a task as translating, and would rejoice to see less versions, and more originals; so the latter were not as bad as many of the first are, through want of encouragement. Some indeed have deservedly gained esteem by translating ; yet not many condescend to translate, but such as cannot invent ; though, to do the first well, requires often as much genius as to do the latter.

[1] The gracious acknowledgment of Cardinal Ippolite d'Este, to Ariosto, on dedicating to him his Orlando Furioso.

The Translator's Preface

I wish, reader, thou mayest be as willing to do my author justice, as I have strove to do him right. Yet, if thou art a brother of the quill, it is ten to one thou art too much in love with thy own dear productions, to admire those of one of thy trade. However, I know three or four who have not such a mighty opinion of themselves; but I'll not name them, lest I should be obliged to place myself among them. If thou art one of those, who, though they never write, criticise every one that does; avaunt!—Thou art a professed enemy of mankind and of thyself who wilt never be pleased, nor let anybody be so, and knowest no better way to fame, than by striving to lessen that of others; though wouldst thou write thou mightst be soon known, even by the butter-women, and fly through the world in band-boxes. If thou art of the dissembling tribe, it is thy office to rail at those books which thou huggest in a corner. If thou art one of those eavesdroppers, who would have their moroseness be counted gravity, thou wilt condemn a mirth which thou are past relishing; and I know no other way to quit the score, than by writing (as like enough I may) something as dull, or duller than thyself, if possible. If thou art one of those critics in dressing, those extempores of fortune, who, having lost a relation, and got an estate, in an instant, set up for wit and every extravagance, thou'lt either praise or discommend this book, according to the dictates of some less foolish than thyself, perhaps of one of those, who being lodged at the sign of the box and dice, will know better things, than to recommend to thee a work which bids thee beware of his tricks. This book might teach thee to leave thy follies: but some will say, it does not signify much to some fools whether they are so or not; for when was there a fool that thought himself one? If thou art one of those who would put themselves upon us for learned men in Greek and Hebrew, yet are mere blockheads in English, and patch together old pieces of the ancients, to get themselves clothes out of them, thou art too severely mauled in this work to like it. Who then will? some will cry. Nay, besides these, many societies that make a great figure in the world are reflected on in this book; which caused Rabelais to study to be dark, and even bedaub it with many loose expressions, that he might not be thought to have any other design than to droll; in a manner beraying his book, that his enemies might not bite it. Truly, though now the riddle is expounded, I would advise those who read it, not to reflect on the author, lest he be thought to have been beforehand with them, and they be ranked among those who have nothing to show for their honesty, but their money; nothing for their religion, but their dissembling, or a fat benefice; nothing for their wit, but their dressing; for their nobility, but their title; for their gentility, but their sword; for their courage, but their huffing; for their preferment, but their assurance; for their learning, but their degrees; or for their gravity, but their wrinkles or dulness. They had better laugh at one another here, as it is the custom of the world. Laughing is of all professions: the miser may hoard, the spendthrift squander, the politician plot, the lawyer wrangle, and the gamester cheat; still their main design is to be able to laugh at one another; and here they may do it at a cheap and easy rate. After all, should this work fail to please the greater number of readers, I am sure it cannot miss being liked by those who are for witty mirth, and a chirping bottle; though not by those solid sots, who seem to have

Preface] **The Translator's Preface**

drudged all their youth long, only that they might enjoy the sweet blessing of getting drunk every night in their old age. But those men of sense and honour, who love truth, and the good of mankind in general above all other things, will undoubtedly countenance this work. I will not gravely insist upon its usefulness, having said enough of it in the preface to the first part. I will only add, that as Homer in his Odyssey makes his hero wander ten years through most parts of the then known world, so Rabelais, in a three months' voyage, makes Pantagruel take a view of almost all sorts of people and professions: with this difference, however, between the ancient mythologist and the modern, that while the Odyssey has been compared to a setting sun, in respect to the Iliads, Rabelais' last work, which is this Voyage to the Oracle of the Bottle (by which he means truth) is justly thought his masterpiece; being wrote with more spirit, salt, and flame, than the first part of his works. At near seventy years of age, his genius, far from being drained, seemed to have acquired fresh vigour, and new graces, the more it exerted itself; like those rivers which grow more deep, large, majestic, and useful by their course. Those who accuse the French of being as sparing of their wit, as lavish of their words, will find an Englishman in our author. I must confess indeed that my countrymen, and other southern nations, temper the one with the other, in a manner, as they do their wine with water, often just dashing the latter with a little of the first. Now here men love to drink their wine pure; nay, sometimes it will not satisfy, unless in its very quintessence, as in brandies; though an excess of this betrays want of sobriety, as much as an excess of wit betrays a want of judgment. But I must conclude, lest I be justly taxed with wanting both. I will only add, that as every language has its peculiar graces, seldom or never to be acquired by a foreigner, I cannot think I have given my author those of the English in every place; but as none compelled me to write, I fear to ask a pardon which yet the generous temper of this nation makes me hope to obtain. Albinus, a Roman, who had written in Greek, desired in his preface to be forgiven his faults of language: but Cato asked him in derision, whether any had forced him to write in a tongue of which he was not an absolute master. Lucullus wrote a history in the same tongue, and said, He had scattered some false Greek in it, to let the world know it was the work of a Roman. I will not say as much of my writings, in which I study to be as little incorrect as the hurry of business and shortness of time will permit; but I may better say, as Tully did of the history of his consulship, which he also had written in Greek, that what errors may be found in the diction, are crept in against my intent. Indeed Livius Andronicus and Terence, the one a Greek, the other a Carthaginian, wrote successfully in Latin, and the latter is perhaps the most perfect model of the purity and urbanity of that tongue; but I ought not to hope for the success of those great men. Yet am I ambitious of being as subservient to the useful diversion of the ingenious of this nation as I can, which I have endeavoured in this work, with hopes to attempt some greater tasks, if ever I am happy enough to have more leisure. In the meantime it will not displease me, if it is known that this is given by one, who, though born and educated in France, has the love and veneration of a loyal subject for this nation; one who, by a fatality, which with many more made him say,

Epistle] *The Epistle Dedicatory*

'Nos patriam fugimus et dulcia linquimus arva,'

is obliged to make the language of these happy regions as natural to him as he can, and thankfully say with the rest, under this Protestant government,

'Deus nobis hæc otia fecit.'

THE AUTHOR'S EPISTLE DEDICATORY

TO THE MOST ILLUSTRIOUS PRINCE, AND MOST REVEREND LORD ODET, CARDINAL DE CHASTILLON

You are not unacquainted, most illustrious prince, how often I have been, and am daily pressed and required by great numbers of eminent persons, to proceed in the Pantagruelian fables : they tell me that many languishing, sick, and disconsolate persons, perusing them, have deceived their grief, passed their time merrily, and been inspired with new joy and comfort. I commonly answer, that I aimed not at glory and applause, when I diverted myself with writing; but only designed to give by my pen, to the absent who labour under affliction, that little help which at all times I willingly strive to give to the present that stand in need of my art and service. Sometimes I at large relate to them, how Hippocrates in several places, and particularly in lib. 6, Epidem., describing the institution of the physician, his disciple, and also Soranus of Ephesus, Oribasius, Galen, Hali Abbas, and other authors, have descended to particulars, in the prescription of his motions, deportment, looks, countenance, gracefulness, civility, cleanliness of face, clothes, beard, hair, hands, mouth, even his very nails ; as if he were to play the part of a lover in some comedy, or enter the lists to fight some potent enemy. And indeed the practice of physic is properly enough compared by Hippocrates to a fight, and also to a farce acted between three persons, the patient, the physician, and the disease. Which passage has sometimes put me in mind of Julia's saying to Augustus, her father.[1] One day she came before him in a very gorgeous, loose, lascivious dress, which very much displeased him, though he did not much discover his discontent. The next day she put on another, and in a modest garb, such as the chaste Roman ladies wore, came into his presence. The kind father could not then forbear expressing the pleasure which he took to see her so much altered, and said to her : Oh! how much more this garb becomes, and is commendable in the daughter of Augustus ! But she, having her excuse ready, answered : This day, sir, I dressed myself to please my father's eye ; yesterday, to gratify that of my husband. Thus disguised in looks and garb, nay even, as formerly was the fashion, with a rich and pleasant gown with four sleeves, which was called *philonium* according to Petrus Alexandrinus in 6, Epidem., a physician might answer to such as might find the metamorphosis indecent : Thus have I accoutred myself, not that I am proud of appearing in such a dress; but for the sake of my patient, whom alone I wholly design to please, and no ways offend or dissatisfy. There is also a passage in our father Hippocrates, in the book I have named, which causes some to sweat, dispute, and labour :

---

[1] See Macrobius, l. 9, c. 5, of his *Saturnalia*.

Epistle] **The Epistle Dedicatory**

not indeed to know whether the physician's frowning, discontented, and morose Catonian look render the patient sad, and his joyful, serene, and pleasing countenance rejoice him; for experience teaches us that this is most certain; but whether such sensations of grief, or pleasure, are produced by the apprehension of the patient observing these motions and qualities in his physician, and drawing from thence conjectures of the end and catastrophe of his disease; as, by his pleasing look, joyful and desirable events, and by his sorrowful and unpleasing air, sad and dismal consequences; and whether those sensations be produced by a transfusion of the serene or gloomy, aerial or terrestrial, joyful or melancholic spirits of the physician, into the person of the patient, as is the opinion of Plato and Averroes.

Above all things, the fore-cited authors have given particular directions to physicians about the words, discourse, and converse, which they ought to have with their patients; every one aiming at one point, that is, to rejoice them without offending God, and in no ways whatsoever to vex or displease them. Which causes Herophilus[2] much to blame the physician Callianax, who, being asked by a patient of his, Shall I die? impudently made him this answer:

> Patroclus died, whom all allow,
> By much a better man than you.

Another, who had a mind to know the state of his distemper, asking him, after our merry Patelin's way: Well, doctor, does not my water tell you I

---

[2] Rabelais forgets himself. It was not Herophilus that blamed Callianax, but another. Callianax, in the place from whence this is quoted, is only said to be an Herophilian. See Galen on lib. 6 of *Hippocrates de Epidem.*

shall die? He foolishly answered, No; if Latona, the mother of those lovely twins, Phœbus and Diana, begot thee. Galen, lib. 4, *Comment.* 6, Epidem., blames much also Quintus, his tutor, who, a certain nobleman of Rome, his patient, saying to him, You have been at breakfast, my master, your breath smells of wine; answered arrogantly, Yours smells of fever: which is the better smell of the two, wine or a putrid fever? But the calumny of certain cannibals, misanthropes, perpetual eavesdroppers,[3] has been so foul and excessive against me, that it had conquered my patience, and I had resolved not to write one jot more. For the least of their detractions were, that my books are all stuffed with various heresies, of which, nevertheless, they could not show one single instance: much, indeed, of comical and facetious fooleries, neither offending God nor the King (and truly I own they are the only subject, and only theme of these books); but of heresy, not a word, unless they interpreted wrong, and against all use of reason, and common language, what I had rather suffer a thousand deaths, if it were possible, than have thought: as who should make bread to be stone, a fish to be a serpent, and an egg to be a scorpion. This, my lord, emboldened me once to tell you, as I was complaining of it in your presence, that if I did not esteem myself a better Christian, than they show themselves towards me, and if my life, writings, words, nay thoughts, betrayed to me one single spark of heresy, or I should in a detestable manner fall into the snares of the spirit of detraction, Διάβολος, who, by their means, raises such crimes against me; I would then, like the phœnix, gather dry wood, kindle a fire, and burn myself in the midst of it.

---

[3] *Agelastes, i.e.,* one that never laughs; a Greek word.

The Epistle Dedicatory

You were then pleased to say to me, that King Francis, of eternal memory, had been made sensible of those false accusations; and that having caused my books (mine, I say, because several, false and infamous, have been wickedly laid to me) to be carefully and distinctly read to him by the most learned and faithful anagnost in this kingdom, he had not found any passage suspicious; and that he abhorred a certain envious, ignorant, hypocritical informer,[4] who grounded a mortal heresy on an *n* put instead of an *m* [5] by the carelessness of the printers.

As much was done by his son, our most gracious, virtuous, and blessed sovereign, Henry, whom Heaven long preserve: so that he granted you his royal privilege, and particular protection for me, against my slandering adversaries.

You kindly condescended since, to confirm me these happy news at Paris; and also lately, when you visited my Lord Cardinal du Bellay, who, for the benefit of his health, after a lingering distemper, was retired to St Maur, that place (or rather paradise) of salubrity, serenity, conveniency, and all desirable country pleasures.

Thus, my lord, under so glorious a patronage, I am emboldened once more to draw my pen, undaunted now and secure; with hopes that you will still prove to me, against the power of detrac-

---

[4] The original has it only a snake-eater, by which word Rabelais designs the monks; whom, in chap. 46, he compares to the Troglodytes, who, Pliny tells us, lib. 5, cap. 8, lived in caverns and fed on snakes.

[5] As there are instances enough that formerly they wrote *asme* with an *s*, for *ame*, the soul; this might be an impious allusion of *asme* to *asne*, an ass, which so often is mentioned, l. 3, c. 22 and 23, in the old editions. Those of Lyons, and that of 1626, corrected, as is said in the title, according to the censure passed in 1552, removed the scandal.

tion, a second Gallic Hercules in learning, prudence, and eloquence; an Alexicacos in virtue, power, and authority; you, of whom I may truly say what the wise monarch Solomon saith of Moses, that great prophet and captain of Israel, Ecclesiast. 45. A man fearing and loving God, who found favour in the sight of all flesh, well-beloved both of God and man; whose memorial is blessed. God made him like to the glorious saints, and magnified him so, that his enemies stood in fear of him; and for him made wonders; made him glorious in the sight of kings, gave him a commandment for his people, and by him showed his light: He sanctified him in his faithfulness, and meekness, and chose him out of all men. By him he made us to hear His voice, and caused by him the law of life and knowledge to be given.

Accordingly, if I shall be so happy as to hear any one commend those merry composures, they shall be adjured by me to be obliged, and pay their thanks to you alone, as also to offer their prayers to Heaven, for the continuance and increase of your greatness; and to attribute no more to me, than my humble and ready obedience to your commands; for by your most honourable encouragement, you at once have inspired me with spirit, and with invention; and without you my heart had failed me, and the fountain-head of my animal spirits had been dry. May the Lord keep you in His blessed mercy.

My Lord,
Your Most Humble and Most Devoted Servant,
FRANCIS RABELAIS, *Physician*.

PARIS, *this 28th of January MDLII.*

THE AUTHOR'S PROLOGUE

GOOD people, God save and keep you! Where are you? I can't see you:[1] stay—I'll saddle my nose with spectacles—oh, oh! it will be fair anon,[2] I see you.[3] Well, you have had a good vintage, they say: this is no bad news to Frank, you may swear. You have got an infallible cure against thirst: rarely performed of you, my friends! You, your wives, children, friends, and families are in as good case as hearts can wish; it is well, it is as I would have it : God be praised for it, and if such be His will, may you long be so. For my part, I am thereabouts, thanks to His blessed goodness; and by the means of a little Pantagruelism (which you know is a certain jollity of mind, pickled in the scorn of fortune), you see me now hale and cheery, as sound as a bell, and ready to drink, if you will. Would you know why I'm thus, good people? I will even give you a positive answer—Such is the Lord's will, which I obey and revere; it being said in His word, in great derision to the physician neglectful of his own health, Physician, heal thyself.

Galen had some knowledge of the Bible, and had conversed with the Christians of his time, as appears

---

[1] He can't see good people, they are so scarce. So Aristophanes, in his Plutus, makes Cremylus say.

[2] It should be Englished, 'Soft and fair, Lent is drawing to an end: I see you.'

[3] Rabelais, who but a moment before saw none of these good people, to whom he addresses his prologue or preface, sees numbers of them all of a sudden; which he ascribes to Lent drawing to a conclusion. And, indeed, as soon as Easter approaches, in obedience to the Church's command, everybody is forward to receive the communion, in order to seem at least to be good people.

lib. 11, *De Usu Partium: lib.* 2, *De Differentiis Pulsuum, cap.* 3, and *ibid, lib.* 3, *cap.* 2, *and lib. De Rerum Affectibus* (if it be Galen's). Yet it was not for any such veneration of holy writ that he took care of his own health. No, it was for fear of being twitted with the saying so well known among physicians:

Ιητρὸς ἄλλων αὐτὸς ἕλκεσι βρύων.[4]
He boasts of healing poor and rich,
Yet is himself all over itch.

This made him boldly say, that he did not desire to be esteemed a physician, if from his twenty-eighth year to his old age he had not lived in perfect health, except some ephemerous fevers, of which he soon rid himself: yet he was not naturally of the soundest temper, his stomach being evidently bad. Indeed, as, he saith, *lib.* 5, *De Sanitate tuenda*, that physician will hardly be thought very careful of the health of others, who neglects his own. Asclepiades boasted yet more than this; for he said that he had articled with fortune not to be reputed a physician, if he could be said to have been sick, since he began to practise physic, to his latter age, which he reached, lusty in all his members, and victorious over fortune; till at last the old gentleman unluckily tumbled down from the top of a certain ill-propped and rotten staircase, and so there was an end of him.

If by some disaster health is fled from your worships to the right or to the left, above or below, before or behind, within or without, far or near, on this side or the other side, wheresoever it be, may you presently, with the help of the Lord, meet with

[4] A sentence ascribed by Plutarch to a certain tragic poet. See his discourses against Colotes, the Epicurean.

The Author's Prologue

it. Having found it, may you immediately claim it, seize it, and secure it. The law allows it: the king would have it so: nay, you have my advice for it. Neither more nor less than the law-makers of old did fully empower a master to claim and seize his runaway servant, wherever he might be found. Ods-bodikins, is it not written and warranted by the ancient customs of this so noble, so rich, so flourishing realm of France, that the dead [5] seizes the quick? See what has been declared very lately in that point by that learned, wise, courteous,[6] humane and just civilian, Andrew Tiraqueau, counsellor of the great, victorious, and triumphant [7] Henry II., in the most honourable court of Parliament at Paris. Health is our life, as Ariphron,[8] the Sicyonian, wisely has it; without health life is not life, it is not living life: 'ΑΒΙ'ΟΣ ΒΙ'ΟΣ, ΒΙ'ΟΣ ΑΒΙ'ΩΤΟΣ.[9] Without health life is only a languishment, and an image of death. Therefore, you that want your health, that is to say, That are dead, seize the quick; secure life to yourselves, that is to say, health.

[5] That is, the death of a person gives a right to his heir to seize what he has left, *i.e.*, to give him, as it were, livery and *seisin* of it.
[6] When Tiraqueau was lieutenant-general of the bailiwick of Fontenay-le-Comte, he released Rabelais out of prison, into which the Cordeliers of the place had cast him. Rabelais here testifies his gratitude to him.
[7] M. Duchat says, the author having published this his fourth book, before Henry II. had seized the three bishoprics (Metz, Toul, and Verdun, I suppose he means), the eulogium we see here of that monarch was inserted after the first edition, and only out of regard to that conquest.
[8] See Athenæus, l. 15, c. ultim.
[9] To these Greek words should be added, χωρὶς ὑγιείας, and then the sentence is complete, otherwise not. Here it may not be amiss to observe, that the great Pyrrhus, King of Epirus (now Albania Inferior), never prayed the gods to give him anything but health; and Menage used to say, 'Sanitas, sanitatum, omnia sanitas.'

I have this hope in the Lord, that he will hear our supplications, considering with what faith and zeal we pray, and that he will grant this our wish, because it is moderate and mean. Mediocrity was held by the ancient sages to be golden, that is to say, precious, praised by all men, and pleasing in all places. Read the Sacred Bible, you will find, the prayers of those who asked moderately were never unanswered. For example, little dapper Zaccheus, whose body and reliques the monks of St Garlick,[10] near Orleans, boast of having, and nicknamed him St Sylvanus;[11] he only wished to see our blessed Saviour near Jerusalem. It was but a small request, and no more than anybody then might pretend to. But alas! he was but low-built; and one of so diminutive a size, among the crowd, could not so much as get a glimpse of Him. Well then he struts, stands on tip-toes, bustles, and bestirs his stumps, shoves and makes way, and with much ado clambers up a sycamore. Upon this, the Lord, Who knew his sincere affection, presented himself to His sight, and was not only seen by him, but heard also; nay, what is more, he came to his house, and blessed his family.

One of the sons of the prophets in Israel felling wood near the river Jordan, his hatchet forsook the helve, and fell to the bottom of the river; so he prayed to have it again (it was but a small request, mark ye me), and having a strong faith, he did not

[10] Or rather St Onion; for Rabelais, who was a dear lover of puns (and the worse the pun the better, as Mr Dryden used to say), quibbles upon the similitude between *ainan* and *onion;* for near Orleans there is an abbey called St Aignan, or Anian, as it is pronounced, and so sounds just like Oignon.

[11] From *sylva*, a wood. Zaccheus might be so called from his climbing up a tree, the better to behold the Messias, as he passed by.

The Author's Prologue

throw the hatchet after the helve, as some spirits of contradiction say by way of scandalous blunder, but the helve after the hatchet, as you all properly have it. Presently two great miracles were seen: up springs the hatchet from the bottom of the water, and fixes itself to its old acquaintance the helve. Now had he wished to coach it to heaven in a fiery chariot like Elias, to multiply in seed like Abraham, be as rich as Job, strong as Sampson, and beautiful as Absalom, would he have obtained it, do you think? In troth, my friends, I question it very much.

Now I talk of moderate wishes in point of hatchet (but harkee me, be sure you do not forget when we ought to drink), I will tell you what is written among the apologues of wise Æsop, the Frenchman. I mean the Phrygian and Trojan, as Max. Planudes makes him; from which people, according to the most faithful chroniclers, the noble French are descended. Ælian writes that he was of Thrace; and Agathais, after Herodotus, that he was of Samos; it is all one to Frank.

In his time lived a poor honest country fellow of Gravot, Tom Wellhung by name, a wood-cleaver by trade, who in that low drudgery made shift so to pick up a sorry livelihood. It happened that he lost his hatchet. Now tell me who ever had more cause to be vexed than poor Tom? Alas, his whole estate and life depended on his hatchet; by his hatchet he earned many a fair penny of the best wood-mongers or log merchants, among whom he went a-jobbing; for want of his hatchet he was like to starve; and had death but met with him six days after without a hatchet, the grim fiend would have mowed him down in the twinkling of a bed-staff. In this sad case he began to be in a heavy taking, and called upon Jupiter with the most eloquent prayers—for you know necessity was the mother of eloquence. With the whites of his eyes turned up towards heaven, down on his marrow-bones, his arms reared high, his fingers stretched wide, and his head bare, the poor wretch without ceasing was roaring out, by way of litany, at every repetition of his supplications, My hatchet, lord Jupiter, my hatchet! my hatchet! only my hatchet, O Jupiter, or money to buy another, and nothing else! alas, my poor hatchet!

Jupiter happened then to be holding a grand council, about certain urgent affairs, and old gammer Cybele was just giving her opinion, or, if you would rather have it so, it was young Phœbus the beau; but, in short, Tom's outcries and lamentations were so loud, that they were heard with no small amazement at the council-board, by the whole consistory of the gods. What a devil have we below, quoth Jupiter, that howls so horridly? By the mud of Styx, have not we had all along, and have not we here still enough to do, to set to rights a world of damned puzzling businesses of consequence? We made an end of the fray between Presthan, King of Persia, and Soliman, the Turkish Emperor; we have stopped up the passages between the Tartars and the Muscovites; answered the Xeriff's petition; done the same to that of Golgots Rays;[12] the state of Parma's dispatched; so is that of Maydenburg, that of Mirandola, and that of Africa, that town on the Mediterranean which we call Aphrodisium; Tripoli by carelessness has got a new master; her hour was come.

[12] The famous corsair Dragut.

The Author's Prologue

Here are the Gascons cursing and damning, demanding the restitution of their bells.[13] In yonder corner are the Saxons, Easterlings, Ostrogoths, and Germans, nations formerly invincible, but now aberkeids,[14] bridled, curbed, and brought under by a paltry diminutive crippled fellow: they ask us revenge, relief, restitution of their former good sense, and ancient liberty.

But what shall we do with this same Ramus and this Galland, with a pox to them, who, surrounded with a swarm of their scullions, blackguard ragamuffins, sizers, vouchers, and stipulators, set together by the ears the whole university of Paris? I am in a sad quandary about it, and for the heart's blood of me cannot tell yet with whom of the two to side.

Both seem to me notable follows, and as true cods as ever pissed. The one has rose nobles,[15] I say fine and weighty ones; the other would gladly have some too.[16] The one knows something; the

[13] King Francis I. had introduced the tax on salt throughout the country of Guienne. The people, especially the peasants, who could not brook this new imposition, took their opportunity, and when the new king, Henry II., was in Piedmont with most of his forces, rose in arms, and crowded into Bordeaux, when they massacred the king's lieutenant of the province, Tristan de Monnins, a kinsman of the high constable's. This rebellion too much concerned the first (military) officer of the crown for him to sit still, and not take immediate measures to punish it with severity. He hastened towards Bordeaux with some troops, and a good train of artillery, in 1549, and the gates being thrown open, on the bare terror of his name, among other disgraceful penalties which he inflicted on the people of Bordeaux, he took away all their bells; nor were they restored to them again till three months afterwards, together with their privileges.

[14] It was the Emperor Charles V. who, though he had for many years been crippled with the gout, yet held the German noses to the grindstone, and had so done even from the time he obtained the victory over the Protestants at Mulberg in 1547.

[15] Ramus who was rich.

[16] Rabelais seems here to tax Peter Gallandus with having no

other is no dunce. The one loves the better sort of men; the other is beloved by them. The one is an old cunning fox; the other with tongue and pen, tooth and nail, falls foul on the ancient orators and philosophers, and barks at them like a cur.

What thinkest thou of it, say, thou bawdy Priapus? I have found thy counsel just before now, *et habet tua mentula mentem.*

King Jupiter, answered Priapus, standing up and taking off his cowl, his snout uncased and reared up, fiercely and stiffly propped, since you compare the one to a yelping snarling cur, and the other to sly Reynard the fox, my advice is, with submission, that without fretting or puzzling your brains any further about them, without any more ado, even serve them both as, in the days of yore, you did the dog and the fox. How? asked Jupiter; when? who were they? where was it? You have a rare memory, for aught I see, returned Priapus! This right worshipful father Bacchus, whom we have here nodding with his crimson phiz, to be revenged on the Thebans, had got a fairy fox, who, whatever mischief he did, was never to be caught or wronged by any beast that wore a head.

The noble Vulcan here present had framed a dog of Monesian brass, and with long puffing and blowing, put the spirit of life into him: he gave it to you, you gave it your Miss Europa, Miss Europa gave it Minos, Minos gave it Procris, Procris gave it Cephalus. He was also of the fairy kind; so that, like the lawyers of our age, he was too hard for all other sorts of creatures; nothing could escape the dog. Now who should happen to meet but these

other view in writing against Ramus, in behalf of the old philosophy, but only to get patrons that might make him rich too.

Prologue] **The Author's Prologue**

two? What do you think they did? Dog by his destiny was to take fox, and fox by his fate was not to be taken.

The case was brought before your council: you protested that you would not act against the fates; and the fates were contradictory. In short, the end and result of the matter was, that to reconcile two contradictions was an impossibility in nature. The very pang put you into a sweat, some drops of which happening to light on the earth, produced what the mortals call cabbage. All our noble consistory, for want of a categorical resolution, were seized with such a horrid thirst, that above seventy-eight hogsheads of nectar were swilled down at that sitting. At last you took my advice, and transmogrified them into stones; and immediately got rid of your perplexity and a truce with thirst was proclaimed through this vast Olympus. This was the year of flabby rods, near Teumessus, between Thebes and Chalcis

After this manner, it is my opinion, that you should petrify this dog and this fox. The metamorphosis will not be incongruous:[17] for they both bear the name of Peter.[18] And because, according to the Imosin proverb, to make an oven's mouth there must be three stones, you may associate them with Master Peter du Coignet,[19] whom you formerly petrified for the same cause. Then those three dead pieces shall be put in an equilateral trigone, somewhere in the great temple at Paris; in the

---

[17] Read, instead of not incongruous, not unprecedented, there having been one before.
[18] *Pierre*, in French, signifies both Peter and a stone.
[19] Or De Coigneres, a knight and advocate-general of the parliament of Paris in the reign of Philip de Valois. [See Motteux' Note at end of this Prologue.]

23

middle of the porch, if you will; there to perform the office of extinguishers, and with their noses put out the lighted candles, torches, tapers, and flambeaux; since, while they lived, they still lighted, ballock-like, the fire of faction, division, ballock sects,[20] and wrangling among those idle bearded boys, the students. And this will be an everlasting monument to show, that those puny self-conceited pedants, ballock-framers, were rather contemned than condemned by you. Dixi, I have said my say.

You deal too kindly by them, said Jupiter, for aught I see, Monsieur Priapus. You do not use to be so kind to everybody, let me tell you; for as they seek to eternize their names, it would be much better for them to be thus changed into hard tones, than to return to earth and putrefaction. But now to other matters. Yonder behind us, towards the Tuscan Sea, and the neighbourhood of Mount Appenine, do you see what tragedies[21] are stirred up by certain topping ecclesiastical bullies.[2] This hot fit will last its time, like the Limosins ovens, and then will be cooled, but not so fast.

We shall have sport enough with it but I foresee one inconveniency; for methinks we have but little store of thunder ammunition, since the

[20] If because it is Priapus that speaks here, we should take this word *couilloniques* in an obscene sense, we should fall to the very snare Rabelais had a mind to catch his less judicious readers in. These *couillonic* sects are not properly any other thing than the different orders of monks, or cucullated, *i.e.*, hoodgentry; for the word may come from the Latin cucullus, a hood, as well as from *couillon*, the cod. Among these monks there are generally subsisting, divisions and factions, about things of much the same weight as those which then divided the university of Paris.

[21] An allusion to the massacres of Cabrières, and Merindol, in 1547, by the orders of the Parliament of Aix.

[22] *Pastophores* in the original, *i.e.*, sacred priests, who carried the Shrine of Isis in the processions of the Mysteries.

Prologue]   *The Author's Prologue*

time that you, my fellow gods, for your pastime, lavished them away to bombard new Antioch [23] by my particular permission; as since, after your example, the stout champions, who had undertaken to hold the fortress of Dindenarois [24] against all comers, fairly wasted their powder with shooting at sparrows; and then, not having wherewith to defend themselves in time of need, valiantly surrendered to the enemy, who were already packing up their awls, full of madness and despair, and thought on nothing but a shameful retreat. Take care this be remedied, son Vulcan: rouse up your drowsy Cyclopes, Asteropes, Brontes, Arges, Polyphemus, Steropes, Pyracmon, and so forth; set them at work, and make them drink as they ought.

Never spare liquor to such as are at hot work. Now let us despatch this bawling fellow below. You, Mercury, go see who it is, and know what he wants. Mercury looked out at heaven's trap-door, through which, as I am told, they hear what is said here below. By the way, one might well enough mistake it for the scuttle of a ship; though Icaromenippus said it was like the mouth of a

[23] New Antioch must be the city of Rome. The word Antioch means nothing but preposterous venery, ἀντι, *contra, et* οχela, *concubitus*. The thunder darted against this Antioch, may be the sacking of it in 1527, as also the considerable diminution of the extent of her Church by the introduction of the Protestant religion; misfortunes which befel her when Rabelais wrote.

[24] The German *dinten-narr* signifies one possessed with the demon of scribbling. I fancy, Rabelais, by this, means certain scholastics, who being furiously bent on debating with one another upon questions of no moment, were mute when they should have strenuously defended the doctrine and worship of the Romish Church against the Lutherans, whose party, humanly speaking, could never have subsisted, if at the beginning it had been attacked by some preachers of the crusades.

well.²⁵ The light-heeled deity saw that it was honest Tom, who asked for his lost hatchet; and accordingly he made his report to the synod. Marry, said Jupiter, we are finely helped up, as if we had now nothing else to do here but to restore lost hatchets. Well, he must have it then for all this, for so it is written in the book of fate (do you hear?), as well as if it was worth the whole duchy of Milan. The truth is, the fellow's hatchet is as much to him as a kingdom to a king. Come, come, let no more words be scattered about it, let him have his hatchet again.

Now, let us make an end of the difference betwixt the levites and mole-catchers of Landerousse.²⁶ Whereabouts were we? Priapus was standing in the chimney-corner, and having heard what Mercury had reported, said in a most courteous and jovial manner: King Jupiter, while by your order and particular favour, I was garden-keeper-general on earth, I observed that this word hatchet is equivocal to many things: for it signifies a certain instrument, by the means of which men fell and cleave timber. It also signifies (at least I am sure

---

²⁵ See Lucian's Icaromenippus.

²⁶ I think it should rather be translated, their moleships the monks of Landerousse; for Rabelais elsewhere, more than once, calls the monks moles (not mole-catchers) from their living as it were under ground. The original runs, 'Resolvons le different du clergé et de la taulpetiere de Landerousse.' This difference between these two bodies of ecclesiastics, M. Duchat says, may have been the famous law suit between the chapter of St Gatien of Tours, and the chapter of St Martin of the same city, about the dirt (or *pus*) of St Martin. The last were in possession of this pretended relic; but the property of it had been claimed by the former for the space of between threescore and fourscore years, and it was not till ten years after Rabelais' death, that the Huguenots cut this Gordian knot. See Beza's Ecclesiast. Hist. on the year 1563, and M. du Thou, l. 30.

The Author's Prologue

it did formerly) a female soundly and frequently thumpthumpriggletickletwiddletobyed. Thus I perceived that every cock of the game used to call his doxy his hatchet; for with that same tool (this he said lugging out and exhibiting his nine-inch knocker) they so strongly and resolutely shove and drive in their helves, that the females remain free from a fear epidemical amongst their sex, viz., that from the bottom of the male's belly the instrument should dangle at his heel for want of such feminine props. And I remember (for I have a member, and a memory too, ay, and a fine memory, large enough to fill a butter-firkin); I remember, I say, that one day of tubilustre [27] [horn-fair] at the festivals of good-man Vulcan in May, I heard Josquin Des Prez, [28] Ockeghem, Hobrecht, Agricola, Brumel, Camelin, Vigoris, De la Fage, Bruyer, Prioris, Seguin, De la Rue, Midy, Moulu, Mouton, Gascogne, Loysel, Compere, Penet, Fevin, Rousée, Richard Fort, Rousseau, Consilion, Constantio Festi, Jacquet Bercan, melodiously singing the following catch on a pleasant green:

> 'Long John to bed went to his bride,
> And laid a mallet by his side:
> What means this mallet, John, saith she?
> Why! it is to wedge thee home, quoth he.
> Alas! cried she, the man's a fool:
> What need you use a wooden tool?
> When lusty John does to me come,
> He never shoves but with his bum.'

Nine Olympiads, and an intercalary year after (I

---

[27] From *tuba*, a trumpet, and *lustrum*, a sacrifice. M. Motteux, in his merry way, calls it horn-fair.

[28] Ten of those many musicians named here, were the disciples of this excellent musician, who was of Cambray. There are several books of songs of his composing, printed with the music notes at Paris, Lyons, Antwerp, etc.

have a rare member, I would say memory; but I often make blunders in the symbolisation and colligance of those two words) I heard Adrian Villart, Gombert, Janequin, Arcadet, Claudin, Certon, Manchicourt, Auxerre, Villiers, Sandrin, Sohier, Hesdin, Morales, Passereau, Maille, Maillart, Jacotin, Heurteur, Verdelot, Carpentras, l'Heritier, Cadeac, Doublet, Vermont, Bouteiller, Lupi, Pagnier, Millet, Du Moulin, Alaire, Maraut, Morpain, Gendre, and other merry lovers of music, in a private garden,[29] under some fine shady trees, round about a bulwark of flagons, gammons, pasties, with several coated quails, and laced mutton, waggishly singing:

> 'Since tools without their hafts are useless lumber,
> And hatchets without helves are of that number;
> That one may go in t'other, and may match it,
> I'll be the helve, and thou shalt be the hatchet.'

Now would I know what kind of hatchet this bawling Tom wants? This threw all the venerable gods and godesses into a fit of laughter, like any microcosm of flies; and even set limping Vulcan a-hopping and jumping smoothly[30] three or four times for the sake of his dear. Come, come, said Jupiter to Mercury, run down immediately, and cast at the poor fellow's feet three hatchets; his own, another of gold, and a third of massy silver, all of one size: then having left it to his will to take his choice, if he take his own, and be satisfied with it, give him the other two: if he take another, chop his head off with his own; and henceforth

[29] Belon, l. 4, c. 26, of his Ornithologia, seems to speak of this adventure, and dates it in 1552.
[30] He danced the trihori of Bretagne. This, says Cotgrave, is a kind of Breton, and peasantly or boorish dance, consisting of three steps, and performed by those hobbling youths, commonly in a round.

The Author's Prologue

serve me all those losers of hatchets after that manner. Having said this, Jupiter, with an awkward turn of his head, like a jackanapes swallowing of pills, made so dreadful a phiz, that all the vast Olympus quaked again. Heaven's foot messenger, thanks to his low-crowned narrow-brimmed hat, his plume of feathers, heel-pieces, and running stick with pigeon wings, flings himself out at heaven's wicket through the empty deserts of the air, and in a trice nimbly alights on the earth, and throws at friend Tom's feet the three hatchets, saying unto him: Thou hast bawled long enough to be a-dry; thy prayers and request are granted by Jupiter; see which of these three is thy hatchet, and take it away with thee. Wellhung lifts up the golden hatchet, peeps upon it, and finds it very heavy: then staring on Mercury, cries, Codszouks this is none of mine; I will not have it! the same he did with the silver one, and said, It is not this neither, you may even take them again. At last, he takes up his own hatchet, examines the end of the helve, and finds his mark there; then, ravished with joy, like a fox that meets some straggling poultry, and sneering from the tip of his nose, he cried, By the mass, this is my hatchet, master god; if you will leave it me, I will sacrifice to you a very good and huge pot of milk, brim full, covered with fine strawberries, next ides, *i.e.*, the 15th of May.

Honest fellow, said Mercury, I leave it thee: take it; and because thou hast wished and chosen moderately, in point of hatchet, by Jupiter's command, I give thee these two others; thou hast now wherewith to make thyself rich: be honest. Honest Tom gave Mercury a whole cartload of thanks, and revered the most great Jupiter. His old hatchet he fastens close to his leathern girdle, and girds it above his breech like Martin of Cambray : [30] the two others, being more heavy, he lays on his shoulder. Thus he plods on, trudging over the fields, keeping a good countenance amongst his neighbours and fellow-parishioners, with one merry saying or other after Patelin's way. The next day, having put on a clean white jacket, he takes on his back the two precious hatchets, and comes to Chinon, the famous city, noble city, ancient city, yea, the first city in the world, according to the judgment and assertion of the most learned massorets. At Chinon he turned his silver hatchet into fine testons, crown pieces, and other white cash; his golden hatchet into fine angels, curious ducats, substantial ridders, spankers, and rose nobles : then with them purchases a good number of farms, barns, houses, outhouses, thatched houses, stables, meadows, orchards, fields, vineyards, woods, arable lands, pastures, ponds, mills, gardens, nurseries, oxen, cows, sheep, goats, swine, hogs, asses, horses, hens, cocks, capons, chickens, geese, ganders, ducks, drakes, and a world of all other necessaries, and in a short time became the richest man in the country, nay, even richer than that limping scrape-good Maulevrier. His brother bumpkins, and the other yeomen and country-puts thereabouts, perceiving his good fortune, were not a little amazed insomuch that their former pity of Tom was soon changed into an envy of his so great and unexpected rise ; and as they could not for their souls devise how this came about, they made it their business to

[31] Martin and Martine are the names which are given to two figures, who each with a (*marteau*) hammer, strike the hours on the clock at Cambray. And Martin being represented as a peasant in a jacket, girded about the waist very tight; thence comes it that when a man is ridiculously girt with a belt over his clothes, people say, proverbially, he is girt like Martin of Cambray.

Prologue] **The Author's Prologue**

pry up and down, and lay their heads together, to inquire, seek, and inform themselves by what means, in what place, on what day, what hour, how, why, and wherefore, he had come by his great treasure.

At last, hearing it was by losing his hatchet, Ha! ha! said they, was there no more to do but to lose a hatchet to make us rich? Mum for that; it is as easy as pissing a bed, and will cost but little. Are then at this time the revolutions of the heavens, the constellations of the firmament, and aspects of the planets such, that whosoever shall lose a hatchet, shall immediately grow rich? Ha, ha, ha! by Jove, you shall even be lost, an it please you, my dear hatchet. With this they all fairly lost their hatchets out of hand. The devil of one that had a hatchet left: he was not his mother's son, that did not lose his hatchet. No more was wood felled or cleaved in that country, through want of hatchets. Nay, the Æsopian apologue even saith, that certain petty country gents,[32] of the lower class, who had sold Wellhung their little mill and little field, to have wherewithal to make a figure at the next muster, having been told that his treasure was come to him by this only means, sold the only badge of their gentility, their swords, to purchase hatchets to go lose them, as the silly clodpates did, in hopes to gain store of chink by that loss.

You would have truly sworn they had been a parcel of your petty spiritual usurers, Rome-bound, selling their all, and borrowing of others to buy store of mandates, a pennyworth of a new-made Pope.

Now they cried out and brayed, and prayed and bawled, and invoked Jupiter: My hatchet! my hatchet! Jupiter, my hatchet! on this side; my

[32] *Janspillhommes*, a sort of small gentry, a little given to pillage; thence the word.

hatchet! on that side, my hatchet! ho, ho, ho, ho, Jupiter, my hatchet! The air round about rung again with the cries and howlings of these rascally losers of hatchets.

Mercury was nimble in bringing them hatchets; to each offering that which he had lost, as also another of gold, and a third of silver.

Every he still was for that of gold, giving thanks in abundance to the great giver, Jupiter; but in the very nick of time, that they bowed and stooped to take it from the ground, whip, in a trice, Mercury lopped off their heads, as Jupiter had commanded; and of heads, thus cut off, the number was just equal to that of the lost hatchets.

You see how it is now; you see how it goes with those, who in the simplicity of their hearts wish and desire with moderation. Take warning by this, all you greedy, fresh-water shirks, who scorn to wish for anything under ten thousand pounds: and do not for the future run on impudently, as I have sometimes heard you wishing, Would to God, I had now one hundred seventy-eight millions of gold! Oh! how I should tickle it off. The deuce on you, what more might a king, an emperor, or a Pope wish for? For that reason, indeed, you see that after you have made such hopeful wishes, all the good that comes to you of it is the itch or the scab, and not a cross in your breeches to scare the devil that tempts you to make these wishes: no more than those two mumpers, wishers after the custom of Paris;[33] one of whom only wished to have in good old gold as much as hath been spent, bought, and sold in Paris, since its first foundations were laid, to this hour; all

[33] At Paris everything goes by grandeur: divine service lasts longer there than it does anywhere else, and the ell here exceeds in measure the ell of other places.

Prologue] **The Author's Prologue**

of it valued at the price, sale, and rate of the dearest year in all that space of time. Do you think the fellow was bashful? Had he eaten sour plums unpeeled? Were his teeth on edge, I pray you? The other wished Our Lady's Church brimful of steel needles, from the floor to the top of the roof, and to have as many ducats as might be crammed into as many bags as might be sewed with each and every one of these needles, till they were all either broke at the point or eye. This is to wish with a vengeance! What think you of it? What did they get by it, in your opinion? Why, at night both my gentlemen had kibed-heels, a tetter in the chin, a churchyard cough in the lungs, a catarrh in the throat, a swingeing boil at the rump, and the devil of one musty crust of a brown george the poor dogs had to scour their grinders with. Wish therefore for mediocrity, and it shall be given unto you, and over and above yet; that is to say, provided you bestir yourself manfully, and do your best in the meantime.

Ay, but say you, God might as soon have given me seventy-eight thousand as the thirteenth part of one-half: for He is omnipotent, and a million of gold is no more to Him than one farthing. Oh, oh! pray tell me who taught you to talk at this rate of the power and predestination of God, poor silly people? Peace, tush, st, st, st, fall down before His sacred face, and own the nothingness of your nothing.

Upon this, O ye that labour under the affliction of the gout, I ground my hopes; firmly believing, that if it so pleases the divine goodness, you shall obtain health; since you wish and ask for nothing else, at least for the present. Well, stay yet a little longer with half an ounce of patience.

The Genoese do not use, like you, to be satisfied, with wishing health alone, when after they have all the live-long morning been in a brown study, talked, pondered, ruminated, and resolved in the counting-houses, of whom and how they may squeeze the ready, and who by their craft must be hooked in, wheedled, bubbled, sharped, over-reached, and choused; they go to the exchange, and greet one another with a *Sanità et guadagno, messer;* [34] health and gain to you, sir. Health alone will not go down with the greedy curmudgeons: they over and above must wish for gain, with a pox to them; ay, and for the fine crowns, or *scudi di Guadaigne* [35] whence, heaven be praised, it happens many a time, that the silly wishers and woulders are baulked, and get neither.

Now, my lads, as you hope for good health, cough once aloud with lungs of leather; take me off three swingeing bumpers; prick up your ears; and you shall hear me tell wonders of the noble and good Pantagruel.

ON THE AUTHOR'S PROLOGUE.—The main design of this prologue is to teach us to be moderate in our wishes. The author brings several examples to prove what advantages arise from it; particularly he makes use of a fable, in which (after some long but most diverting excursions) the moderation of a poor country fellow, who had lost his hatchet, and wished only to have it again, was largely rewarded; and others, who lost theirs on purpose, to be thus made rich, were undone. This is thought by some, to mean a gentleman of Poictou, who came to Paris with his wife about some business, where Francis the First fell in love with her; and having bestowed large sums of money on the husband, who some time after returned into the country, some of

---

[34] At Florence, and throughout Italy, the middling sort of people scarce ever salute one another any otherwise.

[35] Thomas de Guadaigne, who is said to have lent Francis the First fifty thousand crowns, when he was first imprisoned. See Moreri, at the word Guadaigne.

Prologue] *The Author's Prologue*

the neighbouring gentlemen, who had handsome wives or daughters, made their appearance with them at court, in hopes of the like fortune; but instead of it were forced to sneak into the country, after they had spent their estates, which was all they got for their pains.   ᴄᵛᵉʳᵒʰ

Jupiter is brought in complaining of Ramus and Galland, who, surrounded with a swarm of their scullions, ragamuffins, sizers, vouchers, etc., set together by the ears the whole university of Paris. Petrus Ramus, or De la Ramée, was royal philosophy and oratory professor at that time; and Petrus Gallandus or Galland, royal Greek professor; both were learned men, and Ramus particularly famous for rhetoric and oratory; he also wrote three books of dialectic institutions. But what divided the university, was his elegant, but too passionate animadversions on Aristotle's physics and metaphysics. Carpentarius, Schekius, and Riolanus answered him, and particularly the first. I cannot find that Gallandus wrote against Ramus; yet either he has done it, or opposed him *viva voce*. Priapus is of opinion, they ought to be turned into stone, and associated to their namesake, Master Peter de Coignet, formerly petrified for such a reason. This Du Coignet can be no other than Peter de Coigneres, the king's advocate in his parliament, mentioned by Pasquier.[36] In 1329 he caused all the prelates of France to be summoned before King Philip, who sat in his court of parliament attended by several princes and lords. There the advocate represented many abuses committed by the ecclesiastical court, which had encroached upon the parliament's rights, and used to take cognisance of all civil matters, under divers pretences of conscience, and unjustly favoured those that appealed or removed their causes to the spiritual court. The Archbishop of Sens, and the Bishop of Autun, spoke in behalf of the Church's right, grounded on custom, time out of mind, and of equal validity of the law; then proffered to rectify everything; and in short, so cunningly worked upon the king, that he told them he would make no innovations, nor would show his successors a way to molest the Church. This made the clergy triumph, as if they had gained their point; and to be revenged on Pierre de Coigneres, they got a monkey hewed out of stone, and had it set up in a corner of Notre Dame at Paris: which figure, says Pasquier, by a kind of pun, was called Maitre Pierre du Coignet.[37] So Priapus advises Jupiter to petrify Ramus and Galland, saying, that Peter

---

[36] Recherches de Pasquier, lib. iii. chap. xxvii.
[37] That is, the chief corner-stone.

du Coignet had been turned into stone for the same cause, that is, for setting the learned at variance. Though after all, France is much obliged to that advocate, who seems to have laid the foundation of the liberties of the Gallican Church.

In the same council of the gods, Jupiter says, Here are the Gascons cursing and damning, demanding the restitution of their bells. I find in Du Tillet, that they had been taken from them in 1548. It appears that this prologue was written in 1548 or 1549; and I am apt to believe that these are the bells for whose recovery Master Janotus de Bragmardo made the comical speech in the 19th chapter of the first book; the rather, because Henry d'Albret, King of Navarre (Rabelais' Gargantua) was then governor of Guienne, and acted against the rebels.—*M.*

CHAPTER I

HOW PANTAGRUEL WENT TO SEA TO VISIT THE ORACLE OF BACBUC, ALIAS THE HOLY BOTTLE

In the month of June, on Vesta's Holiday,[1] the very numerical day on which Brutus, conquering Spain, taught its strutting dons to truckle under him, and that niggardly miser Crassus was routed and knocked on the head by the Parthians, Pantagruel took his leave of the good Gargantua, his royal father. The old gentleman, according to the laudable custom of the primitive Christians, devoutly prayed for the happy voyage of his son and his whole company, and then they took shipping at the port of Thalassa. Pantagruel had with him Panurge, Friar John des

[1] The 9th of June: Ovid, l. 6 of the Fasti.

Entomeures, alias of the Funnels,[2] Epistemon,[3] Gymnast, Eusthenes,[4] Rhizotomus,[5] Carpalim,[6] *cum multis aliis*, his ancient servants and domestics: also Xenomanes, the great traveller, who had crossed so many dangerous roads, dikes, ponds, seas, and so forth, and was come some time before, having been sent for by Panurge.

For certain good causes and considerations him thereunto moving, he had left with Gargantua, and marked out, in his great and universal hydrographical chart, the course which they were to steer to visit the Oracle of the Holy Bottle Bacbuc. The number of ships were such as I described in the third book, convoyed by a like number of triremes,[7] men-of-war,[8] galleons, and feluccas, well-rigged, caulked, and stored with a good quantity of Pantagruelion.

[2] I should rather translate it Friar John of the Chopping-knives, that being the true meaning of *entomeures*, as the anonymous Dutch scholiast rightly says on the words *entomeur*, and *entomer*: instead of the modern French word *entamer*, which signifies to have the first cut of a loaf or a joint of meat, or anything else, from the Greek ἐντομή, ἐντέμνειν, to cut, slice, sliver; all very agreeable and suitable virtues to Friar John des Entomeures, who loved to be perpetually running his nose into every kitchen, and playing at snicker-snee with any edible that came in his way; as the author describes him in chap. 10 and 11 of lib. 4 and lib. 1, chap. 27.

[3] *Epistemon.*—With the accent on the last syllable but one: Ἐπιστήμων, *scientiâ præditus*; a man of learning.

[4] *Eusthenes.*—Robust, strong, well-proportioned: or a brave man. Εὐσθενής, *validus*.

[5] *Rhizotomus.*—Was a young page that served Gargantua as an apothecary, lib. 1, c. 23. It comes from the Greek ῥιζοτόμος, root-cutter, as apothecaries and druggists are.

[6] *Carpalim.*—Pantagruel's lacquey; thus named from the Greek καρπαλίμως, *i.e.*, suddenly, swiftly, the properties of a lackey, l. 2, c. 9. Carpalim's swiftness has already appeared.

[7] A galley with three banks of oars, one above another; or with three oars (*tres remi*) on each side or bank.

[8] *Remberges* in the original. Both by its name and make, it

All the officers, dragomen (interpreters), pilots, captains, mates, boatswains, midshipmen, quartermasters, and sailors, met in the Thalamege, Pantagruel's principal flag-ship, which had in her stern, for her ensign, a huge large bottle, half silver, well polished, the other half gold, enamelled with carnation, whereby it was easy to guess that white and red were the colours of the noble travellers, and that they went for the word of the Bottle.

On the stern of the second was a lantern, like those of the ancients, industriously made with diaphanous stone, implying that they were to pass by Lanternland. The third ship had for her device a fine deep China ewer. The fourth, a double-handed jar of gold, much like an ancient urn. The fifth, a famous can made of sperm of emerald.[9] The sixth, a monk's mumping bottle made of the four metals together. The seventh, an ebony funnel, all embossed and wrought with gold after the tauchic manner. The eighth, an ivy goblet, very precious, inlaid with gold. The ninth, a cup of fine obriz gold. The tenth, a tumbler of aromatic agoloch (you call it lignum aloes) edged with Cyprian gold, after the Azemine make.[10] The eleventh, a golden vine-tub of mosaic work. The twelfth, a runlet of unpolished gold, covered with a small vine of large Indian pearl of topiarian work. Insomuch that there was not a man, however, in the dumps, musty, sour-looked, or melancholic he were, not even excepting that blubbering whiner Heraclitus, had he

should be but a sort of row-barge, not man-of-war. Howell's Cotgrave says, it is a long ship or sea-vessel, narrower than a galley, but swift and easy to be governed.
[9] The *Prasius lapis* of Pliny, l. 37, c. 8, 'root of emerald.'
[10] Persian make or work. From Azem, the name by which the Arabians call Persia.

been there, but seeing this noble convoy of ships and their devices, must have been seized with present gladness of heart, and smiling at the conceit, have said, that the travellers were all honest topers, true pitcher men; and have judged by a most sure prognostication, that their voyage, both outward and homeward bound, would be performed in mirth and perfect health.

In the Thalamege, where was the general meeting, Pantagruel made a short but sweet exhortation, wholly backed with authorities from Scripture upon navigation; which being ended, with an audible voice prayers were said in the presence and hearing of all the burghers of Thalassa, who had flocked to the mole to see them take shipping. After the prayers, was melodiously sung a psalm of the holy King David, which begins, '*When Israel went out of Egypt;*' [11] and that being ended, tables were placed upon deck, and a feast speedily served up. The Thalassians, who had also borne a chorus in the psalm, caused store of bellytimber and vinegar to be brought out of their houses. All drank to them: they drank to all: which was the cause that none of the whole company gave up what they had eaten, nor were sea-sick, with a pain at the head and stomach; which inconveniency they could not so easily have prevented by drinking, for some time before, salt water, either alone or mixed with wine; using quinces, citron peel, juice of pomegranates, sourish sweetmeats, fasting a long time, covering their stomachs with paper, or following such other idle remedies, as foolish physicians prescribe to those that go to sea.

---

[11] In Rabelais' time, the Psalms of David were sung publicly at court, being newly put into rhyme by Marot.

Having often renewed their tipplings, each mother's son retired on board his own ship, and set sail all so fast with a merry gale at south-east; to which point of the compass the chief pilot, James Brayer by name, had shaped his course, and fixed all things accordingly. For seeing that the Oracle of the Holy Bottle lay near Cathay, in the Upper India, his advice, and that of Xenomanes also, was not to steer the course which the Portuguese use, who sailing through the torrid zone, and by Cape Bona Speranza, at the south point of Africa, beyond the equinoctial line, and losing sight of the northern pole, their guide, make a prodigious long voyage; but rather to keep as near the parallel of the said India as possible, and to tack to the westward of the said pole, so that winding under the north, they might find themselves in the latitude of the port of Olone, without coming nearer it for fear of being shut up in the frozen sea; whereas, following this canonical turn, by the said parallel, they must have that on the right to the eastward, which at their departure was on their left.

This proved a much shorter cut; for without shipwreck, danger, or loss of men, with uninterrupted good weather, except one day near the island of the Macreons, they performed in less than four months the voyage of Upper India, which the Portuguese, with a thousand inconveniences and innumerable dangers, can hardly complete in three years. And it is my opinion, with submission to better judgments, that this course was perhaps steered by those Indians who sailed to Germany, and were honourably received by the King of the Swedes,[12] while Quintus Metellus Celer was pro-

[12] Of the three passages concerning this piece of history, in as many ancient authors, the first in date is lost, namely, that of

Chap. i.]　　　　　　　　　　　　*Pantagruel*

consul of the Gauls; as Cornelius Nepos, Pomponius Mela, and Pliny after them tell us.

ON CHAP. I.—By Pantagruel and his attendants, who embarked for the Oracle of the Holy Bottle, we may understand Anthony Duke of Vendome, afterwards King of Navarre, setting out of the world of error, to search after truth; which Rabelais places in the bottle, because, drinking its wine, we are inspired with spirit and invention, and freely imparting our sentiments, discover those of others.

As much is implied by the Greek proverb, ἐν οἴνῳ ἀλήθεια; by the Latin, *in vino veritas;* and as some have it among us, True philosophy lies in the bottle. Our author, like skilful dramatic writers, gives us a hint of his design in the first chapter, when just before Pantagruel sets sail, he makes him and his men go to prayers, and sing the 114th Psalm, 'When Israel went out of Egypt,' which country all know is generally taken, in a mystical sense, for error, or being a slave to it.

Bacbuc is a bottle in Hebrew, and the ships have all bottles, cups, or wine vessels on their stern, to show that the whole fleet are for wine: only one has a lantern, to confirm what is said, that the guidance of good lights, *i.e.*, learned men, is requisite in such an attempt. If we had a mind to say that our author had a double meaning all along, as he has in many places, we might suppose one easily; for this was written at the time of the Council of Trent, in which the restitution of the cup to the laity, and of marriage to the clergy were debated. Panurge goes to the Oracle of the Bottle, near Lanternland, where the lanterns, which may be the clergy, who think themselves the lights of the world, held then their provincial chapter. His business is, with the Bottle, to know whether he should marry or no; all his company there are made to drink water, which had the taste of wine; the word of the bottle is *trinck*, which is drink in High Dutch; and Panurge, having drunk, foretells that he shall be married; as indeed Montluc, Bishop of Valence, whom I take to be Rabelais' Panurge, is owned by all the historians of his age to have been: the application is easy.—*M.*

Corn. Nepos, whom Pomp. Mela has but copied, l. 3, c. 5, *De Situ Orbis.*

CHAPTER II

HOW PANTAGRUEL BOUGHT MANY RARITIES IN THE ISLAND OF MEDAMOTHY

THAT day and the two following, they neither discovered land nor anything new; for they had formerly sailed that way: but on the fourth they made an island called Medamothy, of a fine and delightful prospect, by reason of the vast number of lighthouses, and high marble towers in its circuit, which is not less than that of Candia. Pantagruel, inquiring who governed there, heard that it was King Philophanes, absent at that time upon account of the marriage of his brother Philotheamon with the infanta of the kingdom of Engys.

Hearing this, he went ashore in the harbour, and while every ship's crew watered, passed his time in viewing divers pictures, pieces of tapestry, animals, fishes, birds, and other exotic and foreign merchandises, which were along the walks of the mole, and in the markets of the port. For it was the third day of the great and famous fair of the place, to which the chief merchants of Africa and Asia resorted. Out of these Friar John bought him two rare pictures; in one of which, the face of a man that brings in an appeal (or that calls out to another) was drawn to the life; and in the other a servant that wants a master, with every needful particular, action, countenance, look, gait, feature, and deportment, being an original, by Master Charles Charmois, principal painter to King Megistus;[1] and he paid for

---

[1] The King of France, whom in chap. 35, of lib. 3, Rabelais calls the great king, and whom he here represents under the idea of the greatest king in Christendom.

them in the court fashion, with congé and grimace.² Panurge bought a large picture, copied and done from the needlework formerly wrought by Philomela, showing to her sister Progne how her brother-in-law Tereus had by force handselled her copyhold, and then cut out her tongue, that she might not (as women will) tell tales. I vow and swear by the handle of my paper lantern, that it was a gallant,³ a mirific, nay, a most admirable piece. Nor do you think, I pray you, that in it was the picture of a man playing the beast with two backs with a female; this had been too silly and gross: no, no; it was another-guise thing, and much plainer. You may, if you please, see it at Theleme, on the left hand, as you go into the high gallery. Epistemon bought another, wherein were painted to the life, the ideas of Plato, and the atoms of Epicurus. Rhizotomus purchased another, wherein Echo was drawn to the life. Pantagruel caused to be bought, by Gymnast, the life and deeds of Achilles, in seventy-eight pieces of tapestry, four fathoms long, and three fathoms broad, all of Phrygian silk, embossed with gold and silver; the work beginning at the nuptials of Peleus and Thetis, continuing to the birth of Achilles: his youth, described by Statius Papinius; his warlike achievements, celebrated by Homer; his death and obsequies, written by Ovid and Quintus Calaber; and ending at the appearance of his ghost, and Polyxena's sacrifice, rehearsed by Euripides.

² *En monnoye de singe*, monkey's money, that is, in mumbling over (like a chattering monkey) some prayers on behalf of the merchant, who was satisfied with that sort of cash.
³ This puts one in mind of that other picture in Tiberius' closet, not unlike it both for the subject and artifice, mentioned by Suetonius and Martial.

He also caused to be bought three fine young unicorns; one of them a male of a chesnut colour, and two gray dappled females; also a tarand, whom he bought of a Scythian of the Gelones' country.

A tarand is an animal as big as a bullock, having a head like a stag, or a little bigger, two stately horns with large branches, cloven feet, hair long like that of a furred Muscovite; I mean a bear, and a skin almost as hard as steel armour. The Scythian said that there are but few tarands to be found in Scythia, because it varieth in colour according to the diversity of the places where it grazes and abides, and represents the colour of the grass, plants, trees, shrubs, flowers, meadows, rocks, and generally of all things near which it comes. It hath this common with the sea-pulp, or polypus, with the thoes, with the wolves of India, and with the chameleon; which is a kind of a lizard so wonderful, that Democritus hath written a whole book of its figure, and anatomy, as also of its virtue and property in magic. This I can affirm, that I have seen it change its colour, not only at the approach of things that have a colour, but by its own voluntary impulse, according to its fear or other affections; as for example, upon a green carpet, I have certainly seen it become green; but having remained there some time, it turned yellow, blue, tanned, and purple in course, in the same manner as you see a turkey-cock's comb change colour according to its passions. But what we find most surprising in this tarand is, that not only its face and skin, but also its hair could take whatever colour was about it. Near Panurge, with his kersey coat, its hair used to turn gray: near Pantagruel, with his scarlet mantle, its hair and skin grew red; near the pilot, dressed after the fashion of the Isiaci of Anubis, in Egypt, its hair seemed all white; which two last colours the chameleon cannot borrow.

When the creature was free from any fear or affection, the colour of its hair was just such as you see that of the asses of Meung.[4]

ON CHAP. II.—As our author satirises all conditions of men in this voyage, he thought he could not begin better than by reflecting on the follies and lies of travellers; which he does in this chapter. The first place at which our travelling Pantagruelists touch, is the island of Medamothy. All the countries in this voyage are islands, and he styled himself *Caloier des isles hierres*, in the editions of 1553.

The island Medamothy, Μηδαμόθι *nusquam nullo in loco*, means an island that is nowhere, and so cannot be found; and indeed most travellers and seafaring men are for going where no other went before, still bent on discoveries: and accordingly our Pantagruelion journalist tells us, that till they came to that island, they saw nothing new. Philophanes, who is king of the country, signifies one who desires to be seen. He is made absent from home (as travellers are) on account of his brother Philotheamon's marriage with the infanta of Engys; that is the neighbourhood. Philotheamon signifies, One who desires to see things: thus many travel either to see, or be seen, or for both. Now as this kingdom of Medamothy is nowhere, so those exotic rarities, which our travellers purchase there, are nothing but fictions and chimeras. As for example: the voice of a man who brings in an appeal; the picture of a servant who wants a master; that of echo drawn to the life; that of the ideas of Plato, and the atoms of Epicurus; that copied from Philomela's needlework; Achilles' deeds in seventy-eight pieces of tapestry, all of Phrygian silk, embossed with gold and silver, some twenty-four feet long, and twenty broad; things which either are not, never were, or cannot be expressed with the pencil.

---

[4] All this *quasi* Natural History is derived from Pliny.

CHAPTER III

HOW PANTAGRUEL RECEIVED A LETTER FROM HIS FATHER GARGANTUA, AND OF THE STRANGE WAY TO HAVE SPEEDY NEWS FROM FAR DISTANT PLACES

WHILE Pantagruel was taken up with the purchase of those foreign animals, the noise of ten guns and culverins, together with a loud and joyful cheer of all the fleet, was heard from the mole. Pantagruel looked towards the haven, and perceived that this was occasioned by the arrival of one of his father Gargantua's celoces, or advice-boats, named the Chelidonia ; because on the stern of it was carved, in Corinthian brass, a sea swallow ; which is a fish as large as a dare-fish of Loire, all flesh, without scale, with cartilaginous wings (like a bat's), very long and broad, by the means of which I have seen them fly a fathom above water, about a bow-shot. At Marseilles this flying fish is called lendole. And indeed that ship was as light as a swallow ; so that it rather seemed to fly on the sea than to sail. Malicorne, Gargantua's esquire carver, was come in her, being sent expressly by his master to have an account of his son's health and circumstances, and to bring him credentials. When Malicorne had saluted Pantagruel, and the prince had embraced him about the neck, and showed him a little of the cap-courtesy, before he opened the letters, the first thing he said to him, was, Have you here the gozal,[1] the heavenly messenger ?[2] Yes, sir, said

[1] Hebrew word for a (homing) pigeon.
[2] This piece of ingenuity, or political contrivance, was not unknown to the ancients. See Pliny, l. 10, c. 24, and Frontinus,

Pantagruel

he, here it is swaddled up in this basket. It was a gray pigeon, taken out of Gargantua's dove-house, whose young ones were just hatched when the advice-boat was going off.

If any ill fortune had befallen Pantagruel, he would have fastened some black riband to his feet; but because all things had succeeded happily hitherto, having caused it to be undressed, he tied to its feet a white riband, and, without any further delay, let it loose. The pigeon presently flew away, cutting the air with an incredible speed; as you know that there is no flight like a pigeon's, especially when it hath eggs or young ones, through the extreme care which nature hath fixed in it to relieve and be with its young; insomuch, that in less than two hours it compassed in the air the long tract which the advice-boat, with all her diligence, with oars and sails, and a fair wind, could not go through in less than three days and three nights, and was seen as it was going into the dove-house to its nest. Whereupon the worthy Gargantua, hearing that it had the white riband on, was joyful and secure of his son's welfare. This was the custom of the noble Gargantua and Pantagruel, when they would have speedy news of something of great concern; as the event of some battle, either by sea or land; the surrendering or holding out of some strong place; the determination of some difference of moment; the safe or unhappy delivery of some queen or great lady; the death or recovery of their sick friends or allies, and so forth. They used to take the gozal, and had it carried from one to another by the post, to the places whence they desired to have news. The gozal, bearing either a black or white riband, according to the

l. 3, but it was most happily practised, in 1573, by the Dutch, when the Spaniards were besieging Harlem.

occurrences and accidents, used to remove their doubts at its return, making, in the space of one hour, more way through the air, than thirty post-boys could have done in one natural day. May not this be said to redeem and gain time with a vengeance, think you? For the like service, therefore, you may believe, as a most true thing, that, in the dove-houses of their farms, there were to be found, all the year long, store of pigeons hatching eggs, or rearing their young. Which may be easily done in aviaries and voleries, by the help of saltpetre and the sacred herb vervain.

The gozal being let fly, Pantagruel perused his father Gargantua's letter, the contents of which were as followeth :

My dearest Son,—The affection that naturally a father bears to a beloved son, is so much increased in me, by reflecting on the particular gifts which by the divine goodness have been heaped on thee, that since thy departure it hath often banished all other thoughts out of my mind; leaving my heart wholly possessed with fear, lest some misfortune has attended thy voyage : for thou knowest that fear was ever the attendant of true and sincere love. Now because, as Hesiod sayeth, A good beginning of any thing is the half of it ; or, Well begun is half done, according to the old saying; to free my mind from this anxiety, I have expressly dispatched Malicorne,[3] that he may give me a true account of thy health at the beginning of thy voyage. For if it be good, and such as I wish it, I shall easily foresee the rest.

I have met with some diverting books, which the bearer will deliver thee; thou mayest read them when thou wantest to unbend and ease thy mind

[3] There was one Sieur de Malicorne, etc., as appears by the records of Touraine, in 1559.

from thy better studies. He will also give thee at large the news at court. The peace of the Lord be with thee. Remember me to Panurge, Friar John, Epistemon, Xenomanes, Gymnast, and the other principal domestics, my good friends. Dated at our paternal seat, this 13th day of June.
Thy father and friend,
GARGANTUA.

CHAPTER IV

HOW PANTAGRUEL WRIT TO HIS FATHER GARGANTUA, AND SENT HIM SEVERAL CURIOSITIES

PANTAGRUEL, having perused the letter, had a long conference with the esquire Malicorne; insomuch, that Panurge at last interrupting them, asked him, Pray, sir, when do you design to drink? when shall we drink? When shall the worshipful esquire drink? What a devil! have you not talked long enough to drink? It is a good motion, answered Pantagruel; go, get us something ready at the next inn; I think it is The Satyr on Horseback. In the meantime he writ to Gargantua as followeth, to be sent by the aforesaid esquire.

Most gracious Father,—As our senses and animal faculties are more discomposed at the news of events unexpected, though desired (even to an immediate dissolution of the soul from the body), than if those accidents had been foreseen; so the coming of

Malicorne hath much surprised and disordered me. For I had no hopes to see any of your servants, or to hear from you, before I had finished our voyage; and contented myself with the dear remembrance of your august majesty, deeply impressed in the hindmost ventricle of my brain, often representing you to my mind.

But since you have made me happy beyond expectation, by the perusal of your gracious letter, and the faith I have in your esquire hath revived my spirits by the news of your welfare; I am, as it were, compelled to do what formerly I did freely, that is, first to praise the Blessed Redeemer, Who by His divine goodness preserves you in this long enjoyment of perfect health; then to return you eternal thanks for the fervent affection which you have for me your most humble son and unprofitable servant.

Formerly a Roman, named Furnius, said to Augustus, who had received his father into favour, and pardoned him after he had sided with Anthony, that by that action the emperor had reduced him to this extremity, that for want of power to be grateful, both while he lived and after it, he should be obliged to be taxed with ingratitude. So I may say, that the excess of your fatherly affection drives me into such a strait, that I should be forced to live and die ungrateful; unless that crime be redressed by the sentence of the Stoics, who say, that there are three parts in a benefit, the one of the giver, the other of the receiver, the third of the remunerator; and that the receiver rewards the giver, when he freely receives the benefit, and always remembers it; as on the contrary, that man is most ungrateful who despises and forgets a benefit. Therefore, being overwhelmed with infinite favours, all proceeding from your extreme goodness, and on the other side wholly incapable of making the smallest return, I hope, at least, to free myself from the imputation of ingratitude, since they can never be blotted out of my mind; and my tongue shall never cease to own, that, to thank you as I ought, transcends my capacity.

As for us, I have this assurance in the Lord's mercy and help, that the end of our voyage will be answerable to its beginning, and so it will be entirely performed in health and mirth. I will not fail to set down in a journal a full account of our navigation, that, at our return, you may have an exact relation of the whole.

I have found here a Scythian tarand, an animal strange and wonderful for the variations of colour on its skin and hair, according to the distinction of neighbouring things: it is as tractable and easily kept as a lamb; be pleased to accept of it.

I also send you three young unicorns, which are the tamest of creatures.

I have conferred with the esquire, and taught him how they must be fed. These cannot graze on the ground, by reason of the long horn on their forehead, but are forced to browse on fruit trees, or on proper racks, or to be fed by hand, with herbs, sheaves, apples, pears, barley, rye, and other fruits and roots, being placed before them.

I am amazed that ancient writers should report them to be so wild, furious, and dangerous, and never seen alive: far from it, you will find that they are the mildest things in the world, provided they are not maliciously offended. Likewise I send you the life and deeds of Achilles, in curious tapestry; assuring you, whatever rarities of animals, plants, birds, or precious stones, and others, I shall be able to find and purchase in our travels, shall be brought to you, God willing, whom I beseech, by His blessed grace, to preserve you.

From Medamothy, this 15th of June. Panurge, Friar John, Epistemon, Xenomanes, Gymnast, Eusthemes, Rhizotomus, and Carpalim, having most humbly kissed your hand, return your salute a thousand times.

Your most dutiful son and servant,
PANTAGRUEL.

While Pantagruel was writing this letter, Malicorne was made welcome with a thousand goodly good-morrows and howd'ye's: they clung about him so, that I cannot tell you how much they made of him, how many humble services, how many from my love and to my love were sent with him. Pantagruel, having writ his letters, sat down at table with him, and afterwards presented him with a large chain of gold, weighing eight hundred crowns; between whose septenary links, some large diamonds, rubies, emeralds, turquoise stones, and unions were alternately set in. To each of his bark's crew, he ordered to be given five hundred crowns. To Gargantua, his father, he sent the tarand covered with a cloth of satin, brocaded with gold: and the tapestry containing the life and deeds of Achilles, with the three unicorns in frized cloth of gold trappings: and so they left Medamothy; Malicorne, to return to Gargantua; and Pantagruel, to proceed in his voyage; during which, Epistemon read to him the books which the esquire had brought; and because he found them jovial and pleasant, I shall give you an account of them, if you earnestly desire it.

CHAPTER V

HOW PANTAGRUEL MET A SHIP WITH PASSENGERS RETURNING FROM LANTERNLAND

ON the fifth day, beginning already to wind by little and little about the pole, going still farther from the equinoctial line, we discovered a merchantman to the windward of us. The joy for this was not small on both sides; we in hopes to hear news from sea, and those in the merchantman from land. So we bore upon them, and coming up with them we hailed them: and finding them to be Frenchmen of Xaintonge, backed our sails and lay by to talk to them. Pantagruel heard that they came from Lanternland; which added to his joy, and that of the whole fleet. We inquired about the state of that country, and the way of living of the Lanterns: and were told, that about the latter end of the following July, was the time prefixed [1] for the meeting of the general chapter of the Lanterns; and that if we arrived there at that time, as we might easily, we should see a handsome, honourable, and jolly company of Lanterns; and that great preparations

[1] The council of Trent, which, in concert with the Emperor and Pope, at this time continued sitting, in spite of the opposition made to it by the King of France. Rabelais, by the word Lanterns, means the prelates and divines of that assembly; because, instead of enlightening the people (as they would do if they answered the end of their function), they consumed abundance of time in lanterning, as the French say (*i.e.*, trifling and playing the fool), and in no wise healed or composed the differences of religion. To lanternise profoundly, as the author a little lower says they would do at this council, means to put one's self into a deep meditation, as the monks do, when the hood of their habit, being brought over their faces, looks like the top of a lantern.

were making, as if they intended to lanternise there to the purpose. We were told also, that if we touched at the great kingdom of Gebarim, we should be honourably received and treated by the sovereign of that country, King Ohabé, who, as well as all his subjects, speaks Touraine French.

While we were listening to this news, Panurge fell out with one Dingdong, a drover or sheep merchant of Taillebourg. The occasion of the fray was thus:

This same Dingdong, seeing Panurge without a codpiece, with his spectacles fastened to his cap, said to one of his comrades, Prithee, look, is there not a fine medal of a cuckold? Panurge, by reason of his spectacles, as you may well think, heard more plainly by half with his ears than usually; which caused him (hearing this) to say to the saucy dealer in mutton, in a kind of a pet:

How the devil should I be one of the hornified fraternity, since I am not yet a brother of the marriage-noose, as thou art; as I guess by thy ill-favoured phiz?

Yea, verily, quoth the grazier, I am married, and would not be otherwise for all the pairs of spectacles in Europe; nay, not for all the magnifying gimcracks in Africa; for I have got me the cleverest, prettiest, handsomest, properest, neatest, tightest, honestest, and soberest piece of woman's flesh for my wife, that is in all the whole country of Xaintonge; I will say that for her, and a fart for all the rest. I bring her home a fine eleven-inch-long branch of red coral for her Christmas-box. What hast thou to do with it? what is that to thee! who art thou? whence comest thou, O dark lanthorn of Antichrist. Answer, if thou art of God. I ask thee, by the way of question, said Panurge to him

Pantagruel

very seriously, if with the consent and countenance of all the elements, I had gingumbob'd, codpieced, and thumpthumpriggledtickledtwidled [2] thy so clever, so pretty, so handsome, so proper, so neat, so tight, so honest, and so sober female importance, insomuch that the stiff deity that has no forecast, Priapus (who dwells here at liberty, all subjection of fastened codpieces, or bolts, bars, and locks, abdicated), remained sticking in her natural Christmas-box in such a lamentable manner, that it were never to come out, but eternally should stick there, unless thou didst pull it out with thy teeth; what wouldst thou do? Wouldst thou everlastingly leave it there, or wouldst thou pluck it out with thy grinders? Answer me, O thou ram of Mahomet, since thou art one of the devil's gang. I would, replied the sheepmonger, take thee such a woundy cut on this spectacle-bearing lug of thine, with my trusty bilbo, as would smite thee dead as a herring. Thus, having taken pepper in the nose, he was lugging out his sword, but alas! cursed cows have short horns; it stuck in the scabbard; as you know that at sea, cold iron will easily take rust, by reason of the excessive and nitrous moisture. Panurge, so smitten with terror, that his heart sunk down to his midriff, scoured off to Pantagruel for help: but Friar John laid hand on his flashing scimitar that was new ground,[3] and would certainly have dispatched Dingdong to rights, had not the skipper, and some of his passengers, beseeched Pantagruel not to suffer such

---

[2] *Sacsacbezevezinemassé,* in the original. A word not much shorter than *nastypatiturdifacilowzifartical* fellow, which we see quoted in the Cambridge Dictionary.
[3] Friar John had got it new ground, upon Panurge's telling him (l. 3, c. 23) that for want of occupation, it was become more rusty than the keyhole of an old powdering tub.

an outrage to be committed on board his ship. So the matter was made up, and Panurge and his antagonist shaked fists, and drank in course to one another, in token of a perfect reconciliation.

CHAPTER VI

HOW THE FRAY BEING OVER, PANURGE CHEAPENED ONE OF DINGDONG'S SHEEP

THIS quarrel being hushed, Panurge tipped the wink upon Epistemon and Friar John, and taking them aside,—Stand at some distance out of the way, said he, and take your share of the following scene of mirth: you shall have rare sport anon, if my cake be not dough, and my plot do but take. Then addressing himself to the drover, he took off to him a bumper of good lantern wine.[1] The other pledged him briskly and courteously. This done, Panurge earnestly entreated him to sell him one of his sheep.

But the other answered him, Is it come to that, friend and neighbour? Would you put tricks upon travellers? Alas, how finely you love to play upon poor folk! Nay, you seem a rare chapman, that is the truth on it. Oh what a mighty sheep merchant you are! In good faith, you look liker one of the diving trade, than a buyer of sheep. Adzookers, what a blessing it would be to have one's purse, well lined with chink, near your worship at a tripe-house, when it begins to thaw![2] Humph, humph, did

---

[1] Excellent wine, wine theological.
[2] In a thaw, when tripe may be had almost for nothing, it would not be oversafe to be near you in a crowd of poor people

not we know you well, you might serve one a slippery trick! Pray do but see, good people, what a mighty conjuror the fellow would be reckoned. Patience, said Panurge: but waiving that, be so kind as to sell me one of your sheep. Come, how much? What do you mean, master of mine? answered the other. They are long-woolled sheep: from these did Jason take his golden fleece. The order of the house of Burgundy was drawn from them. Zwoons, man, they are oriental sheep, topping sheep, fatted sheep, sheep of quality. Be it so, said Panurge: but sell me one of them, I beseech you, and that for a cause, paying you ready money upon the nail, in good and lawful occidental current cash. Wilt say how much? Friend, neighbour, answered the seller of mutton, hark ye me a little, on the ear.

PANURGE. On which side you please; I hear you.

DINGDONG. You are going to Lanternland, they say.

PAN. Yea, verily.

DING. To see fashions?

PAN. Yea, verily.

DING. And be merry?

PAN. Yea, verily.

DING. Your name is, as I take it, Robin Mutton?

PAN. As you please for that, sweet sir.

DING. Nay, without offence.

PAN. So I understand it.[3]

striving to buy that sort of mouth ammunition. An honest man's purse would stand a bad chance in company of such an odd, ill-looking sort of chap as you.

[3] The first edition of the 2d book of Rabelais, contained nothing injurious against Calvin: but Calvin, in the first of his letters, in the year 1553, having ranked Pantagruel among obscene and prohibited books, the reader has already seen how, in his turn, Rabelais delineates Calvin under the names of predestinator and impostor in the preface to the last editions of the

DING. You are, as I take it, the king's jester; are not you?

PAN. Yea, verily.

DING. Give me your hand—humph, humph, you go to see fashions, you are the king's jester, your name is Robin Mutton!⁴ Do you see this same ram? His name, too, is Robin. Here Robin, Robin, Robin! Baea, baea, baea. Hath he not a rare voice?

PAN. Ay, marry has he, a very fine and harmonious voice.

DING. Well, this bargain shall be made between you and me, friend and neighbour; we will get a pair of scales, then you Robin Mutton shall be put into one of them, and Tup Robin into the other. Now I will hold you a peck of Busch oysters, that in weight, value and price, he shall outdo you, and you shall be found light in the very numerical manner, as when you shall be hanged and suspended.

Patience, said Panurge : but you would do much for me, and your whole posterity, if you would chaffer with me for him, or some other of his inferiors. I beg it of you; good your worship, be so kind. Hark ye, friend of mine, answered the other, with the fleece of these, your fine Rouen cloth is to be made; your Leominster superfine wool is mine arse to it; mere flock in comparison. Of their skins the best cordovan will be made, which shall be sold for Turkey and Montelimart, or for Spanish leather at least. Of the guts shall be made fiddle and harp

said ?d book. Here, from scurrility he passes to raillery, and when he brings in Panurge answering Dingdong by 'So I understand r̩,' and by four 'Yea, verilys' running, it is visible he ridicules he too frequent repitition of words in Calvin's catechism.

⁴ To ca'l any one *un plaisant Robin*, is as much as to call him simpleton, because a sheep is accounted the silliest of all quadrupeds.

strings, that will sell as dear as if they came from Munican [5] or Aquileia. What do you think of it, hah? If you please, sell me one of them, said Panurge, and I will be yours for ever.[6] Look, here is ready cash. What's the price? This he said, exhibiting his purse stuffed with new Henricuses.

CHAPTER VII

WHICH IF YOU READ, YOU WILL FIND HOW PANURGE BARGAINED WITH DINGDONG

NEIGHBOUR, my friend, answered Dingdong, they are meat for none but kings and princes: their flesh is so delicate, so savoury, and so dainty, that one would swear it melted in the mouth. I bring them out of a country where the very hogs, God be with us, live on nothing but myrobalans. The sows in the styes, when they lye-in (saving the honour of this good company) are fed only with orange flowers. But, said Panurge, drive a bargain with me for one of them,[1] and I will pay you for it like a king, upon

---

[5] Some may understand, by this, the city of Munich, the capital of Bavaria; but I rather think the author had in his eye Monaco, in Liguria; the best lutestrings coming from Italy.

[6] It is in the original, 'J'en seray bien fort tenu au courrail de vostre huys.' I shall be so much obliged to you, that for the time to come you shall do with me just what you please, even as if I were for ever fastened to the bolt of your door, and consequently must move forwards and backwards according to the action of your hand upon me.

[1] This is all taken from Merlinus Coccaius, Macaronic XI., at the beginning:

'Fraudifer ergo loquit pastorem Cingar ad unum:
Vis, compagne, mihi castorem vendere grossum?'

the honest word of a true Trojan: come, come, what do you ask? Not so fast, Robin, answered the trader; these sheep are lineally descended from the very family of the ram that wafted Phryxus and Helle over the sea, since called the Hellespont. A pox on it, said Panurge, you are *clericus vel addiscens!*[2] *Ità* is a cabbage, and *verè* a leek, answered the merchant. But rr, rrr, rrrr, rrrrr, hoh Robin, rr, rrrrrrr, you do not understand that gibberish, do you?[3] Now I think of it, over all the fields where they piss corn grows as fast as if the Lord had pissed there; they need neither be tilled nor dunged. Besides, man, your chemists extract the best saltpetre in the world out of their urine. Nay, with their very dung (with reverence be it spoken) the doctors in our country make pills that cure seventy-eight kinds of diseases, the least of which is the evil of St Eutropius of Xaintes, from which, good Lord, deliver us? Now what do you think on't, neighbour, my friend? The truth is, they cost me money, that they do. Cost what they will, cried Panurge, trade with me for one of them, paying you well. Our friend, quoth the quack-like sheep man, do but mind the wonders of nature that are found in those animals, even in a member which one would think were of no use. Take me but these horns, and bray them a little with an iron pestle, or with an andiron, which you please, it is all one to me; then bury them wherever you will, provided it be where the sun may shine, and water them

---

[2] You know so many fine things, that if you are not a clerk, you are at least aspiring to be one.

[3] The canine voice of a shepherd or drover, getting together, or putting forward, a flock of sheep: r, 'litera, quæ in rixando prima est, canina vocatur,' says Erasmus. Note the conclusion of the Author's Prologue to Book III.

frequently; in a few months I will engage you will have the best asparagus in the world, not even excepting those of Ravenna. Now, come and tell me whether the horns of you other knights of the bull's feather have such a virtue and wonderful propriety?

Patience, said Panurge. I do not know whether you be a scholar or no, pursued Dingdong: I have seen a world of scholars, I say great scholars, that were cuckolds, I'll assure you. But hark you me, if you were a scholar, you should know that in the most inferior members of those animals—which are the feet—there is a bone—which is the heel—the astragalus, if you will have it so, wherewith, and with that of no other creature breathing, except the Indian ass, and the dorcades of Libya, they used in old times to play at the royal game of dice, whereat Augustus[4] the emperor won above fifty thousand crowns one evening. Now such cuckolds as you will be hanged ere you get half so much at it. Patience, said Panurge; but let us dispatch. And when, my friend and neighbour, continued the canting sheep-seller, shall I have duly praised the inward members, the shoulders, the legs, the knuckles, the neck, the breast, the liver, the spleen, the tripes, the kidneys, the bladder, wherewith they make footballs; the ribs, which serve in Pigmy-land to make little cross-bows, to pelt the cranes with cherry-stones; the head, which with a little brimstone serves to make a miraculous decoction to loosen and ease the belly of costive dogs? A turd on it! said the skipper to his preaching passenger, what a fiddle-faddle have we here? There is too long a lecture by half: sell him if thou wilt; if thou wilt not, do not let the man lose more time. I hate a gibble-gabble, and a rimble-ramble talk. I am for a man of brevity.

[4] See Suetonius, ch. 71, of the life of Augustus.

I will, for your sake, replied the holder-forth; but then he shall give me three livres, French money, for each pick and choose. It is a woundy price, cried Panurge; in our country, I could have five, nay six for the money: see that you do not overreach me, master. You are not the first man whom I have known to have fallen, even sometimes to the endangering, if not breaking, of his own neck, for endeavouring to rise all at once. A murrain seize thee for a blockheaded booby, cried the angry seller of sheep; by the worthy vow of our lady of Charroux,[5] the worst in this flock is four times better than those which in days of yore the Coraxians in Tuditania,[6] a country of Spain, used to sell for a gold talent each; and how much dost thou think, thou Hibernian fool, that a talent of gold was worth? Sweet sir, you fall into a passion, I see, returned Panurge: well hold, here is your money. Panurge, having paid his money, chose him out of all the flock a fine topping ram; and as he was hauling it along, crying out and bleating, all the rest, hearing and bleating in concert, stared, to see whither their brother ram should be carried. In the meanwhile the drover was saying to his shepherds: Ah! how

[5] Rabelais' words are, *par le digne vœu de Charrous*, *i.e.*, by the worthy vow of Charroux. See more of it in Explanatory Remarks at the end of this chapter.

[6] Rabelais does indeed express himself exactly as it is translated, which would make one believe the Coraxians were a people of Tuditania. They were far from being so: Tuditania is Andalusia: the Coraxians were a people of Colchis. It was a troublesome, expensive, and difficult thing to carry sheep from Colchis to Andalusia (from one end of the Mediterranean to the other). This was what made the Coraxian sheep sell so dear among the Andalusians, who, besides abounding with gold, as they did, stuck at no price, and valued no money, so they could but furnish themselves with a breed of such sheep. See Strabo's Geography, l. 3.

well the knave could choose him out a ram; the whoreson has skill in cattle. On my honest word, I reserved that very piece of flesh for the Lord of Cancale, well knowing his disposition: for the good man is naturally overjoyed when he holds a good-sized handsome shoulder of mutton instead of a left-handed racket, in one hand, with a good sharp carver in the other: got wot how he bestirs himself then.

ON CHAP. VII.—Our author, to ridicule a foolish relique that was in great repute in Poictou in his time, makes Dingdong swear by it. It was called, The worthy vow of Charroux. The people gave that name to a large wooden statue, in the shape of a man, covered with plates of silver, which the monks kept in a corner of their monastery. They used to show it but every seventh year, and then shoals of people thronged to see it; but none of the female sex were suffered to come near to kiss it; th mighty blessing was wholly reserved for men or boys; but the women used to watch to catch the men who had kissed it at unawares, and clipt them about the neck and kissed them; by which means they were persuaded they drew to themselves, an sucked in, the virtuous efficacy which they had got by touching the shrine. A tall lady was so very presumptuous as to dare kiss that blessed worthy vow, and, behold! the angry wooden saint in an instant grew five feet taller than he was before; at least the people said so, and the monks reported it for gospel truth. Yet all its worth and virtue could not protect it against the Sieur Bouganet, and other Protestant gentlemen, who, in the year 1562, stripped it of its silver robes, and since that they were called the valets de chambre of the worthy vow of Charroux.—*M*.

CHAPTER VIII

HOW PANURGE CAUSED DINGDONG AND HIS SHEEP TO BE DROWNED IN THE SEA

ON a sudden you would wonder how the thing was so soon done; for my part I cannot tell you, for I had not leisure to mind it; our friend Panurge, without any further tittle-tattle, throws you his ram overboard into the middle of the sea, bleating and making a sad noise. Upon this all the other sheep in the ship, crying and bleating in the same tone, made all the haste they could to leap nimbly into the sea, one after another; and great was the throng who should leap in first after their leader. It was impossible to hinder them: for you know that it is the nature of sheep always to follow the first, wheresoever it goes; which makes Aristotle, lib. 9, *De Hist. Animal.*, mark them for the most silly and foolish animals in the world. Dingdong, at his wit's end, and stark staring mad, as a man who saw his sheep destroy and drown themselves before his face, strove to hinder and keep them by might and main; but all in vain: they all, one after the other, frisked and jumped into the sea, and were lost. At last he laid hold on a huge sturdy one by the fleece, upon the deck of the ship, hoping to keep it back, and so save that and the rest: but the ram was so strong that it proved too hard for him, and carried its master into the herring-pond in spite of his teeth, where it is supposed he drank somewhat more than his fill; so that he was drowned, in the same manner as one-eyed Polyphemus' sheep carried out of the den Ulysses and his companions. The like happened to the

Pantagruel

shepherds and all their gang, some laying hold on their beloved tup, this by the horns, the other by the legs, a third by the rump, and others by the fleece; till in fine they were all of them forced to sea, and drowned like so many rats. Panurge on the gunnel of the ship, with an oar in his hand, not to help them you may swear, but to keep them from swimming to the ship, and saving themselves from drowning, preached and canted to them all the while, like any little Friar Oliver Maillard, or another Friar John Burgess; laying before them rhetorical commonplaces concerning the miseries of this life, and the blessings and felicity of the next; assuring them that the dead were much happier than the living in this vale of misery, and promising to erect a stately cenotaph and honorary tomb to every one of them, on the highest summit of Mount Cenis, at his return from Lanternland; wishing them, nevertheless, in case they were not disposed to shake hands with this life, and did not like their salt liquor, they might have the good luck to meet with some kind whale which might set them ashore safe and sound, on some land of Gotham, after a famous example.[1]

The ship being cleared of Dingdong and his tups: Is there ever another sheepish soul[2] left lurking on board? cried Panurge. Where are those of Toby Lamb, and Robin Ram, that sleep whilst the rest are a-feeding? Faith I cannot tell myself. This was an old coaster's trick. What thinkest of it, Friar John, hah? Rarely performed, answered Friar John: only methinks that as formerly in war,

[1] *A l'exemple de Jonas*, says Rabelais.
[2] *Sheepish soul.—Ame moutoniere*; alluding to those who, like true sheep, are incapable of determining upon anything of themselves.

on the day of battle, a double pay was commonly promised the soldiers for that day : for if they overcame, there was enough to pay them ; and if they lost, it would have been shameful for them to demand it, as the cowardly foresters[3] did after the battle of Cerizoles : so likewise, my friend, you ought not to have paid your man, and the money had been saved. A fart for the money, said Panurge : have I not had above fifty thousand pounds worth of sport ? Come now, let us be gone ; the wind is fair. Hark you me, my friend John : never did man do me a good turn, but I returned, or at least acknowledged it : no, I scorn to be ungrateful ; I never was, nor ever will be : never did man do me an ill one without rueing the day that he did it, either in this world or the next. I am not yet so much a fool neither. Thou damnest thyself like any old devil, quoth Friar John : it is written, *Mihi vindictam*, etc. Matter of breviary, mark ye me.

ON CHAP. V. TO VIII.—From Panurge's quarrel with Dindenault, the drover, whom I have called Dingdong, and that sheepmonger's misfortune, we may raise this moral ; that the private broils of pastors often prove the ruin of their flocks ; foolish, headstrong, and ready, right or wrong, one and all, to rise and fall with the bell-wether. Dingdong's quack-like

---

[3] *Cowardly foresters.*—*Les fuyars gruyers*, in the original, *Gruyers*, says M. Duchat, were soldiers raised and levied for Swiss, in the county of Gruyere, situated between Berne and the city of Sion, hard by Lausanne and the lake of Geneva. There were some of these Gruyers in the French army at the battle of Cerizol ; and as their bravery was no less depended upon than that of the Swiss themselves, they were posted promiscuously among the true Swiss in the rear ; but they turned tail at the very first onset, which gave occasion to Martin Bellay to say, that it was a very difficult thing to disguise an ass like a war-horse. See his Mem. in the year 1543.

canting stuff does not hinder him from selling the sheep by which he lives.

After all, this may be the relation of some of Montluc's adventures, burlesqued after our author's way. For, as we have observed in the preface to the first three books, that the Bishop of Valence was a Protestant, at least in his opinions : everybody knew it, and the Mareschal de Montluc, his brother, made no mystery of it in his memoirs; he was molested more than once about it, and particularly by the Dean of Valence, of whom we have spoke in the said preface, and for whom the bishop proved too hard by his subtlety and credit, which inclined him to make use of all possible means to be revenged on one who had plagued him so long.—*M.*

CHAPTER IX

HOW PANTAGRUEL ARRIVED AT THE ISLAND OF ENNASIN, AND OF THE STRANGE WAYS OF BEING AKIN IN THAT COUNTRY

WE had still the wind at south-south-west, and had been a whole day without making land. On the third day, at the flies' uprising (which, you know, is some two or three hours after the sun's), we got sight of a triangular island, very much like Sicily for its form and situation. It was called the Island of Alliances.

The people there are much like your carrot-pated Poitevins, save only that all of them, men, women, and children, have their noses shaped like an ace of clubs. For that reason the ancient name of the country was Ennasin.[1] They were all akin, as the mayor of the place told us, at least they boasted so.

[1] *Ennasin.*—Noseless, or flat-nosed.

You people of the other world esteem it a wonderful thing, that, out of the family of the Fabii,[2] at Rome, on a certain day, which was the 13th of February, at a certain gate, which was the Porta Carmentalis, since named Scelerata, formerly situated at the foot of the Capitol, between the Tarpeian Rock and the Tiber, marched out against the Veientes of Etruria, three hundred and six men bearing arms, all related to each other, with five thousand other soldiers, every one of them their vassals, who were all slain near the river Cremera, that comes out of the lake of Beccano. Now from this same country of Ennasin, in case of need, above three hundred thousand, all relations, and of one family, might march out. Their degrees of consanguinity and alliance are very strange: for being thus akin and allied to one another, we found that none was either father or mother, brother or sister, uncle or aunt, nephew or niece, son-in-law or daughter-in-law, godfather or godmother, to the other; unless, truly, a tall, flat-nosed old fellow, who, as I perceived, called a little shitten-arsed girl, of three or four years old, father, and the child called him daughter.

Their distinction of degrees of kindred was thus: a man used to call a woman, my lean bit;[3]

---

[2] *Fabii.*—See Aulus Gellius, l. 17, c. 21.
[3] There is a fish called by the French, by way of antiphrasis, *maigre* (lean bit). It is a sea fish as well as a porpoise, as this last is vulgarly written; though *porc-pisce* is known to be the true spelling: it being a sort of hog fish, or sea hog. Rabelais here quibbles upon the two words. I take the maigre to be a sort of halibut. [It is the *Sciæna aquila* of Cuvier and of Fleming. Paulus Jovius relates a curious story of the migrations of a head of one of these fishes, which, presented by the conservators to the nephew of Pope Sixtus X., finds its way to a courtesan.]

the woman called him, my porpoise. Those, said Friar John, must needs stink damnably of fish, when they have rubbed their bacon one with the other. One smiling on a young buxom baggage, said, Good morrow, dear currycomb. She, to return him his civility, said, The like to you, my steed. Ha! ha! ha! said Panurge, that is pretty well in faith; for indeed it stands her in good stead to curry-comb this steed. Another greeted his buttock with a Farewell, my case. She replied, Adieu, trial. By St Winifred's placket, cried Gymnast, this case has been often tried. Another asked a she-friend of his, How is it, hatchet? She answered him, At your service, dear helve. Odds belly, saith Carpalim, this helve and this hatchet are well matched. As we went on, I saw one who, calling his she-relation, styled her my crumb, and she called him, my crust.

Quoth one to a brisk, plump, juicy female, I am glad to see you, dear tap. So am I to find you so merry, sweet spiggot, replied she. One called a wench, his shovel; she called him, her peel: one named his, my slipper; and she, my foot: another, my boot; she, my shasoon.[4]

In the same degree of kindred, one called his, my butter; she called him, my eggs; and they were akin just like a dish of buttered eggs. I heard one call his, my tripe, and she called him, my faggot. Now I could not, for the heart's blood of me, pick out or discover what parentage, alliance, affinity, or consanguinity was between them, with reference to our custom; only they told us that she was faggot's

[4] *Estivallet.*—A buskin or summer-boot, called so from the High Dutch, *stiefel*, or rather the Latin, *æstivale*, because used in summer (*æstas*).

tripe (*tripe de fagot*, means the smallest sticks in a faggot). Another complimenting his convenient, said, Yours, my shell; she replied, I was yours before, sweet oyster. I reckon, said Carpalim, she hath gutted his oyster. Another long-shanked ugly rogue, mounted on a pair of high-heeled wooden slippers, meeting a strapping, fusty, squobbed dowdy, says he to her, How is it, my top? She was short upon him, and arrogantly replied, Never the better for you, my whip. By St Anthony's hog, said Xenomanes, I believe so; for how can this whip be sufficient to lash this top?

A college professor, well provided with cod, and powdered and prinked up, having a while discoursed with a great lady, taking his leave, with these words, Thank you, sweet-meat; she cried, There needs no thanks, sour-sauce. Saith Pantagruel, This is not altogether incongruous, for sweet meat must have sour sauce. A wooden loggerhead said to a young wench, It is long since I saw you, bag: All the better, cried she, pipe. Set them together, said Panurge, then blow in their arses, it will be a bagpipe. We saw, after that, a diminutive hump-backed gallant, pretty near us, taking leave of a she-relation of his, thus: Fare thee well, friend hole; she reparteed, Save thee, friend peg. Quoth Friar John, What could they say more, were he all peg and she all hole? But now would I give something to know if every cranny of the hole can be stopped up with that same peg.

A bawdy bachelor, talking with an old trot, was saying, Remember, rusty gun. I will not fail, said she, scourer.[5] Do you reckon these two to be akin? said Pantagruel to the mayor: I rather take them to be foes: in our country a woman would take this as

[5] *Scourer.*—Fyste, in the original: (*vesse*).

a mortal affront. Good people of the other world, replied the mayor, you have few such and so near relations as this gun and scourer are to one another; for they both come out of one shop.⁶ What, was the shop their mother?⁷ quoth Panurge. What mother, said the mayor, does the man mean? That must be some of your world's affinity; we have here neither father nor mother: your little paltry fellows, that live on the other side the water, poor rogues, booted with wisps of hay, may indeed have such; but we scorn it. The good Pantagruel stood gazing and listening; but at those words he had like to have lost all patience.

Having very exactly viewed the situation of the island, and the way of living of the Ennaséd nation, we went to take a cup of the creature at a tavern, where there happened to be a wedding after the manner of the country. Bating that shocking custom, there was special good cheer.

While we were there, a pleasant match was struck up betwixt a female called Pear (a tight thing, as we thought, but by some, who knew better things, said to be quaggy and flabby) and a young soft male, called Cheese, somewhat sandy. (Many such matches have been, and they were formerly much commended.) In our country we say, *Il ne fut oncques tel mariage, qu'est de la poire et du fromage;* there is no match like that made between the pear and the cheese: and in many other places good store of such bargains have been driven. Besides, when the women are at their last prayers, it is to this day a noted saying, that after cheese comes nothing.

---

⁶ *One shop.*—One hole, in the original : (*d'ung trou*).
⁷ In the original, was the wind their mother. Alluding, though jestingly, to what the ancient naturalists have advanced concerning the winds making the mares in Spain conceive.

In another room I saw them marrying an old greasy boot to a young pliable buskin. Pantagrue: was told, that young buskin took old boot to have and to hold, because she was of special leather, ir. good case, and waxed, seared, liquored, and greased to the purpose, even though it had been for the fisherman that went to bed with his boots on. In another room below, I saw a young brogue [8] taking a young slipper for better for worse: which, they told us, was neither for the sake of her piety, parts, or person, but for the fourth comprehensive p, portion; the spankers, spur-royals, rose-nobles, and other coriander seed with which she was quilted all over.

ON CHAP. IX.—By the island of Ennasin, where such strange alliances are made, Rabelais at once exposes unequal matches, and the dull jests and stupidity of gross clowns; which, as the Latin hath it, have no nose, that is, no wit. Thus he tells us, that all the men, women, and children, of the Ennaséd, or noseless, island are like your carrot-pated Poictevins, who are a boorish sort of people. I must own that the comments, which Pantagruel's companions make on their ridiculous manner of being akin, are little better than the text. Yet those wretched quibbles and conundrums, are what your country-fellows admire mightily; and all this chapter would be read or (to speak more properly) be heard read by such people with as much pleasure, as I translated most of it with pain. But in the main, the meaning is admirable; for what more deserves a reproof, than the foolish unequal marriages made every day, which are as odd jests, and as improper as some of those in the chapter? The match struck up between the pear (which seemed right and firm, but was known by some to be flabby) and the soft cheese, is more natural, and made very often in our world; and bating its emblem, which is of the nature of the island, there is salt and nose in that conjunction: nor is there less in that of the old greasy boot, and the young pliable buskin; and the brogue and the slipper; which are in a manner a key to the rest.—*M.*

---

[8] *Une jeune escafignon.*—Under the idea of an *escafignon* (*i.e.*, a single-soled shoe of thin leather; a rope-dancer, or tumbler's pump) Rabelais ridicules a young threadbare, single-soled gentleman: a gentleman of low degree.

CHAPTER X

HOW PANTAGRUEL WENT ASHORE AT THE ISLAND OF
CHELY, WHERE HE SAW KING ST PANIGON

WE sailed right before the wind, which we had at west, leaving those odd alliancers with their ace-of-clubs snouts, and having taken height by the sun, stood in for Chely,[1] a large, fruitful, wealthy, and well-peopled island. King St Panigon, first of the name, reigned there, and, attended by the princes, his sons, and the nobles of his court, came as far as the port to receive Pantagruel, and conducted him to his palace; near the gate of which, the queen, attended by the princesses, her daughters, and the court ladies, received us. Panigon directed her and all her retinue to salute Pantagruel and his men with a kiss; for such was the civil custom of the country: and they were all fairly bussed accordingly, except Friar John, who stepped aside, and sneaked off among the king's officers. Panigon used all the entreaties imaginable to persuade Pantagruel to tarry there that day and the next; but he would needs be gone, and excused himself upon the opportunity of wind and weather, which being oftener desired than enjoyed, ought not to be neglected when it comes. Panigon, having heard these reasons, let us go, but

[1] Read (instead of stood in for Chely) stood out to sea. (*Montasmes en haulte mer.*) Read likewise (instead of having taken the height of the sun) about sunset (*sus la declination du soleil, etc.*). As for taking the height of the sun, it is certain that the translator did not take the height of the author's meaning, in this place; his words are, 'feismes scalle en l'isle de Chely.' We landed on the island of Chely. *Faire scale*, is to land, set foot on land, to go ashore, says Cotgrave expressly.

first made us take off some five-and-twenty or thirty bumpers each.

Pantagruel, returning to the port, missed Friar John, and asked why he was not with the rest of the company? Panurge could not tell how to excuse him, and would have gone back to the palace to call him, when Friar John overtook them, and merrily cried, Long live the noble Panigon! As I love my belly, he minds good eating, and keeps a noble house and a dainty kitchen. I have been there, boys. Everything goes about by dozens. I was in good hopes to have stuffed my puddings there like a monk. What! always in a kitchen, friend? said Pantagruel. By the belly of St Crampacon, quoth the Friar, I understand the customs and ceremonies which are used there, much better than all the formal stuff, antic postures, and nonsensical fiddle-faddle that must be used with those women, *magni magna, shittencumshita*, cringes, grimaces, scrapes, bows, and congees; double honours this way, triple salutes that way, the embrace, the grasp, the squeeze, the hug, the leer, the smack, *baso las manos de vostra mercé, de vostra majestá*. You are most *tarabin, tarabas, Stront;* [2] that is downright Dutch. Why all this ado? I do not say but a man might be for a bit by-the-bye and away, to be doing as well as his neighbours; but this little nasty cringing and courtesying made me as mad as any March devil.[3]

[2] *Stront.—Bren c'est merde à Rouen*, i.e., turd, which is the Rouen word. And, indeed, it is hardly used anywhere else but there; nor there but in the suburbs and country round about; a rustical, clownish word.

[3] After this add, St Benedict never dissembled for the matter. *St Benoist n'en mentit jamais* (a rhyme). On this M. Duchat observes, that neither the Benedictine, nor any other monks, ever salute anybody otherwise than by bowing their head and body.

You talk of kissing ladies; by the worthy and sacred frock I wear, I seldom venture upon it, lest I be served as was the Lord of Guyercharois. What was it? said Pantagruel; I know him; he is one of the best friends I have.

He was invited to a sumptuous feast, said Friar John, by a relation and neighbour of his, together with all the gentlemen and ladies in the neighbourhood. Now some of the latter [the ladies] expecting his coming, dressed the pages in women's clothes, and finified them like any babies;[4] then ordered them to meet my lord at his coming near the drawbridge; so the complimenting monsieur came, and there kissed the petticoated lads with great formality.[5] At last the ladies, who minded passages in the gallery, burst out with laughing, and made signs to the pages to take off their dress; which the good lord having observed, the devil a bit he durst make up to the true ladies to kiss them, but said, that since they had disguised the pages, by his great grandfather's helmet, these were certainly the very footmen and grooms still more cunningly disguised. Odds fish! *(da jurandi)* why do not we rather remove our humanities into some good warm kitchen of God, that noble laboratory; and there admire the turning of the spits, the harmonious rattling of the jacks and fenders, criticise on the position of the lard, the temperature of the pottages, the preparation for the dessert, and the order of the wine service? *Beati immaculati in via.*[6] Matter of breviary, my masters.

[4] *Like any babies.—En damoiselles bien pimpantes et atourées.* Like young girls curiously pranked up and dizened out.

[5] It was then the custom for a gentleman, as soon as he lighted among the ladies, to kiss them all on the cheek; and this mode continued in France till Henry the Third's time.

[6] *Beati, etc.—*Blessed are those who are undefiled in their way.

CHAPTER XI

WHY MONKS LOVE TO BE IN KITCHENS

This, said Epistemon, is spoke like a true monk : I mean like a right monking monk,[1] not a bemonked monastical monkling. Truly you put me in mind of some passages that happened at Florence, some twenty years ago, in a company of studious travellers, fond of visiting the learned, and seeing the antiquities of Italy, among whom I was. As we viewed the situation and beauty of Florence, the structure of the dome, the magnificence of the churches and palaces, we strove to outdo one another in giving them their due ; when a certain monk of Amiens, Bernard Lardon by name, quite angry, scandalised, and out of all patience, told us, I do not know what the devil you can find in this same town, that is so much cried up : for my part I have looked and pored and stared as well as the best of you : I think my eyesight is as clear as another body's ; and what can one see after all? There are fine houses, indeed, and that is all. But the cage does not feed the birds. God and Monsieur St Bernard, our good patron, be with us ! in all this

---

The first words of the 119th Psalm, profaned by Friar John, who applies them to such as get no spots on their clothes, when they visit from time to time the convent kitchen.

[1] *Monking monk.—Moine moinant* is he that has the direction and government of the other monks of his convent. Whereas a bemonked monk (*moyne moyné*) means any monk who is obliged to obey the monking monk, and to suffer himself to be led by him. In which sense, when any brother friar seems to make scorn of the post he is advanced to in the house, they tell him jocularly, by way of consolation, it is better, however, to be a horse than a cart.

same town I have not seen one poor lane of roasting cooks; and yet I have not a little looked about, and sought for so necessary a part of a commonwealth: ay, and I dare assure you that I have pried up and down with the exactness of an informer; as ready to number both to the right and left, how many, and on what side, we might find most roasting cooks, as a spy would be to reckon the bastions of a town. Now at Amiens,[2] in four, nay five times less ground than we have trod in our contemplation, I could have shown you above fourteen streets of roasting cooks, most ancient, savoury, and aromatic. I cannot imagine what kind of pleasure you can have taken in gazing on the lions and Africans (so methinks you call their tigers) near the belfry; or in ogling the porcupines and ostriches in the Lord Philip Strozzi's palace. Faith and truth I had rather see a good fat goose at the spit. This porphyry, those marbles are fine; I say nothing to the contrary: but our cheesecakes at Amiens are far better in my mind. These ancient statues are well made; I am willing to believe it: but by St Ferreol of Abbeville,[3] we have young wenches in our country, which please me better a thousand times.

What is the reason, asked Friar John, that monks are always to be found in kitchens; and kings, emperors, and popes are never there? Is there not,

[2] The reason of the vast number of cooks' shops, with which, for a long time, the whole province of Picardy, and especially the city of Amiens, has abounded, is because the inns there find travellers in nothing but a table-cloth, and a cover (*i.e.*, a plate, with a napkin, knife, fork and spoon), with glasses; not forgetting bread and wine, you may be sure.

[3] Friar Bernard Lardon loved the fat-bacon-like lasses of this country, and he swears it too by the saint that has the superintendency of the fattening of geese.

said Rhizotomus, some latent virtue and specific property hid in the kettles and pans, which, as the loadstone attracts iron, draws the monk there, and cannot attract emperors, popes, or kings? Or is it a natural induction and inclination, fixed in the frocks and cowls, which of itself leads and forceth those good religious men into kitchens, whether they will or no? He means, forms following matter, as Averroës calls them, answered Epistemon. Right, said Friar John.

I will not offer to solve this problem, said Pantagruel; for it is somewhat ticklish, and you can hardly handle it without coming off scurvily; but I will tell you what I have heard.[4]

Antigonus, King of Macedon, one day coming to one of his tents where his cooks used to dress his meat, and finding there poet Antagoras frying a conger, and holding the pan himself, merrily asked him, Pray, Mr Poet, was Homer frying congers when he wrote the deeds of Agamemnon? Antagoras readily answered, But do you think, sir, that when Agamemnon did them, he made it his business to know if any in his camp were frying congers? The king thought it an indecency that a poet should be thus a-frying in a kitchen; and the poet let the king know, that it was a more indecent thing for a king to be found in such a place. I will clap another story upon the neck of this, quoth Panurge, and will tell you what Breton Villandry[5] answered one day to the Duke of Guise.

They were saying that at a certain battle of King Francis, against the Emperor, Charles the

[4] What I have read, it should be; *avois leu*. It is in Plutarch's notable sayings of ancient kings, princes, and captains.
[5] John le Breton, Lord of Villandry, favourite of Francis I., and secretary to that prince, and Henry II. in 1537.

Pantagruel

Fifth, Breton, armed cap-a-pé to the teeth, and mounted like St George; yet sneaked off, and played least in sight during the engagement. Blood an 'ouns, answered Breton, I was there, and can prove it easily; nay, even where you, my lord, dared not have been. The duke began to resent this as too rash and saucy: but Breton easily appeased him, and set them all a-laughing, Egad, my lord, quoth he, I kept out of harm's way; I was all the while with your page Jack, skulking in a certain place where you had not dared hide your head, as I did. Thus discoursing, they got to their ships, and left the island of Chely.

ON CHAPS. X. AND XI.—The island of Chely, which comes after that of the Ennaséd alliancers, is as it were its antipodes; and the one is as courtly as the other is clownish. The word Chely is Greek, and signifies the lips $\chi\epsilon\ell\lambda\epsilon a$, $\chi\epsilon\ell\lambda\eta$; thus it may be called the island of the lips, or of compliments. King St Panigon, first of the name, reigned in that large, well-peopled, fruitful kingdom, and being attended by the princes, his sons, and the nobles of his court, comes as far as the port to receive Pantagruel, and conducts him to his palace; the queen, the princesses, the court ladies, receive him at the gate; Panigon makes them all salute Pantagruel and his men with a kiss, according to the civil custom of the country; all the compliments and entreaties imaginable are used to persuade Pantagruel to stay there a day or two; he excuses himself, but is not suffered to go, till he and his men have drank with the king; all this is compliment. Friar John alone inveighs against this formal stuff, antic postures, and nonsensical fiddle-faddle, cringes, grimaces, scrapes, embraces, leers, etc., and slinks into the kitchens, where there was something more substantial for a monk, who does not use to feed on empty talk. So, though the island was populous, fertile, and of large extent, he admires nothing but the culinary laboratories, the turning of the spits, the harmonious rattling of the jacks and fender; and is for criticising on the position of the bacon, the temperature of the pottages, the preparation for the dessert, and the order of the wine service. All the eleventh chapter illustrates that monastical inclination to frequent kitchens. —*M*.

CHAPTER XII

HOW PANTAGRUEL PASSED THROUGH THE LAND OF PETTIFOGGING, AND OF THE STRANGE WAY OF LIVING AMONG THE CATCHPOLES

STEERING our course forwards the next day, we passed through Pettifogging, a country all blurred and blotted, so that I could hardly tell what to make on it. There we saw some pettifoggers and catchpoles, rogues that will hang their father for a groat. They neither invited us to eat or drink; but, with a multiplied train of scrapes and cringes, said they were all at our service, for a consideration.

One of our interpreters related to Pantagruel their strange way of living, diametrically opposite to that of our modern Romans; for at Rome a world of folks get an honest livelihood by poisoning, drubbing, lambasting, stabbing, and murdering; but the catchpoles earn theirs by being thrashed; so that if they were long without a tight lambasting, the poor dogs with their wives and children would be starved. This is just, quoth Panurge, like those who, as Galen tells us, cannot erect the cavernous nerve towards the equinoctial circle, unless they are soundly flogged.[1] By St Patrick's slipper, whoever should jerk me so, would soon, instead of setting me right, throw me off the saddle, in the devil's name.

The way is this, said the interpreter. When a monk, levite, close-fisted usurer, or lawyer owes a grudge to some neighbouring gentleman, he sends to him one of those catchpoles, or apparitors, who nabs, or at least cites him, serves a writ or warrant

[1] See De Lolme's History of the Flagellants.

upon him, thumps, abuses, and affronts him impudently by natural instinct, and according to his pious instructions: insomuch that if the gentleman hath but any guts in his brains,[2] and is not more stupid than a gyrin frog,[3] he will find himself obliged either to apply a faggot-stick or his sword to the rascal's jobbernol, give him the gentle lash, or make him cut a caper out at the window, by way of correction. This done, catchpole is rich for four months at least, as if bastinadoes were his real harvest: for the monk, levite, usurer, or lawyer, will reward him roundly; and my gentleman must pay him such swingeing damages, that his acres must bleed for it, and he be in danger of miserably rotting within a stone doublet, as if he had struck the King.

Quoth Panurge, I know an excellent remedy against this; used by the Lord of Basché.[4] What is it? said Pantagruel. The Lord of Basché, said Panurge, was a brave, honest, noble-spirited gentleman, who, at his return from the long war, in which the Duke of Ferrara, with the help of the French, bravely defended himself against the fury of Pope Julius the Second, was every day cited, warned, and prosecuted at the suit, and for the sport and fancy of the fat prior of St Louant.[5]

One morning, as he was at breakfast with some of his domestics (for he loved to be sometimes among

[2] *Hath but, etc.*—Hath not the dead palsy.
[3] *Gyrin frog.*—A tadpole. An unformed frog; from the Greek γυρῖνοι, frog spawn.
[4] *Lord of Basché.*—Doubtless a descendant of Perron de Basché, steward of the household to King Charles VIII., who sent him into Italy, before he went thither himself at the head of his army. See Commines, l. 7, c. 3.
[5] St Louant. Liventius. The priory of St Louens, in the diocese of Tours, etc.

them) he sent for one Loire, his baker, and his
spouse, and for one Oudart, the vicar of his parish,
who was also his butler, as the custom was then in
France; then said to them before his gentlemen and
other servants : You all see how I am daily plagued
with these rascally catchpoles ; truly, if you do not
lend me your helping hand, I am finally resolved to
leave the country, and go fight for the Sultan, or
the devil, rather than be thus eternally teased.
Therefore to be rid of their damned visits, hereafter,
when any of them come here, be ready you baker
and your wife, to make your personal appearance in
my great hall, in your wedding clothes, as if you
were going to be affianced. Here take these ducats,
which I give you to keep you in a fitting garb. As
for you, Sir Oudart, be sure you make your personal
appearance there in your fair surplice and stole, not
forgetting your holy water, as if you were to wed
them. Be you there also, Trudon, said he to his
drummer, with your pipe and tabor. The form of
matrimony must be read, and the bride kissed at the
beat of the tabor ; then all of you, as the witnesses
used to do in this country, shall give one another
the remembrance of the wedding,—which you know
is to be a blow with your fist, bidding the party
struck remember the nuptials by that token. This
will but make you have the better stomach to your
supper ; but when you come to the catchpole's
turn, thrash him thrice and threefold, as you would
a sheaf of green corn ; do not spare him ; maul
him, drub him, lambast him, swinge him off, I pray
you. Here, take these steel gauntlets, covered with
kid. Head, back, belly, and sides, give him blows
innumerable : he that gives him most, shall be my
best friend. Fear not to be called to an account about
it ; I will stand by you : for the blows must seem

to be given in jest, as it is customary among us at all weddings.

Ay, but how shall we know the catchpole, said the man of God? All sorts of people daily resort to this castle. I have taken care of that, replied the lord. When some fellow, either on foot, or on a scurvy jade, with a large broad silver ring[6] on his thumb, comes to the door, he is certainly a catchpole; the porter, having civilly let him in, shall ring the bell; then be all ready, and come into the hall to act the tragi-comedy, whose plot I have now laid for you.

That numerical day, as chance would have it, came an old, fat, ruddy catchpole. Having knocked at the gate, and then pissed, as most men will do, the porter soon found him out, by his large, greasy spatterdashes, his jaded hollow-flanked mare, his bag full of writs and informations dangling at his girdle, but, above all, by the large silver hoop on his left thumb.

The porter was civil to him, admitted him kindly, and rung the bell briskly. As soon as the baker and his wife heard it, they clapped on their best clothes, and made their personal appearance in the hall, keeping their gravities like a new-made judge. The dominie put on his surplice and stole, and as he came out of his office, met the catchpole, had him in there, and made him suck his face a good while, while the gauntlets were drawing on all hands; and then told him, You are come just in pudding-time; my lord is in his right cue: we shall feast like kings anon, here is to be swingeing doings; we have a wedding in the house; here, drink and cheer up; pull away.

[6] To seal the writs and writings, belike; for they were not signed in those days.

While these two were at hand-to-fist, Basché, seeing all his people in the hall in their proper equipages, sends for the vicar. Oudard comes with the holy water pot, followed by the catchpole, who, as he came into the hall, did not forget to make good store of awkward cringes, and then served Basché with a writ. Basché gave him grimace for grimace, slipped an angel into his mutton fist, and prayed him to assist at the contract and ceremony: which he did. When it was ended, thumps and fisticuffs began to fly about among the assistants; but when it came to the catchpole's turn they all laid on him so unmercifully with their gauntlets, that they at last settled him, all stunned and battered, bruised and mortified, with one of his eyes black and blue, eight ribs bruised, his brisket sunk in, his omoplates in four quarters, his under jawbone in three pieces; and all this in jest and no harm done. God wot how the levite belaboured him, hiding within the long sleeve of his canonical shirt his huge steel gauntlet lined with ermine; for he was a strong-built ball, and an old dog at fisticuffs. The catchpole, all of a bloody tiger-like stripe,[7] with much ado crawled home to L'Isle Bouchart, well pleased and edified, however, with Basché's kind reception; and, with the help of the good surgeons of the place, lived as long as you would have him. From that time to this, not a word of the business; the memory of it was lost with the sound of the bells that rung with joy at his funeral.

[7] Dappled with variety of contusions.

CHAPTER XIII

HOW, LIKE MASTER FRANCIS VILLON, THE LORD OF
BASCHÉ COMMENDED HIS SERVANTS

THE catchpole being packed off on blind Sorrel,—
so he called his one-eyed-mare,—Basché sent for his
lady, her women, and all his servants, into the
arbour of his garden; had wine brought, attended
with good store of pasties, hams, fruit, and other
table ammunition, for a nunchion; drank with them
joyfully, and then told them this story:

Master Francis Villon, in his old age, retired to
St Maxent, in Poictou, under the patronage of a
good, honest abbot of the place. There to make
sport for the mob, he undertook to get 'The Passion'
acted, after the way, and in the dialect of the country.
The parts being distributed, the play having been
rehearsed, and the stage prepared, he told the mayor
and aldermen, that the mystery would be ready after
Niort fair, and that there only wanted properties and
necessaries, but chiefly clothes fit for the parts: so
the mayor and his brethren took care to get them.

Villon, to dress an old clownish father grey-
beard, who was to represent God the Father, begged
of Friar Stephen Tickletoby, sacristan to the
Franciscan friars of the place, to lend him a cope
and a stole. Tickletoby refused him, alleging, that
by their provincial statutes, it was rigorously for-
bidden to give or lend anything to players. Villon
replied, that the statute reached no farther than
farces, drolls, antics, loose and dissolute games, and
that he asked no more than what he had seen
allowed at Brussels and other places. Tickletoby,
notwithstanding, peremptorily bid him provide him-

self elsewhere if he would, and not to hope for anything out of his monastical wardrobe. Villon gave an account of this to the players, as of a most abominable action ; adding, that God would shortly revenge himself, and make an example of Tickletoby.

The Saturday following, he had notice given him, that Tickletoby, upon the filly of the convent —so they call a young mare that was never leaped yet—was gone a-mumping to St Ligarius, and would be back about two in the afternoon. Knowing this, he made a cavalcade of his devils of 'The Passion' through the town. They were all rigged with wolves', calves', and rams' skins,[1] laced and trimmed with sheep's heads, bull's feathers, and large kitchen tenterhooks, girt with broad leathern girdles; whereat hanged dangling huge cow-bells and horse-bells, which made a horrid din. Some held in their claws black sticks full of squibs and crackers: others had long lighted pieces of wood, upon which, at the corner of every street, they flung whole handfuls of rosin-dust, that made a terrible fire and smoke. Having thus led them about, to the great diversion of the mob, and the dreadful fear of little children, he finally carried them to an entertainment at a summer-house, without the gate that leads to St Ligarius.

As they came near to the place, he espied Tickletoby afar off, coming home from mumping, and told them in macaronic verse :

> Hic est de patria, natus, de gente belistra,[2]
> Qui solet antiquo bribas portare bisacco.[3]

---

[1] This masquerade which generally was performed on New Year's day, was prohibited as impious; but Villon gave himself very little concern about that.
[2] A beggarly race.
[3] A monk's double pouch.

A plague on his friarship, said the devils then; the lousy beggar would not lend a poor cope to the fatherly father; let us fright him. Well said, cried Villon; but let us hide ourselves till he comes by, and then charge him home briskly with your squibs and burning sticks. Tickletoby being come to the place, they all rushed on a sudden into the road to meet him, and in a frightful manner threw fire from all sides upon him and his filly foal, ringing and tingling their bells, and howling like so many real devils. Hho, hho, hho, hho, brrou, rrou, rrourrs, rrrourrs, hoo, hou, hou, hho, hho, hhoi. Friar Stephen, don't we play the devils rarely? The filly was soon scared out of her seven senses, and began to start, to funk it, to squirt it, to trot it, to fart it, to bound it, to gallop it, to kick it, to spurn it, to calcitrate it, to wince it, to frisk it, to leap it, to curvet it, with double jerks, and bum-motions; insomuch that she threw down Tickletoby, though he held fast by the tree of the pack-saddle with might and main. Now his straps and stirrups were of cord; and on the right side, his sandals were so entangled and twisted, that he could not for the heart's blood of him get out his foot. Thus he was dragged about by the filly through the road, scratching his bare breech all the way; she still multiplying her kicks against him, and straying for fear over hedge and ditch; insomuch that she trepanned his thick skull so, that his cockle brains were dashed out near the Osanna or high-cross. Then his arms fell to pieces, one this way, and the other that way; and even so were his legs served at the same time. Then she made a bloody havoc with his puddings; and being got to the convent, brought back only his right foot and twisted sandal, leaving them to guess what had become of the rest.

Villon, seeing that things had succeeded as he intended, said to his devils, You will act rarely, gentlemen devils, you will act rarely; I dare engage you will top your parts. I defy the devils of Saumur, Douay, Montmorillon, Langez, St Espain, Angers; nay, by gad! even those of Poictiers, for all their bragging and vapouring, to match you.

Thus, friends, said Basché, I foresee, that hereafter you will act rarely this tragical farce, since the very first time you have so skilfully hampered, bethwacked, belammed, and bebumped the catchpole. From this day I double your wages. As for you, my dear, said he to his lady, make your gratifications as you please; you are my treasurer, you know. For my part, first and foremost, I drink to you all. Come on, box it about, it is good and cool. In the second place, you, Mr Steward, take this silver basin, I give it you freely. Then you, my gentlemen of the horse, take these two silver gilt cups, and let not the pages be horse-whipped these three months. My dear, let them have my best white plumes of feathers, with the gold buckles to them. Sir Oudart, this silver flagon falls to your share: this other I give to the cooks. To the valets de chambre I give this silver basket; to the grooms, this silver gilt boat; to the porter, these two plates; to the hostlers, these ten porringers. Trudon, take you these silver spoons and this sugar box. You, footman, take this large salt. Serve me well, and I will remember you. For on the word of a gentleman, I had rather bear in war one hundred blows on my helmet in the service of my country, than be once cited by these knavish catchpoles, merely to humour this same gorbellied prior.

CHAPTER XIV

A FURTHER ACCOUNT OF CATCHPOLES WHO WERE DRUBBED AT BASCHÉ'S HOUSE

Four days after, another, young, long-shanked, rawboned catchpole, coming to serve Basché with a writ at the fat prior's request, was no sooner at the gate, but the porter smelt him out, and rung the bell; at whose second pull, all the family understood the mystery. Loire was kneading his dough; his wife was sifting meal; Oudart was toping in his office; the gentlemen were playing at tennis; the Lord Basché at in and out with my lady; the waiting-men and gentlewomen at push-pin; the officers at lanterlue, and the pages at hot-cockles, giving one another smart bangs. They were all immediately informed that a catchpole was housed.

Upon this Oudart put on his sacerdotal, and Loire and his wife their nuptial badges: Trudon piped it, and then tabored it like mad: all made haste to get ready, not forgetting the gauntlets. Basché went into the outward yard: there the catchpole meeting him fell on his marrow-bones, begged of him not to take it ill, if he served him with a writ at the suit of the fat prior; and in a pathetic speech let him know that he was a public person, a servant to the monking tribe, apparitor to the abbatial mitre, ready to do as much for him, nay, for the least of his servants, whensoever he would employ and use him.

Nay, truly, said the lord, you shall not serve your writ till you have tasted some of my good quinquenays wine, and been a witness to a wedding which we are to have this very minute. Let him drink and refresh himself, added he, turning towards the levitical butler, and then bring him into the hall. After which, catchpole, well stuffed and moistened, came with Oudart to the place where all the actors in the farce stood ready to begin. The sight of their game set them a-laughing, and the messenger of mischief grinned also for company's sake. Then the mysterious words[1] were muttered to and by the couple, their hands joined, the bride bussed, and all besprinkled with holy water. While they were bringing wine and kickshaws, thumps began to trot about by dozens. The catchpole gave the levite several blows. Oudart, who had his gauntlet hid under his canonical shirt, draws it on like a mitten, and then, with his clenched fist, souse he fell on the catchpole, and mauled him like a devil : the junior gauntlets dropped on him likewise like so many battering-rams. Remember the wedding by this, by that, by these blows, said they. In short, they stroked him so to the purpose, that he pissed blood out at mouth, nose, ears, and eyes, and was bruised, thwacked, battered, bebumped, and crippled at the back, neck, breast, arms, and so forth. Never did the bachelors at Avignon, in carnival time, play more melodiously at raphe, than was then played on the catchpole's microcosm : at last down he fell.

They threw a great deal of wine on his snout, tied round the sleeve of his doublet a fine yellow and green favour, and got him upon his snotty beast, and God knows how he got to L'Isle Bouchart; where I cannot truly tell you whether he was dressed and looked after or no, both by his spouse and the able

[1] Sacramental words.

doctors of the country; for the thing never came to my ears.

The next day they had a third part to the same tune, because it did not appear by the lean catchpole's bag, that he had served his writ. So the fat prior sent a new catchpole, at the head of a brace of bums, for his *garde du corps*, to summon my lord. The porter ringing the bell, the whole family was overjoyed, knowing that it was another rogue. Basché was at dinner with his lady and the gentlemen; so he sent for the catchpole, made him sit by him, and the bums by the women, and made them eat till their bellies cracked with their breeches unbuttoned. The fruit being served, the catchpole arose from table, and before the bums cited Basché. Basché kindly asked him for a copy of the warrant, which the other had got ready: he then takes witness, and a copy of the summons. To the catchpole and his bums he ordered four ducats for civility money. In the meantime all were withdrawn for the farce. So Trudon gave the alarm with his tabor. Basché desired the catchpole to stay and see one of his servants married, and witness the contract of marriage, paying him his fee. The catchpole slap dash was ready, took out his ink-horn, got paper immediately, and his bums by him.

Then Loire came into the hall at one door, and his wife with the gentlewomen at another, in nuptial accoutrements. Oudart, in pontificalibus, takes them both by their hands, asketh them their will, giveth them the matrimonial blessing, and was very liberal of holy water. The contract written, signed, and registered, on one side was brought wine and comfits; on the other, white and orange-tawny-coloured favours were distributed: on another, gauntlets privately handed about.

CHAPTER XV

HOW THE ANCIENT CUSTOM AT NUPTIALS IS RENEWED BY THE CATCHPOLE

THE catchpole, having made shift to get down a swingeing sneaker of Breton wine, said to Basché, Pray, Sir, what do you mean? You do not give one another the memento of the wedding. By St Joseph's wooden shoe, all good customs are forgot. We find the form, but the hare is scampered; and the nest, but the birds are flown. There are no true friends nowadays. You see how, in several churches, the ancient laudable custom of tippling, on account of the blessed saints O O, at Christmas,[1] is come to nothing. The world is in its dotage, and doomsday is certainly coming all so fast. Now

[1] It was formerly a custom throughout France, and is still in some parts of it, to make, in the parish church, about seven o'clock in the evening for the nine days next before Christmas day, certain prayers or anthems called the Christmas O O's, because in the books which prescribe these anthems they begin with O O, as 'O sapientia, O adonai, O radix,' etc. To him that was last married in the parish, especially if he be one in good circumstances, is carried a very large O, represented in burnished gold on a large piece of very thick parchment, with several ornaments of gold or other fine colours. This O was every evening of the nine days put on the top of the lutrin; there stayed the O all the time that the anthem was singing. The person to whom the O had been sent, was wont, in return, to make a present of a piece of money to the curate, who, on his part, spent some of it in regaling his friends. After the holidays, the O was carried back to the new-married man, who set it up in the most honourable place of his house. It was this ancient custom the catchpole laments the loss of, because most commonly he had a share in the booty, either from the curate or the married man.

come on; the wedding, the wedding, the wedding; remember it by this. This he said, striking Basché and his lady; then her women and the levite. Then the tabor beat a point of war, and the gauntlets began to do their duty: insomuch that the catchpole had his crown cracked in no less than nine places. One of the bums had his right arm put out of joint, and the other his upper jawbone or mandibule dislocated; so that it hid half his chin, with a denudation of the uvula, and sad loss of the molar, masticatory, and canine teeth. Then the tabor beat a retreat; the gauntlets were carefully hid in a trice, and sweetmeats afresh distributed to renew the mirth of the company. So they all drank to one another, and especially to the catchpole and his bums. But Oudart cursed and damned the wedding to the pit of hell, complaining that one of the bums had utterly disincornifistibulated his nether shoulderblade. Nevertheless, he scorned to be thought a flincher, and made shift to tope to him on the square.

The jawless bum shrugged up his shoulders, joined his hands, and by signs begged his pardon; for speak he could not. The sham bridegroom made his moan, that the crippled bum had struck him such a horrid thump with his shoulder-of-mutton fist on the nether elbow, that he was grown quite esperruquanchuzelubelouzerireliced down to his very heel, to the no small loss of mistress bride.

But what harm had poor I done? cried Trudon, hiding his left eye with his kerchief, and showing his tabor cracked on one side: they were not satisfied with thus poaching, black and blueing, and morrambouzevezengouzequoquemorgasacbaquevezinemaffreliding my poor eyes, but they have also broke my harmless drum. Drums indeed are commonly beaten at weddings,—and it is fit they should; but drummers are well entertained, and never beaten. Now let Belzebub even take the drum, to make his devilship a nightcap.² Brother, said the lame catchpole, never fret thyself; I will make thee a present of a fine, large, old patent, which I have here in my bag, to patch up thy drum, and for Madame St Ann's sake I pray thee forgive us. By Our Lady of Riviere, the blessed dame, I meant no more harm than the child unborn. One of the querries, who hopping and halting like a mumping cripple, mimicked the good limping Lord de la Roche Posay, directed his discourse to the bum with the pouting jaw, and told him, What, Mr Manhound, was it not enough thus to have morcrocastebezasteverestegrigeligoscopapopondrillated us all in our upper members with your botched mittens, but you must also apply such morderegripippiatabirofreluchamburelurecaquelurintimpaniments on our shin-bones with the hard tops and extremities of your cobbled shoes. Do you call this children's play? By the mass! it is no jest. The bum, wringing his hands, seemed to beg his pardon, muttering with his tongue, Mon, mon, mon, vrelon, von, von, like a dumb man. The bride crying laughed, and laughing cried, because the catchpole was not satisfied with drubbing her without choice or distinction of members, but had also rudely roused and toused her; pulled off her topping, and not having the fear of her husband before his eyes, treacherously trepignemanpenillorifrizonoufresterfumbledtumbled and squeezed her lower parts. The devil go with it, said Basché; there was much need indeed that this same Master King³ (this was

² Either top or bottom was beat out.
³ In chap. 5. of l. 3 of Fœneste, the serjeant of Doué, who came to serve a writ on La Roche Bosseau, is likewise named

the catchpole's name) should thus break my wife's back : however, I forgive him now ; these are little nuptial caresses. But this I plainly perceive, that he cited me like an angel, and drubbed me like a devil.⁴ He hath something in him of Friar Thumpwell. Come, for all this, I must drink to him, and to you likewise his trusty esquires. But, said his lady, why hath he been so very liberal of his manual kindness to me, without the least provocation ? I assure you, I by no means like it: but this I dare say for him, that he hath the hardest knuckles that ever I felt on my shoulders. The steward held his left arm in a scarf, as if it had been rent and torn in twain : I think it was the devil, said he, that moved me to assist at these nuptials ; shame on ill luck ; I musts needs be meddling with a pox, and now see what I have got by the bargain, both my arms are wretchedly engoulevezinemassed and bruised. Do you call this a wedding ? By St Bridget's tooth, I had rather be at that of a Tom Turdman. This is, on my word, even just such another feast as was that of the Lapithæ, described by the philosopher⁵ of Samosata. One of the bums had lost his tongue. The two others, though they had more need to complain, made their excuse as well as they could, protesting that they had no ill design in this dumbfounding ; begging that, for goodness' sake, they would forgive them ; and so, though they could hardly budge a foot, or wag along, away they crawled. About a mile from

Monsieur le Roy (Mr King,) either because all of that profession execute their commission in the king's name, or because, as is said before, he that strikes one of them had as good strike the king.
⁴ They call the ushers and serjeants angels of the court. To drub, *dauber*, from *delapare*, is properly what that angel of Satan did who buffeted St Paul.
⁵ Lucian, in his Lapithæ.

Basché's seat, the catchpole found himself somewhat out of sorts. The bums got to L'Isle Bouchart, publicly saying, that since they were born, they had never seen an honester gentleman than the Lord of Basché, or civiller people than his, and that they had never been at the like wedding (which I verily believe); but that it was their own faults if they had been tickled off, and tossed about from post to pillar, since themselves had begun the beating. So they lived I cannot exactly tell you how many days after this. But from that time to this it was held for a certain truth, that Basché's money was more pestilential, mortal, and pernicious to the catchpoles and bums, than were formerly the aurum Tholosanum[6] and the Seian horse to those that possessed them. Ever since this, he lived quietly, and Basché's wedding grew into a common proverb.[7]

CHAPTER XVI

HOW FRIAR JOHN MADE TRIAL OF THE NATURE OF THE CATCHPOLES

This story would seem pleasant enough, said Pantagruel, were we not to have always the fear of God before our eyes. It had been better, said Epistemon, if those gauntlets had fallen upon the fat prior. Since he took a pleasure in spending his money partly to vex Basché, partly to see those

[6] See Cicero, *de Nat. Deorum*, l. 3; Justin, l. 22.; Strabo, l. 4. It became a Latin proverb.
[7] See d'Aubigne, Baron de Fœneste, l. 3, c. 5.

catchpoles banged, good lusty thumps would have done well on his shaven crown, considering the horrid concussions nowadays among those puny judges. What harm had done those poor devils the catchpoles? This puts me in mind, said Pantagruel, of an ancient Roman named L. Neratius.[1] He was of noble blood, and for some time was rich; but had this tyrannical inclination, that whenever he went out of doors, he caused his servants to fill their pockets with gold and silver, and meeting in the street your spruce gallants and better sort of beaux, without the least provocation, for his fancy, he used to strike them hard on the face with his fist; and immediately after that, to appease them, and hinder them from complaining to the magistrates, he would give them as much money as satisfied them according to the law of the twelve tables. Thus he used to spend his revenue, beating people for the price of his money. By St Bennet's sacred boot, quoth Friar John, I will know the truth of it presently.

This said, he went on shore, put his hand in his fob, and took out twenty ducats; then said with a loud voice, in the hearing of a shoal of the nation of catchpoles, Who will earn twenty ducats, for being beaten like the devil? Io, Io, Io, said they all: you will cripple us for ever, sir, that is most certain; but the money is tempting. With this they were all thronging who should be first, to be thus preciously beaten. Friar John singled him out of the whole knot of these rogues in grain, a red-snouted catchpole, who upon his right thumb wore a thick, broad silver hoop, wherein was set a good large toad-stone. He had no sooner picked him out from the rest, but I perceived that they all muttered and grumbled;

---

[1] See Aulus Gellius, l. 20, c. 1.

and I heard a young thin-jawed catchpole, a notable scholar, a pretty fellow at his pen, and, according to public report, much cried up for his honesty to Doctors - Commons,[2] making his complaint, and muttering, because this same crimson phiz carried away all the practice; and that if there were but a score and a half of bastinadoes[3] to be got, he would certainly run away with eight-and-twenty of them. But all this was looked upon to be nothing but mere envy.

Friar John so unmercifully thrashed, thumped, and belaboured Red-snout, back and belly, sides, legs, and arms, head, feet, and so forth, with the home and frequently repeated application of one of the best members of a faggot, that I took him to be a dead man : then he gave him the twenty ducats; which made the dog get on his legs, pleased like a little king or two. The rest were saying to Friar John, Sir, sir, brother devil, if it please you to do us the favour to beat some of us for less money, we are all at your devilship's command, bags, papers, pens, and all. Red-snout cried out against them, saying, with a loud voice, Body of me, you little prigs, will you offer to take the bread out of my mouth ? will you take my bargain over my head ? would you draw and inveigle from me my clients and customers ? Take notice, I summon you before the official this day sevennight ; I will law and claw you like any old devil of Vauverd,[4] that I will. Then turning himself towards Friar John, with a smiling and joyful look, he said to him, Reverend father in the devil, if you have found

[2] In the ecclesiastical court ; *en court d'ecclise :* the old way of spelling *eglise* (church).
[3] See Racine, *Les Plaideurs,* act. i., sc. 5.
[4] The palace of Vauvert, built by King Robert, on the actual site of the rue d'Enfer (street of Hell) was abandoned, as a rookery of devils, after the excommunication of its founder.

me a good hide, and have a mind to divert yourself once more, by beating your humble servant, I will bate you half in half this time, rather than lose your custom: do not spare me, I beseech you : I am all, and more than all yours, good Mr Devil; head, lungs, tripes, guts and garbage ; and that at a pennyworth, I'll assure you. Friar John never heeded his proffers, but even left them. The other catchpoles were making addresses to Panurge, Epistemon, Gymnast, and others, entreating them charitably to bestow upon their carcasses a small beating, for otherwise they were in danger of keeping a long fast : but none of them had a stomach to it. Some time after, seeking fresh water for the ship's company, we met a couple of old female catchpoles of the place, miserably howling and weeping in concert. Pantagruel had kept on board, and already had caused a retreat to be sounded. Thinking that they might be related to the catchpole that was bastinadoed, we asked them the occasion of their grief. They replied, that they had too much cause to weep ; for that very hour from an exalted triple tree, two of the honestest gentlemen in Catchpole-land had been made to cut a caper on nothing. Cut a caper on nothing! said Gymnast; my pages used to cut capers on the ground : to cut a caper on nothing, should be hanging and choking, or I am out. Ay, ay, said Friar John, you speak of it like St John de la Palisse.

We asked them why they treated these worthy persons with such a choking hempen salad. They told us they had only borrowed, alias stolen, the tools of the mass, and hid them under the handle of the parish.[5] This is a very allegorical way of speaking, said Epistemon.

[5] The belfry. A Poitevin word, used only by the villagers of Poictou, in way of metaphor stupid and coarse as themselves.

ON CHAPS. XII. XIII. XIV. XV. AND XVI.—All these chapters are occasioned by Pantagruel's passing by Pettifogging, and give us an account of the way of living of the apparitors, serjeants, and bailiffs, and such inferior ministers of the law. Nothing can seem dark in what our author has said of them at the opening of chap. XII., because in Francis the First's and Henry the Second's reigns that rascally tribe had no income so beneficial, as that which came to them from a beating. The nobility thought it so great an affront to be cited, or arrested, by that vermin, that they stood too much on their punctilio, and for that reason they severely used those bailiffs or apparitors who came to them to discharge their office, and who sometimes were sent out of malice. So when the man-catchers, who desired nothing more than to be banged, had been misused, they had swingeng damages to make them amends. Rabelais exposes the folly, villainy, and abuse of this practice on both sides; which has been since so well redressed, that if the bailiffs had nothing to depend on but bastinadoes, those necessary evils would long since have all been starved.

As the betrothing or nuptials of Basché grew into a proverb; so from that Villon, who in the reign of Louis the XIth. was as famous for his cheats and villainies as for his poetry, came the word *villoner*, which has been long used to signify to cheat, or play some rogue's trick. I shall have occasion to take notice of him in my remarks on the last chapter of the fourth book.

Pantagruel's companions are told of two of the honestest men in all Catchpole-land, who were made 'to cut a caper on nothing,' for stealing the tools of the mass, and hiding them under the handle of the parish. This must be some sacrilegious theft of church plate in those times; and, by the bye, we may see what esteem Rabelais had for the catchpoles, since he makes those rogues the honestest in all that country. Friar John says, that this was as mysterious a way of speaking as St John's *de la Palisse*. *De la Palisse* is the name of a family in France; but he means, *de l'apocalypse.*—M.

CHAPTER XVII

HOW PANTAGRUEL CAME TO THE ISLANDS OF TOHU AND BOHU; AND OF THE STRANGE DEATH OF WIDE-NOSTRILS, THE SWALLOWER OF WIND-MILLS

THAT day Pantagruel came to the two islands of Tohu and Bohu, where the devil a bit we could find anything to fry with.[1] For one Widenostrils,[2] a huge giant, had swallowed every individual pan, skillet, kettle, frying-pan, dripping-pan, and brass and iron pot in the land, for want of wind-mills, which were his daily food. Whence it happened, that somewhat before day, about the hour of his digestion, the greedy churl was taken very ill, with a kind of a surfeit, or crudity of stomach, occasioned, as the physicians said, by the weakness of the concocting faculty of his stomach, naturally disposed to digest whole wind-mills at a gust, yet unable to consume perfectly the pans and skillets; though it had indeed pretty well digested the kettles and pots; as they said, they knew by the hypostases[3] and eneoremes[4] of four tubs of second-hand drink which he had evacuated at two different times that morning. They made use of divers remedies, according to art, to give him ease: but all would not do; the distemper

[1] Rabelais uses a proverbial phrase; *ne trovasmes que frire*, which properly means, the devil a bit found we there to fry; that is, as Duchat observes, we found neither fish nor flesh.
[2] *Bringuenarilles.*—Nose-slitters, says M. Duchat, from the German *brechen*, and *narilles* for *nasilles*, after the Paris manner of pronouncing that word. Cotgrave, from whom M. Motteux takes it, says it means wide nostrils.
[3] A sediment in urine.
[4] Cotgrave says *encoresmes*, the signs of urine, especially those that swim on the top thereof. I do not think there is any such word as *encoresmes*.

prevailed over the remedies, insomuch that the famous Widenostrils died that morning, of so strange a death, that I think you ought no longer to wonder at that of the poet Æschylus. It had been foretold him by the soothsayers, that he would die on a certain day, by the ruin of something that should fall on him. That fatal day being come in its turn, he removed himself out of town, far from all houses, trees, rocks, or any other things that can fall, and endanger by their ruin; and strayed in a large field, trusting himself to the open sky; there, very secure, as he thought, unless, indeed, the sky should happen to fall, which he held to be impossible. Yet, they say, that the larks are much afraid of it; for if it should fall, they must all be taken.

The Celts that once lived near the Rhine—they are our noble valiant French—in ancient times were also afraid of the sky's falling: for being asked by Alexander the Great, what they feared most in this world, hoping well they would say that they feared none but him, considering his great achievements; they made answer, that they feared nothing but the sky's falling: however, not refusing to enter into a confederacy with so brave a king; if you believe Strabo, lib. 7, and Arrian, lib. 1.

Plutarch also, in his book of the face that appears on the body of the moon, speaks of one Pharnaces, who very much feared the moon should fall on the earth, and pitied those that live under that planet, as the Æthiopians and Taprobanians, if so heavy a mass ever happened to fall on them: and would have feared the like of heaven and earth, had they not been duly propped up and borne by the Atlantic pillars, as the ancients believed, according to Aristotle's testimony, lib. 5, *Metaphys.* Notwithstanding all this, poor Æschylus was killed by the fall of the shell of a tortoise, which falling from betwixt the claws of an eagle high in the air, just on his head, dashed out his brains.

Neither ought you to wonder at the death of another poet, I mean old jolly Anacreon, who was choked with a grape-stone. Nor at that of Fabius, the Roman prætor, who was choked with a single goat's hair, as he was supping up a porringer of milk.[5] Nor at the death of that bashful fool, who by holding in his wind, and for want of letting out a. bumgunshot, died suddenly in the presence of the Emperor Claudius. Nor at that of the Italian, buried on the Via Flaminia at Rome, who, in his epitaph,[6] complains that the bite of a she puss[7] on his little finger was the cause of his death. Nor of that of Q.

[5] Thus far these examples are taken out of Pliny, l. 7, c. 7.

[6] It is to be seen in the church of the monks of St Austin; and Francis Schottus, a senator of Antwerp, gives it in these words in his travels over Italy:

    'Hospes disce novum mortis genus: improba felis
    Dum trahitur, digitum mordet, et intereo.'
    Hear a new kind of death, ye goers-by:
    A cat my finger bit, and lo! I die.

[7] *Fût mort par estre mord d'une chatte, etc.*—Instead of *mordu*, bit, in Rabelais' time they used to say *mords*; and H. Stevens, p. 144, of his Dialogues 'Du Nouveau Lang. Fran. Italianisé,' insists upon it, that according to analogy, that way of speaking was right, and ought to be continued. And indeed for proof that they did not in those days say *mordu*, but *mords*, I shall transcribe honest Clem. Marot's epigram, *Epousée farouche*:

'L'epousé la premiere nuit	One, married to a country flirt
Asseuroit sa femme farouche :	Full skittish, said the youth,
Mordez-moi, dit-il, s'il vous cuit :	'Bite me, my dear, if you I hurt;
Voila mon doigt en vostre bouche.	My finger's in your mouth.'
Elle y consent ; il s'escarmouche ;	When all was o'er, he asked his
Et apres qu'il l'eust deshoussée,	bride,
Or ça, dit-il, tendre rosée,	If anything did sting her?
Vous ay-je fait du mal ains ?	She, by a question too, replied,
Adonc, respondit l'epousée,	'And did I bite your finger?'
Je ne vous ay pas *mords* aussi.'	

Lecanius Bassus, who died suddenly of so small a prick with a needle on his left thumb, that it could hardly be discerned. Nor of Quenelault, a Norman physician, who died suddenly at Montpellier, merely for having side-ways took a worm out of his hand with a penknife. Nor of Philomenes,[8] whose servant having got him some new figs for the first course of his dinner, whilst he went to fetch wine, a straggling well-hung ass got into the house, and seeing the figs on the table, without further invitation, soberly fell to. Philomenes coming into the room, and nicely observing with what gravity the ass eat its dinner, said to his man, who was come back, Since thou hast set figs here for this reverend guest of ours to eat, methinks it is but reason thou also give him some of this wine to drink. He had no sooner said this, but he was so excessively pleased, and fell into so exorbitant a fit of laughter, that the use of his spleen took that of his breath utterly away, and he immediately died. Nor of Spurius Saufeius,[9] who died supping up a soft-boiled egg as he came out of a bath. Nor of him who, as Boccaccio tells us, died suddenly by picking his grinders with a sage-stalk.[10] Nor of Phillipot Placut, who being brisk and hale, fell dead as he was paying an old debt; which causes, perhaps, many not to pay theirs, for fear of the like accident. Nor of the painter Zeuxis, who killed himself with laughing at the sight of the antic jobbernol of an old hag drawn by him. Nor, in short, of a thousand more of which authors write; as

[8] See Valerius Maximus and Lucian.
[9] Rabelais might as well have called him by his right name, Appius Saufeius, as Pliny does, l. 7, c. 33, but having a mind to bamboozle his readers, and lead them a wild-goose chase, he chooses to err with Fulgosus, who gives this Saufeius the prænomen of Spurius, l. 9, c. 12.
[10] A huge toad had just before cast his venom upon it.

Varrius, Pliny, Valerius, J. Baptista Fulgosus, and Bacabery the elder.[11] In short, Gaffer Widenostrils choked himself with eating a huge lump of fresh butter at the mouth of a hot oven, by the advice of physicians.

They likewise told us there, that the King of Cullan in Bohu had routed the grandees of King Mecloth, and made sad work with the fortresses of Belima.

After this, we sailed by the islands of Nargues and Zargues; also by the islands of Teleniabin and Geleniabin, very fine and fruitful in ingredients for clysters; and then by the islands of Enig and Evig,[12]

[11] There are two Bacou-berys on the river Oise. Perhaps the person who relates this comical death of Phillipot Placut was born at one of them; as writers often assume the name of the place of their birth.

[12] Enig (einige) is a pronoun, and signifies any (and I am apt to think our any comes from enig). As for evig (ewige), it is an adjective and signifies everlasting (perhaps too from evig we have our word ever). However this matter stands, the case Rabelais referred to was this. One clause of the treaty between Charles V. and the Landgrave of Hesse was, That the latter should remain in the court of the former among his retinue *ohne einige gefangniss*, without any confinement; as much as to say, it was by no means as a prisoner that the landgrave should be obliged to abide a certain time about the Emperor, but purely and only that the conqueror might be sure the conquered would undertake nothing to the prejudice of the said treaty. Instead of the word *einige*, any, which joined with the particle *ohne*, without, manifestly means without any; the Emperor had got the word *ewige*, perpetual, slipped into the act. So that the landgrave, who reckoned on being obliged to follow the Emperor no longer than till the agreement made between them was fully executed, was filled with surprise when he was given to understand, that by virtue of the word *ewige*, foisted into the place of *einige*, he had made and owned himself the Emperor's prisoner for as many years as it should please that monarch to have him continue so. This is the foul play which Rabelais calls the *estifilade*, or being swinged off as it were with leather straps; for that is the proper meaning of *estifilade*.

on whose account formerly the Landgrave of Hesse was swinged off with a vengeance.

ON CHAP. XVII.—From Catchpole-land Pantagruel comes to two islands, which the author calls *Tohu* and *Bohu*, from two Hebrew words, which, I am told, are taken out of the first chapter of Genesis, where it is said, the earth was *tohu va bohu*, that is, void, and in confusion, without form or beauty, and, in short, a chaos. This may well be applied to a country that is ruined by war; the fury of the soldiers on one side, and exactions of chiefs, many times leaving little or nothing behind them. This makes Rabelais say, that the devil a bit they could find anything there to fry; which is an expression often used by the French, when they would say, there is no subsisting in a place.

The giant Bringuenarilles, or Widenostrils, had taken away the means of frying there by devouring every individual pan, skillet, kettle, frying-pan, dripping-pan, and brass and iron pot in the land, for want of wind-mills, which used to be his daily food. By this giant we may understand those gigantic bodies of men, vast armies, that bring terror and destruction with them wherever they come; and in particular, those roaring hectors, freebooters, desperadoes, and bullying huff-snuffs, for the most part like those whom Tacitus styles *hospitibus tantum metuendi*, who at the beginning of the war or campaign, live profusely at the husbandman's cost; but when the poor boor has been ruined by those unwelcome guests, they even destroy, and in a manner devour, the straw of the beds, and the pans, kettles, and, in short, whatever comes in their way.

Rabelais tells us, that at last Gaffer Widenostrils was choked with eating a huge lump of fresh butter at the mouth of a hot oven, by the advice of physicians; which very well represents the destiny of those swaggering bravos, who, when the war is over, too often either take to the highway, and other bad courses, for which they are choked sometimes for as inconsiderable matters as a lump of butter taken from a higgler; or else, being reduced to live obscurely on a narrow fortune, waste and pine away by the chimney-corner, half-starved with their small pittance, and lead a lingering sorrowful life, worn out with their former excesses, the fatigues of war, and old age; as little regarded as they were feared much, when by open violence they lived in riot and luxury at the expense of the unfortunate. —*M.*

CHAPTER XVIII

HOW PANTAGRUEL MET WITH A GREAT STORM AT SEA

THE next day we espied nine sail[1] that came spooming before the wind: they were full of Dominicans, Jesuits, Capuchins, Hermits, Austins, Bernardins, Egnatins, Celestins, Theatins, Amadeans,[2] Cordeliers, Carmelites, Minims, and the devil-and-all of other holy monks and friars, who were going to the Council of Chesil, to sift and garble some new articles of faith against the new heretics. Panurge was overjoyed to see them, being most certain of good luck for that day, and a long train of others. So having courteously saluted the blessed fathers, and recommended the salvation of his precious soul to their devout prayers and private ejaculations, he caused seventy-eight dozen of Westphalia hams, units of pots of caviare, tens of Bolonia sausages, hundreds of botargoes, and thousands of fine angels, for the souls of the dead, to be thrown on board their ships. Pantagruel seemed metagrabolized, dozing, out of sorts, and as melancholic as a cat. Friar John, who soon perceived it, was inquiring of him whence should come this unusual sadness? when the master, whose watch it was, observing the fluttering of the

[1] M. Duchat says, and it is manifested by the next chapter, that there was but one sail, which Rabelais calls *une orque*. An ourk is properly a sea-fish, enemy to the whale, of a prodigious, and, indeed, monstrous size, and almost round, known in Saintonge by the name of epaulart. From the largeness of this fish, perhaps, it comes about that the biggest sort of ships, designed for the ocean, are called ourks.
[2] Augustin monks, founded at Rapaille by Amadæus, Duke of Savoy, 1448, after he had renounced the Papacy in favour of Nicholas V. They are a branch of the Franciscans.

ancient above the poop, and seeing that it began to overcast, judged that we should have wind; therefore he bid the boatswain call all hands upon deck, officers, sailors, foremast-men, swabbers, and cabin-boys, and even the passengers; made them first settle their top-sails, take in their sprit-sail; then he cried, In with your top-sails, lower the fore-sail, tallow under the parrels, brade up close all them sails, strike your top-masts to the cap, make all sure with your sheepsfeet, lash your guns fast. All this was nimbly done. Immediately it blowed a storm; the sea began to roar, and swell mountain high: the rut of the sea was great, the waves breaking upon our ship's quarter; the north-west wind blustered and overblowed; boisterous gusts, dreadful clashing and deadly scuds of wind whistled though our yards, and made our shrouds rattle again. The thunder grumbled so horridly, that you would have thought heaven had been tumbling about our ears; at the same time it lightned, rained, hailed; the sky lost its transparent hue, grew dusky, thick, and gloomy, so that we had no other light than that of the flashes of lightning, and rending of the clouds: the hurricanes, flaws, and sudden whirlwinds began to make a flame about us, by the lightnings, fiery vapours, and other aerial ejaculations. Oh how our looks were full of amazement and trouble, while the saucy winds did rudely lift up above us the mountainous waves of the main! Believe me, it seemed to us a lively image of the chaos, where fire, air, sea, land, and all the elements were in a refractory confusion. Poor Panurge having, with the full contents of the inside of his doublet, plentifully fed the fish, greedy enough of such odious fare, sat on the deck all in a heap with his nose and arse together, most sadly cast down, moping and half dead; invoked and called to his assistance all the blessed he and she saints he could muster up; swore and vowed to confess in time and place convenient, and then bawled out frightfully, Steward, maitre d'hotel, see hoe! my friend, my father, my uncle, prithee, let us have a piece of powdered beef or pork; we shall drink but too much anon, for aught I see. Eat little and drink the more, will hereafter be my motto, I fear. Would to our dear Lord, and to our blessed, worthy, and sacred Lady, I were now, I say, this very minute of an hour, well on shore, on terra firma, hale and easy! O twice and thrice happy those that plant cabbages! O Destinies, why did you not spin me for a cabbage-planter? O how few are there to whom Jupiter hath been so favourable, as to predestinate them to plant cabbages! They have always one foot on the ground, and the other not far from it. Dispute who will of felicity and *summum bonum;* for my part, whosoever plants cabbages, is now, by my decree, proclaimed most happy; for as good a reason as the philosopher Pyrrho, being in the same danger, and seeing a hog near the shore, eating some scattered oats, declared it happy in two respects; first, because it had plenty of oats, and besides that, was on shore. Ha, for a divine and princely habitation, commend me to the cows' floor.

Murder! This wave will sweep us away, blessed Saviour! O my friends! a little vinegar. I sweat with mere agony. Alas, the mizzen-sail is split, the gallery is washed away, the masts are sprung, the main-top-mast-head dives into the sea; the keel is up to the sun; our shrouds are almost all broke, and blown away. Alas! alas! where is our main course? *Al is verlooren, by Godt;*[3] our top-mast is run adrift.

[3] Low German; all is lost by God. It is in the original ' tout est frelore, bigoth,' which means the same thing. When

Rabelais' Works [Book iv.

Alas! who shall have this wreck? Friend, lend me here behind you one of these whales. Your lanthorn is fallen, my lads. Alas! do not let go the main tack nor the bowline. I hear the block crack; is it broke? For the Lord's sake, let us have the hull, and let all the rigging be damned. Be, be, be, bous, bous, bous. Look to the needle of your compass, I beseech you, good Sir Astrophil, and tell us, if you can, whence comes this storm. My heart's sunk down below my midriff. By my troth, I am in a sad fright, bou, bou, bou, bous, bous, I am lost for ever. I conskite myself for mere madness and fear. Bou, bou, bou, bou, Otto to to to to ti. Bou, bou, bou, ou, ou, ou, bou, bou, bous. I sink, I am drowned, I am gone, good people, I am drowned.

the Swiss were beaten at the battle of Marignan, there was a song for four voices, set to music by the famous Clement Jannequin, and reprinted at Venice, by Jer. Scot. 1550, the burden of which was :
> Tout est frelore,
> La tintelore,
> Tout est frelore, bigot.

After the farce of Patelin, which has these words in it, they became French, and the late gay Mademoiselle de Limueil sung them as she was dying. Bigot, or by God, is the St Picaut of Panurge, l. 3, c. 29. Peter Larrivey, act 2nd, last scene of his comedy called Morfondu, calls him St Picot : so, to save the oath, they make the oath itself a saint ; for there is no such saint as St Picault in reality, nor ever was.

CHAPTER XIX

WHAT COUNTENANCES PANURGE AND FRIAR
JOHN KEPT DURING THE STORM

PANTAGRUEL, having first implored the help of the great and Almighty Deliverer, and prayed publicly with fervent devotion, by the pilot's advice held tightly the mast of the ship. Friar John had stripped himself to his waistcoat, to help the seamen. Epistemon, Ponocrates, and the rest did as much. Panurge alone sat on his breech upon deck, weeping and howling. Friar John espied him going on the quarter-deck, and said to him, Odzoons! Panurge the calf, Panurge the whiner, Panurge the brayer, would it not become thee much better to lend us here a helping hand, than to lie lowing like a cow, as thou dost, sitting on thy stones like a baldbreeched baboon? Be, be, be, bous, bous, bous, returned Panurge; Friar John, my friend, my good father, I am drowning, my dear friend! I drown! I am a dead man, my dear father in God, I am a dead man, my friend: your cutting hanger cannot save me from this: alas! alas! we are above ela.[1] Above the pitch, out of tune, and off the hinges. Be, be, be, bou, bous. Alas! we are now above *g sol re ut*. I sink, I sink, ha, my father, my uncle, my all. The water is got into my shoes by the collar; bous, bous, bous, paish, hu, hu, hu, he, he, he, ha, ha, I drown. Alas! alas! Hu, hu, hu, hu, hu, hu, hu, be, be, bous, bous, bobous, bobous, ho, ho, ho, ho, ho, alas! alas! Now I am like your tumblers,

[1] Allusion from (helas) alas, to ela, a term in music. Panurge's meaning is, that in their present imminent danger of death, their alas's would do no good.

III

my feet stand higher than my head. Would to heaven I were now with those good holy fathers bound for the council, whom we met this morning,[2] so godly, so fat, so merry, so plump, and comely. Holos, bolos, holas, holas, alas! This devilish wave (*mea culpa Deus*), I mean this wave of God,[3] will sink our vessel. Alas, Friar John, my father, my friend, confession. Here I am down on my knees; *confiteor;* your holy blessing. Come hither and be damned, thou pitiful devil, and help us, said Friar John,—who fell a-swearing and cursing like a tinker,—in the name of thirty legions of black devils, come; will you come! Do not let us swear at this time, said Panurge; holy father, my friend, do not swear, I beseech you; to-morrow as much as you please. Holos, holas, alas, our ship leaks. I drown, alas, alas! I will give eighteen hundred thousand crowns to any one that will set me on shore, all bewrayed and bedaubed as I am now. If ever there was a man in my country in the like pickle. *Confiteor*, alas! a word or two of testament or codicil at least. A thousand devils seize the cuckoldy cow-hearted mongrel, cried Friar John. Ods belly, art thou talking here of making thy will, now we are in danger, and it behoveth us to bestir our stumps lustily, or never? Wilt thou come, ho devil? Midshipman, my friend; O the rare lieutenant; here Gymnast, here on the poop. We are, by the mass, all beshit now, our light is out. This is hastening to the devil as fast as it can. Alas, bou, bou, bou, bou, bou, alas, alas, alas, alas, said Panurge, was it here we were

[2] Add in the ork, *dedans l'orque*. This confirms M. Duchat's assertion, that there was but one sail loaded with monks. See the first line of the preceding chapter.

[3] Panurge, who had just uttered a profane expression, corrects himself in complaisance to a friend, who represents to him the danger they are all in.

born to perish? Oh! ho! good people, I drown, I die. *Consummatum est.* I am sped—*Magna, gna, gna,* said Friar John. Fye upon him, how ugly the shitten howler looks. Boy, younker, see hoyh. Mind the pumps, or the devil choke thee. Hast thou hurt thyself? Zoons, here fasten it to one of these blocks. On this side, in the devil's name, hay —so my boy. Ah, Friar John, said Panurge, good ghostly father, dear friend, do not let us swear, you sin.. Oh ho, oh ho, be, be, be, bous, bous, bhous, I sink, I die, my friends. I die in charity with all the world. Farewell, *in manus.* Bohus, bohous, bhousow-auswaus. St Michael of Aure! St Nicholas! now, now or never, I here make you a solemn vow, and to our Saviour, that if you stand by me this time, I mean if you set me ashore out of this danger, I will build you a fine large little chapel or two, between Candé and Monsoreau,[4] where neither cow nor calf shall feed. Oh ho, oh ho. Above eighteen pailfuls or two of it are got down my gullet; bous, bhous, bhous, bhous, how damned bitter and salt it is! By the virtue, said Friar John, of the blood, the flesh, the belly, the head, if I hear thee again howling,[5]

[4] Panurge would say, a fine large chapel, or two little ones, but fear had disordered his sense. What he adds, viz., Where neither cow nor calf shall feed, alludes to the proverb:

'Entre Candé et Monsoreau
La ne paist brebis ne veau.'

Between Candé and Montsorrow,
There feeds nor sheep, nor calf, nor cow.

By this proverb we are informed that there is but a very small extent of land, and that too very barren, between the manor of Monsoreau and the village of Candé, which are only parted by the Vienne, and the sands on each side of that river.
[5] It runs thus in Rabelais, If I hear thee again pieping like a chicken, I will scratch thy back worse than a file.

thou cuckoldy cur, I will maul thee worse than any sea-wolf. Ods fish, why do not we take him up by the lugs and throw him overboard to the bottom of the sea? Here, sailor, ho honest fellow. Thus, thus, my friend, hold fast above. In truth here is a sad lightning and thundering; I think that all the devils are got loose; it is holiday with them; or else Madame Proserpine is in child's labour: all the devils dance a morrice.

CHAPTER XX

HOW THE PILOTS WERE FORSAKING THEIR SHIPS IN THE GREATEST STRESS OF WEATHER

OH, said Panurge, you sin, Friar John, my former crony! former, I say, for at this time I am no more, you are no more. It goes against my heart to tell it you : for I believe this swearing doth your spleen a great deal of good; as it is a great ease to a woodcleaver to cry hem at every blow; and as one who plays at nine pins is wonderfully helped, if, when he hath not thrown his bowl right, and is like to make a bad cast, some ingenious stander-by leans and screws his body half way about, on that side which the bowl should have took to hit the pin. Nevertheless you offend, my sweet friend. But what do you think of eating some kind of cabirotadoes?[1] Would not this

[1] Mind how our author drolls upon the name of this dish of meat, equivocating to that of the gods Cabiri; and how amidst a storm he brings in their priests, who were always miraculously preserved in storms at sea, how violent soever they were, says the commentator of Apollonius. These Cabiri were gods highly revered in Samothrace, as being the penates of those islanders. Cabir, in Syriac, signifies potent. Not only the priests belonging

secure us from this storm? I have read, that in a storm at sea no harm ever befel the ministers of the gods Cabiri, so much celebrated by Orpheus, Apollonius, Pherecides, Strabo, Pausanias, and Herodotus.[2] He doats, he raves, the poor devil! A thousand, a million, nay, a hundred millions of devils seize the hornified doddipole. Lend us a hand here, hoh, tiger, wouldst thou? Here, on the starboard side. Ods me, thou buffalo's head stuffed with relics, what ape's paternoster art thou muttering and chattering here between thy teeth? That devil of a sea-calf is the cause of all this storm, and is the only man who doth not lend a helping hand. By God, if I come near thee, I'll fetch thee out by the head and ears with a vengeance, and chastise thee like any tempestative devil. Here, mate, my lad, hold fast, till I have made a double knot. O brave boy! Would to heaven thou wert abbot of Talemouze, and that he that is were guardian of Croullay. Hold, brother Ponocrates, you will hurt yourself, man. Epistemon, pray thee stand off out of the hatchway. Methinks I saw the thunder fall there but just now. Con the ship, so ho—Mind your steerage. Well said, thus, thus, steady, keep her thus, get the longboat clear—

to the Cabiri, but all others of that sodality, were secure in time of storm, though the sea went never so high. As for the dish called cabirotades, or capilotades, according to Boyer, it is a French ragout of remnants of meat.

[2] I am afraid I shall punish the reader with puns. But it is the author's fault, not mine. Rabelais concludes this sentence with Herodotus (*Herodote*) and begins the next with *il radote*: he dotes. Can there be a more manifest pun than *Herodote* and *il radote*, to such as speak French right; nay, it is so plain, that the famous Menage tells us (under the word *radoter*) several have been induced, from this allusion of Rabelais, to believe that *radoter* properly signifies to tell stories as unlikely to be true, as many things seem to be that are related by the historian Herodotus.

steady. Ods fish, the beak-head is staved to pieces. Grumble, devils, fart, belch, shite, a turd on the wave. If this be weather, the devil is a ram. Nay, by God, a little more would have washed me clear away into the current. I think all the legions of devils hold here their provincial chapter, or are polling, canvassing, and wrangling for the election of a new rector. Starboard; well said. Take heed; have a care of your noddle, lad, in the devil's name. So ho, starboard, starboard. Be, be, be, bous, bous, bous, cried Panurge, bous, bous, be, be, be, bous, bous, I am lost. I see neither heaven nor earth; of the four elements we have here only fire and water left. Bou, bou, bou, bous, bous, bous. Would it were the pleasure of the worthy divine bounty, that I were at this present hour in the close at Seville, or at Innocent's, the pastry-cook, over against the painted wine vault at Chinon, though I were to strip to my doublet, and bake the petti-pasties myself.

Honest man, could not you throw me ashore? you can do a world of good things, they say. I give you all Salmigondinois, and my large shore full of whelks, cockles, and periwinkles, if, by your industry, I ever set foot on firm ground. Alas, alas, I drown. Harkee, my friends, since we cannot get safe into port, let us come to an anchor into some road, no matter whither. Drop all your anchors; let us be out of danger, I beseech you. Here, honest tar, get you into the chains, and heave the lead, if it please you. Let us know how many fathom water we are in. Sound, friend, in the Lord Harry's name. Let us know whether a man might here drink easily, without stooping. I am apt to believe one might. Helm a-lee, hoh, cried the pilot. Helm a-lee; a hand or two at the helm; about ships with her; helm a-lee, helm a-lee. Stand off from the leech of the

Chap. xx.] *Pantagruel*

sail. Hoh! belay, here make fast below; hoh, helm a-lee, lash sure the helm a-lee, and let her drive. Is it come to that? said Pantagruel: our good Saviour then help us. Let her lie under the sea, cried James Brahier, our chief mate, let her drive. To prayers, to prayers, let all think on their souls, and fall to prayers; nor hope to escape but by a miracle. Let us, said Panurge, make some good pious kind of vow: alas, alas, alas! bou, bou, be, be, be, bous, bous, bous, oho, oho, oho, oho, let us make a pilgrim: come, come, let every man club his penny towards it, come on. Here, here, on this side, said Friar John, in the devil's name. Let her drive, for the Lord's sake unhang the rudder: hoh, let her drive, let her drive, and let us drink, I say, of the best and most cheering; do you hear, steward, produce, exhibit; for, do you see? this and all the rest will as well go to the devil out of hand. A pox on that wind-broker Æolus, with his fluster-blusters. Sirrah, page, bring me here my drawer (for so he called his breviary); stay a little here, haul, friend, thus. Odzoons, here is a deal of hail and thunder to no purpose. Hold fast above, I pray you. When have we All Saints day? I believe it is the unholy holiday of all the devil's crew. Alas, said Panurge, Friar John damns himself here as black as buttermilk for the nonce. Oh what a good friend I lose in him. Alas, alas, this is another-gats bout than last year's. We are falling out of Scylla into Charybdis. Oho! I drown. *Confiteor;* one poor word or two by way of testament, Friar John, my ghostly father; good Mr Abstractor, my crony, my Achates, Xenomanes, my all. Alas, I drown; two words of testament here upon this ladder.

CHAPTER XXI

A CONTINUATION OF THE STORM, WITH A SHORT DISCOURSE ON THE SUBJECT OF MAKING TESTAMENTS AT SEA

To make one's last will, said Epistemon, at this time that we ought to bestir ourselves and help our seamen, on the penalty of being drowned, seems to me as idle and ridiculous a maggot as that of some of Cæsar's men, who, at their coming into the Gauls, were mightily busied in making wills and codicils; bemoaned their fortune, and the absence of their spouses and friends at Rome; when it was absolutely necessary for them to run to their arms, and use their utmost strength against Ariovistus, their enemy.

This also is to be as silly, as that jolt-headed loblolly of a carter, who, having laid his waggon fast in a slough, down on his marrow-bones, was calling on the strong-backed deity, Hercules, might and main, to help him at a dead lift, but all the while forgot to goad on his oxen, and lay his shoulder to the wheels, as it behoved him: as if a Lord have mercy upon us, alone, would have got his cart out of the mire.

What will it signify to make your will now? for either we shall come off or drown for it. If we escape, it will not signify a straw to us; for testaments are of no value or authority, but by the death of the testators. If we are drowned, will it not be drowned too? Prythee who will transmit it to the executors? Some kind wave will throw it ashore, like Ulysses, replied Panurge; and some king's daughter, going to fetch a walk in the fresco, on the evening, will find it, and take care to have it proved

Chap. xxi.] *Pantagruel*

and fulfilled; nay, and have some stately cenotaph erected to my memory, as Dido had to that of her good man Sichæus;[1] Æneas to Deiphobus,[2] upon the Trojan shore, near Rhœte; Andromache to Hector,[3] in the city of Buthrotus; Aristotle to Hermias and Eubulus;[4] the Athenians to the poet Euripides; the Romans to Drusus[5] in Germany, and to Alexander Severus,[6] their emperor, in the Gauls; Argentier to Callaischre;[7] Xenocrates to Lysidices;[8] Timares to his son Teleutagoras; Eupolis and Aristodice to their son Theotimus; Onestus to Timocles;[9] Callimachus to Sopolis, the son of Dioclides;[10] Catullus to his brother;[11] Statius to his father:[12] Germain of Brie to Hervé, the Breton tarpaulin.[13] Art thou mad, said

---

[1] Whence Rabelais had this, I know not. Perhaps he took for a cenotaph, the funeral pile which gave occasion to Dido to burn herself with the sacrifice she had been offering to the manes of Sichæus. See Justin. l. 18, c. 6.
[2] Æneid, l. 6, v. 505.
[3] Ibid. l. 3, v. 302.
[4] See Diogenes Laertius, in the Life of Aristotle.
[5] See Suetonius, in the Life of the Emperor Claudius.
[6] See Lampridius, in the Life of that Emperor.
[7] Read Callaischrus ; Καλλαίσχρος. He perishing at sea, the poets, doubtless well paid by his heirs, set themselves at work to make cenotaphs (honorary tombs) to his memory : two of which are extant, l. 3, of the Anthologia, c. 22. One by Leonidas, the other by Argentarius.
[8] Read, Xenocrites. See the Anthologia.
[9] See the Anthologia, l. 3, p. 366, Wechel's edition.
[10] See the epigram of Callimachus, Epigram, 22.
[11] See the 103rd epigram of Catullus.
[12] See the Sylvæ of Statius, l. 5, Epiced. 3.
[13] In the year 1512, on St Lawrence's day, there was off St Mahe, in Bretagne, a great sea fight between the French fleet and the English, who were above two to one in number of ships. [So says M. Duchat of the English.] The English seeing their admiral in danger, threw fire into that of France, commanded by Captain Hervé, a Breton. He, after having in vain endeavoured to save his ship, finding the loss of her inevitable, grappled with

Friar John, to run on at this rate? Help, here, in the name of five hundred thousand millions of cartloads of devils, help! may a shanker gnaw thy moustachios, and the three rows of pock-royals and cauliflowers cover thy bum and turd-barrel, instead of breeches and codpiece. Codsooks, our ship is almost overset. Ods death, how shall we clear her? it is well if she do not founder. What a devilish sea there runs! She will neither try nor hull; the sea will overtake her, so we shall never escape; the devil escape me. Then Pantagruel was heard to make a sad exclamation, saying, with a loud voice, Lord save us, we perish; yet not as we would have it, but Thy holy will be done. The Lord and the blessed Virgin be with us, said Panurge. Holos, alas, I drown; be, be, be, bous, be, bous, bous: in manus. Good heavens, send me some dolphin to carry me safe on shore, like a pretty little Arion. I shall make shift to sound the harp, if it be not unstrung. Let nineteen legions of black devils seize me, said Friar John, (The Lord be with us, whispered Panurge, between his chattering teeth). If I come down to thee, I will show thee to some purpose, that the badge of thy humanity dangles at a calf's breech, thou ragged, horned, cuckoldy booby:[14] mgna, mgnan,

the English ship, to which the wind having carried the fire, the Regent of England, and the Cordeliere (Franciscan nun) of France (so were the two ships called) perished with all that were on board. Germain de Brie, in Latin Germanus Brixeus, wrote, upon this occasion, a poem entituled Chordigera (*Cordeliere*), dedicated to Queen Anne, at the conclusion whereof he raised a cenotaph to the memory of Captain Hervé.

[14] Mr Motteux here not only mistakes the meaning of the word cornart (for how could Panurge be a cuckold that was not yet married?) but likewise the rest of the sentence. Rabelais' words are, *veau cocquart, cornart, escorné*. *Veau cornart* is an ignorant doctor, who, to procure the more respect, is never seen abroad without his tippet or hood (*cornette*, in French) to show he

mgnan: come hither and help us, thou great weeping calf, or may thirty millions of devils leap on thee. Wilt thou come, sea-calf? Fie! how ugly the howling whelp looks. What, always the same ditty? Come on now, my bonny drawer. This he said, opening his breviary. Come forward, thou and I must be somewhat serious for a while; let me peruse thee stiffly. *Beatus vir qui non abiit.* Pshaw, I know all this by heart; let us see the legend of Mons. St Nicholas.

Horrida tempestas montem turbavit acutum.

Tempeste[15] was a mighty flogger of lads, at Montaigu College. If pedants be damned for whipping poor little innocent wretches, their scholars, he is, upon my honour, by this time fixed within Ixion's wheel, lashing the crop-eared, bob-tailed cur that gives it motion. If they are saved for having whipped innocent lads, he ought to be above the—[16]

CHAPTER XXII

AN END OF THE STORM

SHORE, shore! cried Pantagruel. Land ho, my friend, I see land! Pluck up a good spirit,[1] boys, it is within

is graduated; *veau escorné*, an arrant scrub, who has, by his base pranks, already loaded himself with contempt and scorn ; *escorno*, in Italian, from whence Rabelais borrows it.

[15] Anthony Tempeste, doctor of Paris, principal of Montaigu College, where his picture is still to be seen. Eutrapel's Tales, ch. 26. The Latin verse alludes to this of Horace.

'Horrida tempestas cœlum contraxit et imbres.'

[16] The period interrupted by Pantagruel's crying out he saw land.

[1] In the original, *couraige de brebis:* on with a sheep's courage. The nearer sheep draw to the fold, the more they bleat. [Com-

a-kenning. So! we are not far from a port.—I see the sky clearing up to the northwards.—Look to the south-east! Courage, my hearts, said the pilot; now she will bear the hullock of a sail: the sea is much smoother; some hands aloft to the main-top. Put the helm a-weather. Steady! steady! Haul your after mizen bowlings. Haul, haul, haul! Thus, thus, and no near. Mind your steering; bring your main tack aboard. Clear your sheets; clear your bowlings; port, port. Helm a-lee. Now to the sheet on the starboard side, thou son of a whore. Thou art mightily pleased, honest fellow, quoth Friar John, with hearing make mention of thy mother. Luff, luff, cried the quartermaster that conned the ship, keep her full, luff the helm. Luff it is, answered the steersman. Keep her thus. Get the bonnets fixed. Steady, steady.

That is well said, said Friar John; now, this is something like a tansey. Come, come, come children, be nimble. Good. Luff, luff, thus. Helm a-weather. That is well said and thought on. Methinks the storm is almost over. It was high time, faith: however, the Lord be thanked. Our devils begin to scamper. Out with all your sails. Hoist your sails. Hoist. That is spoke like a man, hoist, hoist. Here, a God's name, honest Ponocrates; thou art a lusty fornicator; the whoreson will get none but boys. Eusthenes, thou art a notable fellow. Run up to the fore-top-sail. Thus, thus. Well said, i'faith; thus, thus. I dare not fear anything all this while, for it is holiday. Vea, vea, vea! huzza! This shout of the seamen is not amiss, and pleases me, for it is holiday. Keep her full thus. Good. Cheer up, my merry mates, all, cried out Epistemon; I see already

pare Grangousier's encouragement to Gargamelle, Bk. 1. cap. vi.]

Castor on the right.² Be, be, bous, bous, bous, said Panurge, I am much afraid it is the bitch Helen. It is truly Mixarchagenas,³ returned Epistemon, if thou likest better that denomination, which the Argives give him. Ho, ho! I see land too: let her bear in with the harbour: I see a good many people on the beach: I see a light on an obeliscolychny. Shorten your sails, said the pilot; fetch the sounding line; we must double that point of land, and mind the sands. We are clear of them, said the sailors. Soon after, Away she goes, quoth the pilot, and so doth the rest of our fleet: help came in good season.

By St John, said Panurge, this is spoke somewhat like: Oh the sweet word! there is the soul of music in it. Mgna, mgna, mgna, said Friar John; if ever thou taste a drop of it, let the devil's dam taste me, thou ballocky devil. Here, honest soul, here is a full sneaker[4] of the very best. Bring the flaggons: dost hear, Gymnast? and that same large pasty jambic, or gammonic, even as you will have it. Take heed you pilot her in right.

Cheer up, cried out Pantagruel; cheer up, my boys: let us be ourselves again. Do you see yonder, close by our ship, two barks, three sloops, five ships, eight pinks, four yawls, and six frigates, making towards us, sent by the good people of the neighbouring island to our relief? But who is this Ucalegon below, that cried, and makes such a sad moan? Were it not that I hold the mast firmly with both my hands, and keep it straighter than two hundred

---

[2] See Pliny, l. 2, c. 37, and the Scaligerana, at the word *Noctilucæ*.

[3] Read Mixarchagevas; for that is the true reading. See Plutarch, problem 23, question 63.

[4] Rabelais uses our English word tankard, but spells it tanquart.

tacklings—I would— It is, said Friar John, that poor devil, Panurge, who is troubled with a calf's ague; he quakes for fear when his belly is full. If, said Pantagruel, he hath been afraid during this dreadful hurricane and dangerous storm, provided he hath done his part like a man, I do not value him a jot the less for it. For as, to fear in all encounters, is the mark of a heavy and cowardly heart; as Agamemnon did, who, for that reason, is ignominiously taxed by Achilles with having dog's eyes, and a stag's heart:[5] so, not to fear when the case is evidently dreadful, is a sign of want or smallness of judgment. Now, if anything ought to be feared in this life, next to offending God, I will not say it is death. I will not meddle with the disputes of Socrates and the academics, that death of itself is neither bad nor to be feared; but, I will affirm, that this kind of shipwreck is to be feared, or nothing is. For, as Homer saith, it is a grievous, dreadful, and unnatural thing, to perish at sea. And, indeed, Æneas, in the storm that took his fleet near Sicily, was grieved that he had not died by the hand of the brave Diomedes; and said that those were three, nay four times happy, who perished in the conflagration at Troy. No man here hath lost his life, the Lord our Saviour be eternally praised for it: but in truth here is a ship sadly out of order. Well, we must take care to have the damage repaired. Take heed we do not run a-ground and bulge her.

[5] Iliad 1st.

CHAPTER XXIII

HOW PANURGE PLAYED THE GOOD FELLOW WHEN THE STORM WAS OVER

WHAT cheer, ho, fore and aft? quoth Panurge. Oh ho! all is well, the storm is over. I beseech ye, be so kind as to let me be the first that is sent on shore; for I would by all means a little untruss a point. Shall I help you still? Here, let me see, I will coil this rope; I have plenty of courage, and of fear as little as may be. Give it me yonder, honest tar. No, no, I have not a bit of fear. Indeed, that same decumane wave, that took us fore and aft, somewhat altered my pulse. Down with your sails; well said. How now, Friar John? you do nothing. Is it time for us to drink now? Who can tell but St Martin's running footman[1] may still be hatching us some further mischief? Shall I come and help you again? Pork and peas choke me, if I do not heartily repent, though too late, not having followed the doctrine of the good philosopher, who tells us that to walk by the sea, and to navigate by the shore, are very safe and pleasant things: just as it is to go on foot, when we hold our horse by the bridle. Ha! ha! ha! by God all goes well. Shall I help you here too? Let me see, I will do this as it should be, or the devil is in it.

Epistemon, who had the inside of one of his hands all flayed and bloody, having held a tackling with might and main, hearing what Pantagruel had said, told him: You may believe, my lord,

[1] The Devil. The legend of St Martin assigns him the devil for a running footman on a certain occasion.

I had my share of fear as well as Panurge; yet I spared no pains in lending my helping hand. I considered, that since by fatal and unavoidable necessity, we must all die, it is the blessed will of God that we die this or that hour, and this or that kind of death: nevertheless we ought to implore, invoke, pray, beseech, and supplicate Him: but we must not stop there; it behoveth us also to use our endeavours on our side, and, as the holy writ saith, to co-operate with Him.

You know what C. Flaminius the consul said, when by Hannibal's policy he was penned up near the lake of Peruse, alias Thrasymene. Friends, said he to his soldiers, you must not hope to get out of this place barely by vows or prayers to the gods; no, it is by fortitude and strength we must escape and cut ourselves a way with the edge of our swords through the midst of our enemies.

Sallust likewise makes M. Portius Cato say this: The help of the gods is not obtained by idle vows and womanish complaints; it is by vigilance, labour, and repeated endeavours, that all things succeed according to our wishes and designs. If a man, in time of need and danger, is negligent, heartless, and lazy, in vain he implores the gods; they are then justly angry and incensed against him. The devil take me, said Friar John (I'll go his halves, quoth Panurge), if the close of Sevillé had not been all gathered, vintaged, gleaned, and destroyed, if I had only sung *contra hostium insidias* (matter of breviary) like all the rest of the monkish devils, and had not bestirred myself to save the vineyard as I did, dispatching the truant picaroons of Lerné with the staff of the cross.

Let her sink or swim a God's name, said

Panurge, all's one to Friar John; he doth nothing; his name is Friar John Do-little;[2] for all he sees me here sweating and puffing to help with all my might this honest tar, first of the name.—Hark you me, dear soul, a word with you;—but pray be not angry. How thick do you judge the planks of our ship to be? Some two good inches and upwards, returned the pilot; don't fear. Odskilderkins, said Panurge, it seems then we are within two fingers' breadth of damnation.

Is this one of the nine comforts of matrimony?[3] Ah, dear soul, you do well to measure the danger by the yard of fear. For my part, I have none on't; my name is William Dreadnought. As for my heart, I have more than enough on't; I mean none of your sheep's heart; but of wolf's heart;[4] the courage of a bravo. By the pavilion of Mars, I fear nothing but danger.

[2] In opposition to Panurge, whose name comes from factotum, do-all.

[3] A pleasant comparison between a man, however lucky in marrying, and another that is embarked, and on the sea; however good the ship be he has under him, yet is he not sure he shall not be cast away.

He that in wedlock (twice) ventures his carcase
(Twice) ventures a drowning, and faith that is a hard case,

says a merry poet. A small book of the *Fifteen Comforts of Matrimony*, attributed to Antoine de la Sale, was several times reprinted in the sixteenth century.

[4] Forced courage; for a wolf never turns head to fight, but when he cannot run away with his prey.

CHAPTER XXIV

HOW PANURGE WAS SAID TO HAVE BEEN AFRAID WITHOUT REASON DURING THE STORM

GOOD morrow, gentlemen, said Panurge, good morrow to you all: you are in very good health, thanks to heaven and yourselves: you are all heartily welcome, and in good time. Let us go on shore.—Here, cockswain, get the ladder over the gunnel; man the sides: man the pinnace, and get her by the ship's side. Shall I lend you a hand here? I am stark mad for want of business, and would work like any two yokes of oxen. Truly this is a fine place, and these look like a very good people. Children, do you want me still in anything? do not spare the sweat of my body, for God's sake. Adam—that is man—was made to labour and work, as the birds were made to fly. Our Lord's will is, that we get our bread with the sweat of our brows, not idling and doing nothing, like this tatterdamallion of a monk here, this Friar Jack, who is fain to drink to hearten himself up, and dies for fear.—Rare weather.— I now find the answer of Anacharsis, the noble philosopher, very proper: being asked what ship he reckoned the safest? he replied, That which is in the harbour. He made yet a better repartee, said Pantagruel, when somebody inquiring which is greater, the number of the living or that of the dead? he asked them, amongst which of the two they reckoned those that are at sea? ingeniously implying, that they are continually in danger of death, dying alive, and living die. Portius Cato also said, that there were but three things of which he would repent; if ever he had trusted his wife with his secret, if he had idled away a day, and if he had ever gone by sea to a place which he could visit by land. By this dignified frock of mine, said Friar John to Panurge, friend, thou hast been afraid during the storm, without cause or reason: for thou wert not born to be drowned, but rather to be hanged, and exalted in the air, or to be roasted in the midst of a jolly bonfire.[1] My lord, would you have a good cloak for the rain; leave me off your wolf and badger-skin mantle: let Panurge but be flayed, and cover yourself with his hide. But do not come near the fire, nor near your blacksmith's forges, a God's name; for in a moment you will see it in ashes. Yet be as long as you please in the rain, snow, hail, nay, by the devil's maker, throw yourself, or dive down to the very bottom of the water, I'll engage you'll not be wet at all. Have some winter boots made of it, they'll never take in a drop of water: make bladders of it to lay under boys, to teach them to swim, instead of corks, and they will learn without the least danger. His skin, then, said Pantagruel, should be like the herb called true maiden's hair, which never takes wet nor moistness, but still keeps dry, though you lay it at the bottom of the water as long as you please; and for that reason is called Adiantos.

Friend Panurge, said Friar John, I pray thee

[1] After bonfire, add, like a father. 'Pendu ou brulé comme ung père,' are Rabelais' words. M. Duchat tells us that Rabelais, by like a father, means like one of the Lutherans, or first reformers, who in France were denominated fathers (*pères*, in French), because in those days, praying in French (as they still do), most of their prayers begin with, Father everlasting (*Père eternel*).

never be afraid of water : thy life for mine thou art threatened with a contrary element. Ay, ay, replied Panurge, but the devil's cooks dote sometimes, and are apt to make horrid blunders as well as others : often putting to boil in water, what was designed to be roasted on the fire : like the head cooks of our kitchen, who often lard partridges, queests, and stock-doves, with intent to roast them, one would think ; but it happens sometimes, that they even turn the partridges into the pot, to be boiled with cabbages, the queests with leek pottage, and the stock-doves with turnips. But hark you me, good friends, I protest before this noble company, that as for the chapel which I vowed to Mons. St Nicholas, between Candé and Monsoreau, I honestly mean that it shall be a chapel of rose-water,[2] which shall be where neither cow nor calf shall be fed : for between you and I, I intend to throw it to the bottom of the water. Here is a rare rogue for you, said Eusthenes : here is a pure rogue, a rogue in grain, a rogue enough, a rogue and a half. He is resolved to make good the Lombardic proverb, *Passato el pericolo, gabbato el santo.*[3]

> The devil was sick, the devil a monk would be ;
> The devil was well, the devil a monk was he.

ON CHAP. XVIII. AND THE SIX FOLLOWING.—These chapters contain a description of a dreadful storm, which Pantagruel's fleet met with. It began immediately after they came up with

---

[2] A distilling chapel, that is, a limbeck. The word *chapelle*, in the signification of an alembick, is to be found in Nicot and Oudin.

[3] The danger once over, the saint is despised.

Chap. xxiv.] *Pantagruel*

nine sail laden with all sorts of monks, who were going to the Council of Chesil, to sift and garble some articles of faith against the new heretics.

This council can be no other but that of Trent, then sitting, in which such sort of articles were framed. The word chesil, by the transposition of a single letter, makes the Hebrew word *chelis*, three; whence comes *chelism*, thirty, which is *trente* in French: and, if you will keep to the number *chelis*, or three, the name of that town, which is *Tridentum* in Latin, is partly made up of it; so there is no doubt but in one of those senses the author had a mind to let us know his meaning.

The storm in these chapters is undoubtedly the cruel persecution that was raised in France in the reign of Henry II. It began in 1548, by a kind of inquisition to prosecute the Lutherans. These are Du Tillet's words about it. It was ordered that the judges should meet in an extraordinary manner at Paris, to take particular cognisance of the cases of the heretics. Some wretches suffered cruel punishment, inflicted by that assembly with the utmost rigour.

During that storm Pantagruel shows an heroic steadfastness and constancy of mind; Friar John an undaunted courage, and a great activity; all Pantagruel's household do their best to save the ship and help one another: Panurge alone sits on his tail upon deck, weeping and howling, and says a thousand ridiculous things suggested to him by his fear; sometimes he wishes himself with the blessed fathers, whom they met steering their course for the Council of Chesil: presently he proves as great a milksop as most of his brother deists do on such occasions, and is most mightily godly; then he is for making his will. In short, nothing can be more unaccountable than the vows, wishes, and moans of that maudling coward, till the storm abates, and the fleet comes in sight of the island of the Macreons. Then he plays the good fellow, and is as busy as any six, seeming as resolute and active as he was fearful and unmanly before.

The storm begins just as soon as they have been met by monks; mention is made in it of the thunder's falling on a part of the ship; which may mean the ecclesiastical censures, and the Pope's thunderbolts: then, when the storm abates, Friar John says, our devils began to scamper. I will show that by devils Rabelais has meant the monks, and persecuting tempters of the church of Rome. As for Panurge's seeming a Papist in the midst of the storm, it gave us exactly his character; for he was doubtless ready enough to make all the grimaces of a rank Papist in the midst of the persecution; though, as soon as it was past, he laughed at St Nicholas, the water saint, to whom he had promised a chapel, if he escaped, between Candé and Monsoreau, where neither cow nor calf should feed. The word chapel is equivocal in French, signifying a limbeck ; so he says he will throw one in the river, doubtless that which drowns up all the ground between those two towns, and thus he means to fulfil his vow. Perhaps this is also designed to ridicule the vows and behaviour of seamen in a storm.

Pantagruel's holding the mast of the ship tight with both his hands all the while, by the skipper's advice, implies, that as the family of Navarre, and particularly Anthony of Bourbon, was best able to protect the great ones, who were embarked together for a reformation, it was fit he should do it with his power ; and accordingly Du Tillet tells us, that none but *miserables* (poor wretches) suffered. If anyone will say, that perhaps Rabelais did not in this voyage mean any particular persons, I hope at least they will grant he has admirably described the different behaviour of most men in danger, and chiefly in persecuting times.

CHAPTER XXV

HOW, AFTER THE STORM, PANTAGRUEL WENT ON SHORE IN THE ISLANDS OF THE MACREONS

IMMEDIATELY after, he went ashore at the port of an island which they called the island of the Macreons.[1]

[1] Some will have this to be Great Britain ; others will have it take in likewise the province of Bretagne, in France, wherein, as well as in England, the tales of Eutrapel, ch. 33, observe there are still to be seen a world of ancient monuments and singular rarities, as are mentioned in this chapter. The translator of Rabelais into English is of opinion it means England, and no other country ; but, although it is certain that people live there to a very great age, yet that does not determine the question. The sole reason is, those who in Edward the Sixth's time, to avoid persecution in France, fled into England, found the secret there to prolong a life which they had not failed to have lost in their own country. Again, literally taken, may it not mean the Isle of Wight, which, in the Romance of Perceforest, is called the Isle of Life ? and that romance, which extends its heroes' lives to

Chap. xxv.] *Pantagruel*

The good people of the place received us very honourably. An old Macrobius (so they called their eldest elderman) desired Pantagruel to come to the town-house to refresh himself, and eat something: but he would not budge a foot from the mole till all his men were landed. After he had seen them, he gave order that they should all change clothes, and that some of all the stores in the fleet should be brought on shore, that every ship's crew might live well: which was accordingly done, and God wot how well they all toped and caroused. The people of the place brought them provisions in abundance. The Pantagruelists returned them more: as the truth is theirs were somewhat damaged by the late storm. When they had well-stuffed the insides of their doublets, Pantagruel desired every one to lend their help to repair the damage ; which they readily did. It was easy enough to refit there ; for all the inhabitants of the island were carpenters, and all such handicrafts as are seen in the arsenal at Venice. None but the largest island was inhabited, having three ports and ten parishes ; the rest being overrun with wood, and desert, much like the forest of Arden. We entreated the old Macrobius to show us what was worth seeing in the island ; which he did ; and in the desert and dark forest we discovered several old ruined temples, obelisks, pyramids, monuments, and ancient tombs, with divers inscriptions and epitaphs ; some of them in hieroglyphic characters ; others in the Ionic dialect ; some in the Arabic, Agarenian, Sclavonian, and other tongues ; of which Epistemon took an exact account. In the

many ages, makes them live so long for no other reason, but on account of his assigning them that island to reside in ; from whence they are at last forced to be taken, in order to put them into a possibility of dying.

interim, Panurge said to Friar John, is this the island of the Macreons? Macreon signifies in Greek an old man, or one much stricken in years. What is that to me, said Friar John, how can I help it? I was not in the country when they christened it. Now I think on it, quoth Panurge, I believe the name of mackerel (that is a bawd in French) was derived from it: for procuring is the province of the old, as buttock-riggling is that of the young. Therefore I do not know but this may be the bawdy or Mackerel Island, the original and prototype of the island of that name at Paris. Let us go and dredge for cock-oysters. Old Macrobius asked, in the Ionic tongue, How, and by what industry and labour, Pantagruel got to their port that day, there having been such blustering weather, and such a dreadful storm at sea. Pantagruel told him that the Almighty Preserver of mankind had regarded the simplicity and sincere affection of his servants, who did not travel for gain or sordid profit; the sole design of their voyage being a studious desire to know, see, and visit the Oracle of Bacbuc, and take the word of the Bottle upon some difficulties offered by one of the company: nevertheless this had not been without great affliction, and evident danger of shipwreck. After that, he asked him what he judged to be the cause of that terrible tempest, and if the adjacent seas were thus frequently subject to storms; as in the ocean are the Ratz of Sammaieu,[2] Maumusson,[3] and in the Mediterranean Sea the

[2] In Bretagne, a dangerous passage, because of the rapidity of the currents there.
[3] The canal so called, is likewise very dangerous, on account of the numberless banks and quicksands there, which are moving up and down continually. It is two leagues long, and one broad, and separates the isles of Alvert and Oleron.

gulph of Sataly,[4] Montargentan,[5] Piombino, Capo Melio, in Laconia,[6] the Straits of Gibraltar, Faro di Messina, and others.

CHAPTER XXVI

HOW THE GOOD MACROBIUS GAVE US AN ACCOUNT OF THE MANSION AND DECEASE OF THE HEROES

THE good Macrobius then answered,—Friendly strangers, this island is one of the Sporades ; not of your Sporades that lie in the Carpathian Sea, but one of the Sporades of the ocean: in former times rich, frequented, wealthy, populous, full of traffic, and in the dominions of the rulers of Britain, but now, by course of time, and in these latter ages of the world, poor and desolate, as you see. In this dark forest, above seventy-eight thousand Persian leagues in compass, is the dwelling-place of the demons and heroes, that are grown old, and we believe that some one of them died yesterday ; since the comet, which we saw for three days before together, shines no more: and now it is likely, that at his death there arose this horrible storm ; for while they are

[4] Anciently Attalia, in Pamphylia. It is still very dangerous, but nothing near so much as it was heretofore, by reason of a sea-monster, which, if we believe Villamont in his travels, was wont to infest that part of the sea, till the Empress St Helena, in her return from Jerusalem, from whence she was bringing the nails with which our Saviour was fastened to the cross, threw one of them into the waves there ; which has rendered that monster so gentle, that it is but seldom he nowadays meddles with any of the ships that come near the place of his abode. See Villamont's Voyages, l. 2, c. 5.
[5] Porto de Telamone, in Tuscano.
[6] Cabo de Malvasia ; anciently Melleum Promontorium.

alive all happiness attends both this and the adjacent islands, and a settled calm and serenity. At the death of every one of them, we commonly hear in the forest, loud and mournful groans, and the whole land is infested with pestilence, earthquakes, inundations, and other calamities ; the air with fogs and obscurity, and the sea with storms and hurricanes. What you tell us, seems to me likely enough, said Pantagruel. For, as a torch or candle, as long as it hath life enough and is lighted, shines round about, disperses its light, delights those that are near it, yields them its service and clearness, and never causes any pain or displeasure ; but as soon as it is extinguished, its smoke and evaporation infect the air, offend the by-standers, and are noisome to all: so, as long as those noble and renowned souls inhabit their bodies, peace, profit, pleasure, and honour never leave the places where they abide ; but as soon as they leave them, both the continent and adjacent islands are annoyed with great commotions ; in the air fogs, darkness, thunder, hail ; tremblings, pulsations, agitations of the earth ; storms and hurricanes at sea ; together with sad complaints amongst the people, broaching of religions, changes in governments, and ruins of commonwealths.

We had a sad instance of this lately, said Eustemon, at the death of that valiant and learned knight, William du Bellay ; during whose life France enjoyed so much happiness, that all the rest of the world looked upon it with envy, sought friendship with it, and stood in awe of its power ; but now, after his decease, it hath for a considerable time been the scorn of the rest of the world.[1]

[1] Soon after the death of William du Bellay, the Emperor Charles V. forced the Duke of Cleves to depart from the alliance he had made with France ; and as Francis I. was generally

Pantagruel

Thus, said Pantagruel, Anchises being dead at Drepani, in Sicily, Æneas was dreadfully tossed and endangered by a storm; and perhaps for the same reason, Herod, that tyrant and cruel King of Judea, finding himself near the passage of a horrid kind of death,—for he died of a phthiriasis, devoured by vermin and lice; as before him died L. Sylla, Pherecydes, the Syrian, the preceptor of Pythagoras, the Greek poet Alcmæon, and others,—and foreseeing that the Jews would make bonfires at his death, caused all the nobles and magistrates to be summoned to his seraglio, out of all the cities, towns, and castles of Judea, fraudulently pretending that he had some things of moment to impart to them. They made their personal appearance; whereupon he caused them all to be shut up in the hippodrome of the seraglio; then said to his sister Salome, and Alexander her husband: I am certain that the Jews will rejoice at my death; but if you will observe and perform what I tell you, my funeral shall be honourable, and there will be a general mourning. As soon as you see me dead, let my guards, to whom I have already given strict commission to that purpose, kill all the noblemen and magistrates that are secured in the hippodrome. By these means, all Jewry shall, in spite of themselves, be obliged to

---

reckoned to have brought into the Mediterranean, and even before the Castle of Nice, the corsair Barbarossa, the Emperor, at that time almighty in Germany, not only hindered the ambassadors, sent by the King to the diet, from setting foot within the empire, but was going to hang a herald they had dispatched before for passports; so absolute was the Emperor in Germany, after the death of M. de Langey, who, being present in all the diets, never failed to support the glory and interests of France, by representing to the Germans, in those assemblies, their true interest, and the measures they were to take to preserve their liberty. See Sleidan, l. 15.

mourn and lament, and foreigners will imagine it to be for my death, as if some heroic soul had left her body. A desperate tyrant wished as much when he said, When I die, let earth and fire be mixed together; which was as good as to say, Let the whole world perish. Which saying the tyrant Nero altered, saying, While I live, as Suetonius affirms it. This detestable saying, of which Cicero, lib. *De Finib.* and Seneca, lib. 2, *De Clementia,* make mention, is ascribed to the Emperor Tiberius, by Dion Nicæus and Suidas.

CHAPTER XXVII

PANTAGRUEL'S DISCOURSE OF THE DECEASE OF HEROIC SOULS; AND OF THE DREADFUL PRODIGIES THAT HAPPENED BEFORE THE DEATH OF THE LATE LORD DE LANGEY

I WOULD not, continued Pantagruel, have missed the storm that hath thus disordered us, were I also to have missed the relation of these things told us by this good Macrobius. Neither am I unwilling to believe what he said of a comet that appears in the sky some days before such a decease. For some of those souls are so noble, so precious, and so heroic, that heaven gives us notice of their departing some days before it happens. And as a prudent physician, seeing by some symptoms that his patient draws towards his end, some days before, gives notice of it to his wife, children, kindred, and friends, that, in that little time he hath yet to live, they may admonish him to settle all things in his family, to tutor and instruct his children as much as he can, recommend his relict to his friends in her widowhood, and declare what he knows to be necessary about a provision for the orphans ; that he may not be surprised by death without making his will, and may take care of his soul and family : in the same manner the heavens, as it were, joyful for the approaching reception of those blessed souls, seem to make bonfires by those comets and blazing meteors, which they at the same time kindly design should prognosticate to us here, that in a few days one of these venerable souls is to leave her body, and this terrestrial globe. Not altogether unlike this was what was formerly done at Athens, by the judges of the Areopagus. For when they gave their verdict to cast or clear the culprits that were tried before them, they used certain notes according to the substance of the sentences ; by Θ, signifying sentence to death ;[1] by T, absolution ;[2] by A, ampliation[3] or a demur, when the case was not sufficiently examined. Thus having publicly set up those letters, they eased the relations and friends of the prisoners, and such others as desired to know their doom, of their doubts. Likewise by these comets, as in ætherial characters, the

[1] From the Greek Θανατος, death ; and it is to this signification of the theta (in the judgments passed by the Greeks) that this verse of Persius alludes. ' Et potis es vitio nigrum præfigere theta.'

[2] In Greek, τελέωσις.

[3] Rabelais follows the error of Erasmus, who had no correct copy of Asconius to go by. That grammarian says nothing absolutely of what we see here in Rabelais, and in the Adages of Erasmus, chil. 1, cent. 5, ch. 56 ; since A, according to him, is the mark of absolution, C, of condemnation, and the two letters N. L., *i.e.*, *non liquet*, denote ampliation.

heavens silently say to us, Make haste mortals, if you would know or learn of the blessed souls any thing concerning the public good, or your private interest; for their catastrophe is near, which being past, you will vainly wish for them afterwards.

The good-natured heavens still do more : and that mankind may be declared unworthy of the enjoyment of those renowned souls, they fright and astonish us with prodigies, monsters, and other foreboding signs, that thwart the order of nature.

Of this we had an instance several days before the decease of the heroic soul of the learned and valiant Chevalier de Langey, of whom you have already spoken. I remember it, said Epistemon; and my heart still trembles within me, when I think on the many dreadful prodigies that we saw five or six days before he died. For the Lords D'Assier, Chemant, one-eyed Mailly, St Ayl, Villeneufve-la-Guyart, Master Gabriel, physician of Savillan, Rabelais, Cohuau, Massuau, Majorici, Bullou, Cercu, alias Bourguemaistre, Francis Proust, Ferron, Charles Girard, Francis Bourré, and many other friends and servants to the deceased, all dismayed, gazed on each other without uttering one word ; yet not without foreseeing that France would in a short time be deprived of a knight so accomplished, and necessary for its glory and protection, and that heaven claimed him again as its due. By the tufted tip of my cowl, cried Friar John, I am even resolved to become a scholar before I die. I have a pretty good head-piece of my own, you must confess. Now pray give me leave to ask you a civil question, Can these same heroes or demigods you talk of, die ? May I never be damned, if I was not so much a lobcock as to believe they had been immortal, like so many fine angels. Heaven forgive me ! but this most reverend father, Macrobius, tells us they die at last. Not all, returned Pantagruel.

The stoics held them all to be mortal, except one, who alone is immortal, impassible, invisible. Pindar plainly saith, that there is no more thread, that is to say, no more life, spun from the distaff and flax of the hard-hearted fates for the goddesses Hamadryades, than there is for those trees that are preserved by them, which are good, sturdy, downright oaks; whence they derived their original, according to the opinion of Callimachus, and Pausanias in Phoci. With whom concurs Martianus Capella. As for the demigods, fauns, satyrs, sylvans, hobgoblins, ægipanes, nymphs, heroes, and demons, several men have, from the total sum, which is the result of the diver ages calculated by Hesiod, reckoned their life to be 9720 years: that sum consisting of four special numbers orderly arising from one, the same added together, and multiplied by four every way, amounts to forty; these forties, being reduced into triangles by five times, make up the total of the aforesaid number. See Plutarch, in his book about the Cessation of Oracles.

This, said Friar John, is not matter of breviary; I may believe as little or as much of it as you and I please. I believe, said Pantagruel, that all intellectual souls are exempted from Atropos' scissors. They are all immortal, whether they be of angels, of demons, or human: yet I will tell you a story concerning this, that is very strange, but is written and affirmed by several learned historians.

CHAPTER XXVIII

HOW PANTAGRUEL RELATED A VERY SAD STORY OF THE DEATH OF THE HEROES

EPITHERSES, the father of Æmilian the rhetorician, sailing from Greece to Italy, in a ship freighted with divers goods and passengers, at night the wind failed them near the Echinades, some islands that lie between the Morea and Tunis, and the vessel was driven near Paxos. When they got thither, some of the passengers being asleep, others awake, the rest eating and drinking, a voice was heard that called aloud, Thamous! which cry surprised them all. This same Thamous was their pilot, an Egyptian by birth, but known by name only to some few travellers. The voice was heard a second time, calling Thamous! in a frightful tone; and none making answer, but trembling, and remaining silent, the voice was heard a third time, more dreadful than before.

This caused Thamous to answer: Here am I; what dost thou call me for? What wilt thou have me do? Then the voice, louder than before, bid him publish, when he should come to Palodes, that the great god Pan was dead.

Epitherses related that all the mariners and passengers, having heard this, were extremely amazed and frighted; and that consulting among themselves, whether they had best conceal or divulge what the voice had enjoined; Thamous said, his advice was, that if they happened to have a fair wind, they should proceed without mentioning a word of it, but if they chanced to be becalmed, he would publish what he had heard. Now when they were near Palodes, they had no wind, neither were they in any current. Thamous then getting up on the top of the ship's forecastle, and casting his eyes on the shore, said that he had been commanded to proclaim that the great god Pan was dead. The words were hardly out of his mouth, when deep groans, great lamentations, and doleful shrieks, not of one person, but of many together, were heard from the land.

The news of this—many being present—was soon spread at Rome; insomuch that Tiberius, who was then emperor, sent for this Thamous, and having heard him, gave credit to his words. And inquiring of the learned in his court, and at Rome, who was that Pan? he found by their relation that he was the son of Mercury and Penelope, as Herodotus and Cicero in his third book of the Nature of the Gods had written before.

For my part, I understand it of that great saviour of the faithful, who was shamefully put to death at Jerusalem, by the envy and wickedness of the doctors, priests, and monks of the Mosaic law. And methinks, my interpretation is not improper; for he may lawfully be said in the Greek tongue to be *Pan*, since he is our *all*. For all that we are, all that we live, all that we have, all that we hope, is him, by him, from him, and in him. He is the god Pan, the great shepherd, who, as the loving shepherd Corydon affirms, hath not only a tender love and affection for his sheep, but also for their shepherds. At his death, complaints, sighs, fears, and lamentations were spread through the whole fabric of the universe, whether heavens, land, sea or hell.

The time also concurs with this interpretation of mine: for this most good, most mighty Pan, our only Saviour, died near Jerusalem, during the reign of Tiberius Cæsar.

Pantagruel, having ended this discourse, remained silent, and full of contemplation. A little while after, we saw the tears flow out of his eyes[1] as big as ostrich's eggs. God take me presently, if I tell you one single syllable of a lie in the matter.

ON CHAPS. XXV. XXVI. XXVII. AND XXVIII.—The island of the Macreons, where the fleet went into harbour after the storm, signifies the island where men are long-lived. Its eldest elderman is named Macrobius, or Long-lived. We are told in the 26th chapter, that it was in the dominions of the ruler of Britain; consequently it was a safe port against the tempest of persecution, the reformation being openly professed at that time in England under King Edward VI. This causes Rabelais to make his persecuted fleet take shelter there, and to say that men lived long in that island; because none were put to death on account of their religion.

The ruins of temples, obelisks, pyramids, ancient tombs and monuments, which they see there, denote the decay, downfall, and ruin of Popery, unfrequented, and left in dismal solitude. The souls of the heroes, who are lodged in those ruined mansions, are the true Christians who had cast off the yoke of Popery, and of the blind worship of saints, many of them fabulous, to which the superstition of the Papists had made them raise temples, obelisks, and monuments, as formerly the heathens did to their false gods.

The old Macrobius says, that the death of one of those heroes had occasioned the storm. By which our author gives us to understand, that troubles and commotions are often raised in kingdoms at the death of those eminent persons who have governed them under their kings; and probably, he may have had a mind to mark the death of Margaret de Valois, Queen of Navarre, sister to King Francis I., which happened towards the latter end of the year 1549, about a year after the Lady Jane d'Albret, Princess of Navarre, had been married to Anthony de Bourbon, Duke of Vendôme, Rabelais' Pantagruel. That princess, who had always protected the reformers and the re-

---

[1] When before, l. 3, c. 2, Rabelais describes Pantagruel as the best little and great good man that ever girded a sword to his side, he seems to hint that the great qualities of that prince were mixed with abundance of others not so great. Here, he makes him weep, out of the constitutional softness of his temper, and the tenderness of his disposition.

formed, as has been observed in the preface to the first three books, was not less eminent for her piety, wit, learning, and virtue, than for her royal extraction.

CHAPER XXIX

HOW PANTAGRUEL SAILED BY THE SNEAKING ISLAND, WHERE SHROVETIDE REIGNED

THE jovial fleet being refitted and repaired, new stores taken in, the Macreons over and above satisfied and pleased with the money spent there by Pantagruel, our men in better humour than they used to be, if possible, we merrily put to sea the next day, near sunset, with a delicious fresh gale.

Xenomanes showed us afar off the Sneaking Island,[1] where reigned Shrovetide,[2] of whom Pantagruel had heard much talk formerly; for that reason he would gladly have seen him in person, had not Xenomanes advised him to the contrary: first, because this would have been much out of our way; and then for the lean cheer (*manger maigre*), which he told us was to be found at that prince's court, and indeed all over the island.

You can see nothing there for your money, said he, but a huge greedy-guts, a tall woundy swallower of

[1] *L'Isle de Tapinois*, in French, means neither more nor less than the habitation of the monks, which in ch. 46 of l. 3, and in the Prol. of l. 4, Rabelais calls *taupetiers*, and their churches *taupétieres*; properly holes which the moles root in the ground; because the monks are shut up therein like so many moles (*taupes*, in French, from *talpa*, a mole, in Latin). Lent is said to dwell in these monks' convents, where abstinence from flesh is supposed, and ought to reign.

[2] *Quaresme-prenant.*—Rabelais means the beginning of Lent.

hot wardens³ and muscles;⁴ a long-shanked mole-catcher;⁵ an overgrown bottler of hay;⁶ a mossy-chinned demi-giant, with a double shaven crown, of lantern breed;⁷ a very great loitering noddy-peaked youngster,⁸ banner-bearer to the fish-eating tribe,⁹ dictator of mustard land,¹⁰ flogger of little children,¹¹ calciner of ashes,¹² father and foster-father to physicians;¹³ swarming with pardons,¹⁴ indulgences

³ Grey peas, in the original.
⁴ Rabelais rather means herrings; his expression is *ung grand cacquerotier* (not *cacquerolier*). Now *cacquerotier* is *cacqueruptier*; one that makes ruptures in cags (or barrels) of herrings, which in time of Lent the cloistral folks are often doing, because it is a great article of their subsistence.
⁵ Lent is the chief season of the whole year for mole-catching.
⁶ Hay beginning to be scarce in Lent, there is much of it sold by bottles, or trusses.
⁷ Lent is mossy, or downy-chinned, because it has not been long on the footing it now is. Demi-giant, because of its length. Of lantern-breed, and with shaven crown, because Lent was first established by the ecclesiastics, whom Rabelais elsewhere calls lanterniers.
⁸ *Bien grand lanternier*, in French, and that is all. On which word M. Duchat observes : Lent makes fools of (*lanterne*) those that keep it; and furthermore, as there are in Lent many nocturnal devotions, there are lanterns then to be seen trotting about in proportion.
⁹ Rabelais so calls the first day of Lent, because it precedes many other days on which fish is always eaten.
¹⁰ Because in many of the Lent dishes there is mustard used.
¹¹ Partly because fasting, and likewise a melancholy bilious diet, in Lent, is apt to make parents and schoolmasters very peevish to their children; and partly because during the holy week, the whipping part is redoubled among the cucullated gentry.
¹² Both on account of people's going to church on Ash Wednesday, to have ashes put on their heads; and also because in Lent there being plenty of brands on the hearths, then, or never, is the time to reduce the same to ashes, for lye to wash and cleanse their linen with.
¹³ In ch. 29 of l. 5. The food people use in Lent engenders the distempers of the whole year.
¹⁴ In time of Lent people run a *stationing* (*i.e.*, visiting the

and stations; a very honest man; a good catholic, and as brimful of devotion as ever he can hold.

He weeps the three-fourth parts of the day, and never assists at any weddings [15] but, give the devil his due, he is the most industrious larding-stick and skewer-maker [16] in forty kingdoms.

About six years ago, as I passed through Sneakingland, I brought home a large skewer [17] from thence, and made a present of it to the butchers of Quande, who set a great value upon them, and that for a cause. Some time or other, if ever we live to come back to our own country, I will show you two of them fastened on the great church porch. His usual food is pickled coats of mail,[18] salt helmets and head pieces, and salt salads; which sometimes make him piss pins and needles. As for his clothing, it is comical enough of conscience, both for make and colour; for he wears grey and cold,[19] nothing before, and nought behind, with the sleeves of the same.

churches), to gain the pardons and indulgencies each church abounds with.
[15] The church forbids marrying in Lent.
[16] In Lent, especially towards the end, butchers begin to busy themselves to make skewers; and cooks, laiding-sticks, and the like.
[17] It should be a gross of skewers (12 dozen). *J'en emportay une grosse.* Mr Motteux took grosse for the feminine of gros, large.
[18] The original has salt coats of mail, salt casks, salt morrions, and salt salads. On which M. Duchat's note is: all Lent food is high seasoned, and hard of digestion, and the name such meats go by, are those of *salades*, a sort of head-piece so-called; *morions*, another sort of head-piece, &c. (though this latter means, likewise, a small red delicious mushroom, called *morillios*, salted for winter use).
[19] Lent weather is generally grey and cold; but that is not all Rabelais means. His 'nothing before, nothing behind, and sleeves of the same,' alludes to Saint Francis' rule, enjoining the grey friars to wear no shirts, and to reiterate in time of Lent the discipline (whip) on their naked skin.

You will do me a kindness, said Pantagruel, if, as you have described his clothes, food, actions, and pastimes, you will also give me an account of his shape and disposition in all its parts. Prithee do, dear cod, said Friar John, for I have found him in my breviary, and then follows the moveable holy-days. With all my heart, answered Xenomanes; we may chance to hear more of him as we touch at the Wild Island, the dominions of the squob Chitterlings, his enemies; against whom he is eternally at odds: and were it not for the help of the noble Carnival, their protector and good neighbour, this meagre-looking Shrovetide would long before this have made sad work among them, and rooted them out of their habitation. Are these same Chitterlings, said Friar John, male or female, angels, or mortals, women or maids? They are, replied Xenomanes, females in sex, mortal in condition, some of them maids, other not. The devil have me, said Friar John, if I be not for them. What a shameful disorder in nature, is it not, to make war against women? Let us go back, and hack the villain to pieces.—What! meddle with Shrovetide? cried Panurge, in the name of Belzebub, I am not yet so weary of my life. No, I am not yet so mad as that comes to. *Quid juris?* Suppose we should find ourselves pent up between the Chitterlings and Shrovetide? between the anvil and the hammers?[20] Shankers and buboes stand off! godzooks, let us make the best of our way, I bid you good night, sweet Mr Shrovetide; I recommend to you the Chitterlings, and pray don't forget the puddings.

[20] It is Lent (called by the translator Shrovetide), that is the striker and persecutor. The Chitterlings are the sufferers, the party struck and persecuted.

CHAPTER XXX

HOW SHROVETIDE IS ANATOMISED AND DESCRIBED BY XENOMANES

As for the inward parts of Shrovetide, said Xenomanes; his brain is (at least it was in my time) in bigness,[1] colours, substance, and strength, much like the left cod of a he hand-worm.

The ventricles of his said brain like an auger.
The worm-like excrescence, like a christmas-box.
The membranes, like a monk's cowl.
The funnel, like a mason's chisel.
The fornix, like a casket.
The glandula pinealis, like a bag-pipe.
The rete mirabile, like a gutter.
The dug-like processus, like a patch.
The tympanums, like a whirly-gig.
The rocky bones, like a goose wing.
The nape of the neck, like a paper lantern.
The nerves, like a pipkin.
The uvula, like a sackbut.
The palate, like a mitten.
The spittle, like a shuttle.
The almonds, like a telescope.
The bridge of his nose, like a wheelbarrow.
The head of the larynx, like a vintage basket.
The stomach, like a belt.
The pylorus, like a pitchfork.
The wind-pipe, like an oyster knife.
The throat, like a pincushion stuffed with oakum.
The lungs, like a prebend's fur gown.
The heart, like a cope.
The mediastine, like an earthen cup.
The pleura, like a crow's bill.
The arteries, like a watch-coat.
The midriff, like a montero-cap.
The liver, like a double-tongued mattock.
The veins, like a sash window.
The spleen, like a catcal.
The guts, like a trammel.
The gall, like a cooper's adze.
The entrails, like a gantlet.
The mesentery, like an abbot's mitre.
The hungry-gut, like a button.
The blind gut, like a breast-plate.
The colon like a bridle.
The arse-gut like a monk's leathern bottle.
The kidneys, like a trowel.
The loins, like a padlock.
The ureters, like a pot-hook.
The emulgent veins, like two gilliflowers.
The spermatic vessels, like a cully-mully-puff.
The parastata, like an inkpot.

[1] Whoever invented Lent, in Rabelais' opinion, had no great share of wisdom.

The bladder, like a stone-bow,
The neck, like a mill-clapper.
The mirach, or lower parts of the belly, like a high-crowned hat.
The siphach, or its inner rind, like a wooden cuff.
The muscles, like a pair of bellows.
The tendons, like a hawking-glove.
The ligaments like a tinker's budget.
The bones, like three-cornered cheese-cakes.
The marrow, like a wallet.
The cartilages, like a field tortoise (alias a mole).[2]
The glandules in the mouth, like a pruning-knife.
The animal spirits, like swingeing fisty-cuffs.
The blood-fermenting, like a multiplication of flirts on the nose.
The urine, like a fig-pecker.
The sperm, like a hundred tenpenny nails.

And his nurse told me, that being married to Midlent,[3] he only begot a good number of local adverbs, and certain double fasts.

His memory he had like a scarf.
His common sense, like a buzzing of bees.
His imagination, like the chime of a set of bells.
His thoughts, like a flight of starlings.
His conscience, like the unnestling of a parcel of young herons.
His deliberations, like a set of organs.
His repentance,[4] like the carriage of a double cannon.
His undertakings, like the ballast of a galleon.
His understanding, like a torn breviary.
His notions, like snails crawling out of strawberries.
His will, like three filberts in a porringer.
His desire, like six trusses of hay.
His judgment, like a shoeing horn.
His discretion, like the truckle of a pulley.
His reason, like a cricket stool.

---

[2] Alias a mole, is of Mr Motteux's own putting in. Rabelais says, *tortue de guarriges:* which is a sort of land tortoise, nothing of the mole-kind.

[3] During the whole time of Lent, except on mid-Lent day, none, in the Romish communion, are allowed to marry. This suggested to Rabelais the thought of making a match between *la Mi-careme, i.e.,* Mid-lent, and *le Careme, i.e.,* Lent himself; and as Lent, in point of marriages, is barren, thence it comes that, from such a match, can proceed nothing but *local* adverbs, and certain double fasts: the fastings indeed beginning to increase after mid-Lent, and everybody desiring to know, *whither* they must go [*i.e.,* to what church]; *whence* [from what church] they must come; and lastly *through* what church they must pass to gain the indulgences.

[4] Slow, and attended with great preparatives.

CHAPTER XXXI

SHROVETIDE'S OUTWARD PARTS ANATOMISED

SHROVETIDE, continued Xenomanes, is somewhat better proportioned in his outward parts, excepting the seven ribs which he had over and above the common shape of men.

His toes, were like a virginal on an organ.
His nails, like a gimlet.
His feet, like a guitar.
His heels, like a club.
The soles of his feet, like a crucible.
His legs, like a hawk's lure.
His knees, like a joint-stool.
His thighs, like a steel cap.
His hips, like a wimble.
His belly as big as a tun, buttoned after the old fashion, with a girdle riding over the middle of his bosom.
His navel, like a cymbal.
His groin, like a minced pie.
His member, like a slipper.
His purse, like an oil cruet.
His genitals, like a joiner's planer.
Their erecting muscles, like a racket.
The perineum, like a flageolet.
His arse-hole, like crystal looking-glass.
His bum, like a harrow.
His loins, like a butter-pot.
The peritonæum, or caul, wherein his bowels were wrapped, like a billiard table.
His back, like an overgrown rack-bent cross-bow.
The vertebræ, or joints of his back-bone, like a bagpipe.
His ribs, like a spinning-wheel.
His brisket, like a canopy.
His shoulder-blades, like a mortar.
His breast, like a game at nine-pins.
His paps, like a horn-pipe.
His arm-pits, like a chequer.
His shoulders, like a hand-barrow.
His arms, like a riding-hood.
His fingers, like a brotherhood's andirons.
The fibulæ, or lesser bones of his legs, like a pair of stilts.
His shin-bones, like sickles.
His elbows, like a mouse trap.
His hands, like a curry-comb.
His neck, like a talboy.
His throat, like a felt to distil hippocras.
The knob in his throat, like a barrel, where hanged two brazen wens, very fine and harmonious, in the shape of an hour-glass.
His beard, like a lantern.
His chin, like a mushroom.
His ears, like a pair of gloves.
His nose, like a buskin.
His nostrils, like a forehead cloth.
His eyebrows, like a dripping-pan.
On his left brow was a mark of the shape and bigness of an urinal.
His eyelids, like a fiddle.
His eyes, like a comb-box.
His optic nerves, like a tinder-box.

His forehead, like a false cup.
His temples, like the cock of a cistern.
His cheeks, like a pair of wooden shoes.
His jaws, like a caudle cup.
His teeth, like a hunter's staff.[1] Of such colt's teeth as his, you will find one at Colonges les Royaux, in Poictou, and two at la Brosse,[2] in Xaintonge, on the cellar door.
His tongue, like a jew's harp.
His mouth, like a horse-cloth.
His face embroidered like a mule's pack saddle.
His head contrived like a still.
His skull, like a pouch.
The suturæ, or seams of his skull, like the annulus piscatoris, or the fisher's signet.[3]
His skin, like a gabardine.
His epidermis, or outward skin, like a bolting-cloth.
His hair, like a scrubbing-brush.
His fur, such as above said.

CHAPTER XXXII

A CONTINUATION OF SHROVETIDE'S COUNTENANCE, POSTURES, AND WAY OF BEHAVING

It is a wonderful thing, continued Xenomanes, to hear and see the state of Shrovetide.

If he chanced to spit, it was whole baskets full of goldfinches.
If he blowed his nose, it was pickled grigs.
When he wept, it was ducks with onion sauce.
When he trembled, it was large venison pasties.
When he did sweat, it was old ling with butter sauce.
When he belched, it was bushels of oysters.
When he sneezed, it was whole tubs full of mustard.
When he coughed, it was boxes of marmalade.
When he sobbed, it was watercresses.
When he yawned, it was pots full of pickled pease.
When he sighed, it was dried neats' tongues.
When he whistled, it was a whole scuttle full of green apes.

---

[1] Long, by much fasting.

[2] Boccace, in his Genealogy of the Gods, gives an historical account of some giant's teeth, two whereof were found at Drepano, in Sicily, fastened to the roof of our lady's church there, by two iron chains.

[3] The Pope's seal is doubtless meant by this.

When he snored, it was a whole pan full of fried beans.
When he frowned, it was soused hogs' feet.
When he spoke, it was coarse brown russet cloth; so little it was like crimson silk, with which Parisatis desired that the words of such as spoke to her son Cyrus, King of Persia, should be interwoven.
When he blowed, it was indulgence money-boxes.
When he winked, it was buttered buns.
When he grumbled, it was March cats.
When he nodded, it was iron-bound waggons.
When he made mouths, it was broken staves.
When he muttered, it was lawyer's revels.
When he hopped about, it was letters of licence and protections.
When he stepped back, it was sea cockle-shells.
When he slabbered, it was common ovens.
When he was hoarse, it was an entry of morrice-dancers.
When he broke wind, it was dun cows' leather spatterdashes.
When he funcked, it was washed-leather boots.
When he scratched himself it was new proclamations.
When he sung, it was peas in cods.
When he evacuated, it was mushrooms and morilles.
When he puffed, it was cabbages with oil, alias caules amb'olif.[4]
When he talked, it was the last year's snow.
When he dreamt, it was of a cock and a bull.
When he gave nothing, so much for the bearer.
If he thought to himself, it was whimsies and maggots.[5]
If he dozed, it was leases of lands.

What is yet more strange, he used to work doing nothing, and did nothing though he worked; caroused sleeping, and slept carousing, with his eyes open, like

[4] *Caules amb'olif* in Rabelais: on which M. Duchat says, cabbages or coleworts, with oil, is a common dish among the people of Gascony and Languedoc, who abound more with oil than butter. *Ambe d'oli*, *avec d'huile*, is the true Languedocian word, though Rabelais spells it otherwise.

[5] Rabelais says, 'S'il songeoit, c'etoient vits volans et rampans contre une muraille.' If he dreamt, it was whim-whams, flying in the air, or creeping up a wall. Such dreams prove sometimes dangerous, especially to the fair sex, as we learn from Beroalde de Verville's Moyen de Parvenir. Mademoiselle de Lescar, says he, dreaming one night that she was in a ploughed field, where they were sowing such things, she sprung out of bed on a sudden, and broke her arm in straining to catch one of the largest size, as it was falling to the ground. This she confessed to the king's surgeon.

the hares in our country, for fear of being taken naping by the Chitterlings, his inveterate enemies; biting he laughed, and laughing bit; eat nothing fasting, and fasted eating nothing; mumbled upon suspicion, drank by imagination, swam on the tops of high steeples, dried his clothes in ponds and rivers, fished in the air, and there used to catch decumane lobsters; hunted at the bottom of the herring-pond, and caught there ibices, stamboucs,[6] chamois, and other wild goats; used to put out the eyes of all the crows which he took sneakingly;[7] feared nothing but his own shadow, and the cries of fat kids;[8] used to gad abroad some days, like a truant schoolboy; played with the ropes of bells on festival days of saints;[9] made a mallet of his fist, and writ on hairy parchment[10]

[6] From the German word stein-bock, *i.e.*, rock or mountain goats, not unlike a roe-buck.

[7] In the Sneaking Island rather. En Tapinois. By the crows whose eyes he put out, may be meant the monks, who, the moment they make profession, are to see nothing but with their superior's eyes.

[8] Rabelais seems here to point at such monks as long to eat flesh, but are afraid of two things: first, lest their *companion* should betray them; secondly, lest the cries of the kid they have a mind to feast upon, should discover them. Monks usually go abroad in couples to visit the sick or to gather contributions for the sick, etc., etc., etc.

[9] This is far from what Rabelais means by, *se joüoit ès cordes des ceincts*. *Ceinct* (from *cinctus*, in Latin) is one that is girded about or *cinctured*, as the cordeliers are with a cord (*corde*, in French); with which cord or rope they play, and divert themselves, when they are within the walls of their convent; but abroad they trumpet forth its praises, and extol its merit and virtue to the skies. Some of the new editions of Rabelais have it indeed, *se joüoit ès cordes des saincts:* but Rabelais, even in that case, does not allude at all to church bell-ropes, but puns upon the coincidence of sounds between *cordes* and *corps des saincts*; as if he had said, they play with the bodies of saints and reliques, and make use of them as ways and means to get money.

[10] Took a great deal of pains to no purpose. To write with a pen on hairy parchment, is losing one's labour and time too.

prognostications and almanacks with his huge pincase.

Is that the gentleman ?' said Friar John: he is my man: this is the very fellow I looked for; I will send him a challenge immediately. This is, said Pantagruel, a strange and monstrous sort of man, if I may call him a man. You put me in mind of the form and looks of Amodunt and Dissonance. How were they made, said Friar John? May I be peeled like a raw onion, if ever I heard a word of them. I'll tell you what I read of them in some ancient apologues, replied Pantagruel.

Physis—that is to say Nature—at her first burthen begat Beauty and Harmony, without carnal copulation, being of herself very fruitful and prolific. Antiphysis, who ever was the antagonist of Nature, immediately, out of a malicious spite against her for her beautiful and honourable productions, in opposition begot Amodunt and Dissonance,[11] by copulation with Tellumon.[12] Their heads were round like

[11] Or Amodun, that is, says the Dutch scholiast, *sine modo*, from the primitive *a*, and the noun *modus*). A deformed, irregular, enormous thing. Thus, says our author, Amodunt and Discordance were the offspring of Antiphysis, *i.e.*, repugnant to, or against nature.

[12] As all the learned men I have hitherto consulted (says M. Duchat) on this pretended ancient apologue, have confessed themselves to be utterly ignorant who was the author of it: till such time as it is discovered, adds he, supposing it not to be Rabelais himself, which is very possible, I shall only take notice, after Varro, in the fragments of his *De Diis*; S. Augustin, l. 7, c. 23, of the City of God; and *Stuckius de Gentilium sacris, etc.*, Zurich edition, 1598; I say, I shall content myself with observing, that the Romans who made Tellumon one of their divinities, distinguished him from their deity Tellus in this, viz., the latter, Tellus, according to their theology, was the earth, as to conception, and Tellumon the same earth, as to production. [It is copied from Cœlius Calcagninus, *Opera*, Bâle, 1544, folio, page 622.]

a football, and not gently flatted on both sides, like the common shape of men. Their ears stood pricked up like those of asses; their eyes, as hard as those of crabs, and without brows, stared out of their heads, fixed on bones like those of our heels; their feet were round, like tennis-balls; their arms and hands turned backwards towards the shoulders; and they walked on their heads, continually turning round like a ball, topsy-turvey, heels over head.

Yet—as you know that ape esteem their young the handsomest in the world—Antiphysis extolled her offspring, and strove to prove, that their shape was handsomer and neater than that of the children of Physis: saying, that thus to have spherical heads and feet, and walk in a circular manner, wheeling round, had something in it of the perfection of the divine power, which makes all beings eternally turn in that fashion; and that to have our feet uppermost, and the head below them, was to imitate the Creator of the Universe; the hair being like the roots,[13] and the legs like the branches of man: for trees are better planted by their roots, than they could be by their branches. By this demonstration she implied, that her children were much more to be praised for being like a standing tree, than those of Physis, that made a figure of a tree upside down. As for the arms and hands, she pretended to prove that they were more justly turned towards the shoulders, because that part of the body ought not to be without defence, while the forepart is duly fenced with teeth, which a man can not only use to chew, but also to defend himself against those things that offend him. Thus, by the testimony and astipulation of the brute beasts, she drew all the witless herd and mob of fools into her

[13] Hardly intelligible. Read therefore as Rabelais wrote it; seeing the hair is in man like roots, and the legs like branches.

opinion, and was admired by all brainless and nonsensical people.

Since that, she begot the hypocritical tribes of eavesdropping dissemblers, superstitious pope-mongers, and priest-ridden bigots, the frantic Pistolets,[14] the demoniacal Calvins, impostors of Geneva,[15] the scrapers of benefices, apparitors with the devil in them, and other grinders and squeezers of livings, herb-stinking hermits,[16] gulli-gutted dunces of the cowl, church vermin, false zealots, devourers of the substance of men, and many more other deformed and ill-favoured monsters, made in spite of nature.

ON CHAPS. XXIX. XXX. XXXI. AND XXXII.—The Sneaking Island, which Pantagruel sailed by when he left that of the Macreons, is the dwelling of Shrovetide; by which we must understand Lent; for the ecclesiastics of the church of Rome begin their Lent before the laity; Shrove Tuesday is to them a day of humiliation, and is properly the time when men are shriven; our author calls it Quaresmeprenant, that is, the beginning of Quadragesima; in opposition to Mardigras, Shrove Tuesday. His design seems to expose the superstition of the Papists about Lent, and how much the practice of it, their way, shocked good sense; this made him run on for two or three chapters with an odd description of that ridiculous monster; and probably also to secure himself from the informations of his prying enemies, by that mixture of comical-seeming nonsense. For, as in the time of Lent, the superstition, grimaces, and hypocrisy of the Papists are most observable, and they look on it in a manner as the

---

[14] Under the name of Pistolets, Rabelais alludes to the black and white factions, a sort of Guelphs and Ghibellines, who, about the year 1300, sprung up in Italy, in the little town of Pistoia; which place likewise gave name afterwards to *(pistolets de poche)* pocket-pistols.

[15] Rabelais here avenges himself on Calvin, who had attacked him in his work, *De Scandalis*, published in 1550.

[16] *Enraigez putherbes*, it is in Rabelais; who does not thereby allude to any herb-stinking hermits, but to a certain monk, a great enemy to our author, whose name was Puy-Herbaut, calling himself Putherbeus; which, in old French, signifies a well, infected with herbs which make folks mad.

basis of the Christian religion, it would have been dangerous to have attacked them openly in point.

We find that the wise Xenomanes, one of Pantagruel's most experienced companions, advises him not to go where Shrovetide reigned, and says it would be much out of their way to the Oracle of Truth: that there is very lean cheer at this court; that he is a double-shaveling, banner-bearer to the fish-eating tribe, a flogger of little children, because Papists do penance, and whip themselves then; a calciner of ashes, because of Ash Wednesday; that he swarms with pardons, indulgences and stations; which makes the author say, in the 31st chapter, that Shrovetide being married to Mid-Lent, only begot a good number of local adverbs; that is, the stations, the churches, and chapels, whither the gulled mob must go, whence they come, and through which they must pass to gain the indulgences. We are told besides, that he never assists at weddings, but, give the devil his due, is the most industrious larding-stick and skewer-maker in forty kingdoms; because the butchers have then little else to do but to make some. Lent is an enemy to sausages and chitterlings, because, as well as all other flesh (I mean dead flesh), the people are forbid to taste of any then.

Friar John, always daring and hasty, is for destroying Lent; but Panurge, still fearful and wary, is not of his mind. Rabelais calls that island Tapinois; that word in French is generally used adverbially, with the proposition *en*, to signify an underhand way of acting. Some derive it from the Greek verb ταπεινόω, *humilem reddo*; and so it suits with the true design of Lent, to humble man and make him look sneakingly. Besides, Lent, sneaking in some years sooner, and others later, may also for that reason well be said to dwell in Tapinois. The ingenious fable of nature and her counterpart, is brought in to show that those who enjoin things that shock nature, as is the church of Rome's way of keeping Lent, have the confidence to make laws contrary to those of God, and the impudence to pretend to justify them by reason: so Rabelais tells us, that Antiphysis, the mother of Lent, begot also the eavesdropping dissemblers, superstitious pope-mongers and priest-ridden bigots, scrapers of benefices, mad herb-stinking hermits, gulli-gutted dunces of the cowl, church vermin, devourers of the substance of men, and other deformed and ill-favoured monsters, made in spite of nature.—*M*.

CHAPTER XXXIII

HOW PANTAGRUEL DISCOVERED A MONSTROUS PHYSETER, OR WHIRLPOOL, NEAR THE WILD ISLAND

About sunset, coming near the Wild Island, Pantagruel spied afar off a huge monstrous physeter,[1]—a sort of whale, which some call a whirlpool,—that came right upon us, neighing, snorting, raised above the waves higher than our main-tops, and spouting water all the way into the air, before itself, like a large river falling from a mountain: Pantagruel showed it to the pilot, and to Xenomanes.

By the pilot's advice, the trumpets of the Thalamege were sounded, to warn all the fleet to stand close, and look to themselves. This alarm being given, all the ships, galleons, frigates, brigantines,—according to their naval discipline,—placed themselves in the order and figure of a Greek upsilon (Ψ), the letter of Pythagoras, as cranes do in their flight; and like an acute angle,[2] in whose cone and basis the Thalamege placed herself ready to fight smartly. Friar John, with the grenadiers,[3] got on the forecastle.

Poor Panurge began to cry and howl worse than ever: Babillebabou, said he, shrugging up his shoulders, quivering all over with fear, there will be the devil upon dun. This is a worse business

---

[1] A species of whale, seen sometimes off the French coast, particularly towards Bayonne. The Greeks have named this fish Physeter, as much as to say, the blower, on account of the vast quantity of water it blows, as it were, out of a hole in the upper part of his head.

[2] This observation on the manner of the cranes flying, is Plutarch's in the treatise where he examines what creatures show most sense.

[3] Bombardiers in Rabelais.

than that the other day. Let us fly, let us fly; old Nick take me if it is not Leviathan, described by the noble prophet Moses, in the life of patient Job. It will swallow us all, ships and men, shag, rag, and bobtail, like a dose of pills. Alas, it will make no more of us, and we shall hold no more room in its hellish jaws, than a sugar-plum in an ass's throat. Look, look, it is upon us; let us wheel off, whip it away, and get ashore. I believe it is the very individual sea monster that was formerly designed to devour Andromeda: we are all undone. Oh! for some valiant Perseus here now to kill the dog.

I'll do its business presently, said Pantagruel; fear nothing. Odds-belly, said Panurge, remove the cause of my fear then. When the devil would you have a man be afraid, but when there is so much cause? If your destiny be such, as Friar John was saying a while ago,[4] replied Pantagruel, you ought to be afraid of Pyroeis, Eous, Æthon, and Phlegon, the sun's coach horses, that breathe fire at the nostrils; and not of physeters, that spout nothing but water at the snout and mouth. Their water will not endanger your life; and that element will rather save and preserve than hurt or endanger you.

Ay, ay, trust to that, and hang me, quoth Panurge: yours is a very pretty fancy. Odd's fish! did I not give you a sufficient account of the element's transmutation, and the blunders that are made of roast for boiled, and boiled for roast? Alas, here it is; I'll go hide myself below. We are dead men, every mother's son of us: I see upon our main-top

---

[4] In ch. 24, Friar John advises Panurge not so much to fear water as fire.

that merciless hag Atropos,[5] with her scissors new ground, ready to cut our threads all at one snip. Oh! how dreadful and abominable thou art; thou hast drowned a good many beside us, who never made their brags of it. Did it but spout good, brisk, dainty, delicious white wine, instead of this damned bitter salt water, one might better bear with it, and there would be some cause to be patient; like that English lord,[6] who being doomed to die, and had leave to choose what kind of death he would, chose to be drowned in a butt of malmsey. Here it is.—Oh, oh! devil! Sathanas! Leviathan! I cannot abide to look upon thee, thou art so abominably ugly.—Go to the bar, go take the pettifoggers.

CHAPTER XXXIV

HOW THE MONSTROUS PHYSETER WAS SLAIN BY PANTAGRUEL

THE physeter, coming between the ships and the galleons, threw water by whole tuns upon them, as if it had been the cataracts of the Nile in Ethiopia.

[5] The physeter, which Panurge's fear represented to him as lifting up its head higher than the main-top.
[6] George Duke of Clarence, whom his brother, Edward IV., King of England, put to that sort of death in Feb., 1477, or, according to the Roman calendar, 1478, through a conceit that Merlin's prophecies were relative to the Duke of Clarence, as the person that would one day deprive his (the King's) children of the crown. [Lanquet's *Epitome of Chronicles*, 1559 (under date 1478), says, 'George Duke of Clarence, brother to King Edward of England, was secretly put to death, being drowned in a barrel of malmsey within the Tower of London.']

On the other side, arrows, darts, gleaves, javelins, spears, harping-irons, and partizans, flew upon it like hail. Friar John did not spare himself in it. Panurge was half dead for fear. The artillery roared and thundered like mad, and seemed to gall it in good earnest, but did but little good: for the great iron and brass cannon-shot, entering its skin, seemed to melt like tiles in the sun.

Pantagruel then, considering the weight and exigency of the matter, stretched out his arms, and showed what he could do. You tell us, and it is recorded, that Commodus, the Roman emperor, could shoot with a bow so dexterously, that at a good distance he would let fly an arrow through a child's fingers, and never touch them. You also tell us of an Indian archer, who lived when Alexander the Great conquered India, and was so skilful in drawing the bow, that at a considerable distance he would shoot his arrows through a ring, though they were three cubits long, and their iron so large and weighty, that with them he used to pierce steel cutlasses, thick shields, steel breast-plates, and generally what he did hit, how firm, resisting, hard, and strong soever it were. You also tell us wonders of the industry of the ancient Franks, who were preferred to all others in point of archery; and when they hunted either black or dun beasts, used to rub the head of their arrows with hellebore, because the flesh of the venison, struck with such an arrow, was more tender, dainty, wholesome, and delicious —paring off, nevertheless, the part that was touched round about. You also talk of the Parti.. who used to shoot backwards, more dexterously than other nations forwards; and also celebrate the skill of the Scythians in that art, who sent once to Darius, King of Persia, an ambassador, that made

Pantagruel kills the Physeterre.
Book 4. Ch. 34.

him a present of a bird, a frog, a mouse, and five arrows, without speaking one word; and being asked what those presents meant, and if he had commission to say anything, answered, that he had not: which puzzled and gravelled Darius very much, till Gobrias, one of the seven captains that had killed the magi, explained it, saying to Darius: By these gifts and offerings the Scythians silently tell you that except the Persians, like birds, fly up to heaven, or like mice, hide themselves near the centre of the earth, or, like frogs, dive to the very bottom of ponds and lakes, they shall be destroyed by the power and arrows of the Scythians.

The noble Pantagruel was, without comparison, more admirable yet in the art of shooting and darting: for with his dreadful piles and darts, nearly resembling the huge beams that support the bridges of Nantes, Saumur, Bergerac, and at Paris the millers' and the changers' bridges, in length, size, weight, and ironwork, he, at a mile's distance, would open an oyster, and never touch the edges; he would snuff a candle, without putting it out; would shoot a magpie in the eye; take off a boot's undersole, or a riding-hood's lining, without soiling them a bit; turn over every leaf of Friar John's breviary, one after another, and not tear one.

With such darts, of which there was good store in the ship, at the first blow he ran the physeter in at the forehead so furiously, that he pierced both its jaws and tongue: so that from that time to this it no more opened its guttural trap-door, nor drew and spouted water. At the second blow he put out its right eye, and at the third its left: and we had all the pleasure to see the physeter bearing those three horns in its forehead, somewhat leaning forwards in an equilateral triangle.

Meanwhile it turned about to and fro, staggering and straying like one stunned, blinded, and taking his leave of the world. Pantagruel, not satisfied with this, let fly another dart, which took the monster under the tail likewise sloping; then with three other on the chine, in a perpendicular line, divided its flank from the tail to the snout at an equal distance: then he larded it with fifty on one side, and after that, to make even work, he darted as many on its other side: so that the body of the physeter seemed like the hulk of a galleon with three masts, joined by a competent dimension of its beams, as if they had been the ribs and chainwales of the keel; which was a pleasant sight. The physeter then giving up the ghost, turned itself upon its back, as all dead fishes do; and being thus overturned, with the beams and darts upside down in the sea, it seemed a scolopendra or centipede, as that serpent is described by the ancient sage Nicander.

ON CHAPS. XXXIII. AND XXXIV.—The monstrous physeter, or whirlpool, a huge fish which dies of the wounds given him by Pantagruel near the Wild Island, where lived the Chitterlings, Shrovetide's mortal foes, seems to have a relation to the expiration of Lent; about which time in France they have conquered all their stores of salt fish, and after which flesh rules on the tables; and many are so wild for chitterlings, and other meat, that they get flesh dressed on Easter Eve late at night, and fall to like mad, as soon as the clock strikes twelve: for that reason he makes the fish die near a flesh country.—*M.*

CHAPTER XXXV

HOW PANTAGRUEL WENT ON SHORE IN THE WILD ISLAND, THE ANCIENT ABODE OF THE CHITTERLINGS [1]

THE boat's crew of the ship Lantern towed the physeter ashore on the neighbouring shore, which happened to be the Wild Island,[2] to make an anatomical dissection of its body, and save the fat of its kidneys, which, they said, was very useful and necessary for the cure of a certain distemper, which they called want of money. As for Pantagruel, he took no manner of notice of the monster; for he had seen many such, nay, bigger, in the Gallic Ocean. Yet he condescended to land in the Wild Island, to dry and refresh some of his men (whom the physeter had wetted and bedaubed), at a small desert seaport near the south, seated near a fine pleasant grove, out of which flowed a delicious brook of fresh, clear, and purling water. Here they pitched their tents, and set up their kitchens; nor did they spare fuel.

Every one having shifted, as they thought fit, Friar John rang the bell, and the cloth was immediately laid, and supper brought in. Pantagruel

[1] *Andouilles*, which is the word Rabelais has all along used, is properly a big hog's gut stuffed with chitterlings cut small, and other entrails cut into small pieces, and seasoned with pepper and salt, not forgetting sweet herbs.
[2] There is reason to believe, that by the Wild Island Rabelais means culinary fire, fire in the kitchens. The company go thither to dry themselves, and the ships' crews to melt the physeter's fat. What is more; it is the very element of chitterlings; and, lastly, nothing is so wild as fire is, since it devours everything.

eating cheerfully with his men, much about the second course, perceived certain little sly Chitterlings clambering up a high tree near the pantry, as still as so many mice. Which made him ask Xenomanes, what kind of creatures these were; taking them for squirrels, weazels, martins, or ermines. They are · Chitterlings, replied Xenomanes. This is the Wild Island, of which I spoke to you this morning: there hath been an irreconcilable war, this long time, between them and Shrovetide, their malicious and ancient enemy. I believe that the noise of the guns, which we fired at the physeter, hath alarmed them, and made them fear their enemy hath come with his forces to surprise them, or lay the island waste; as he hath often attempted to do, though he still came off but bluely; by reason of the care and vigilance of the Chitterlings, who (as Dido said to Æneas' companions, that would have landed at Carthage without her leave or knowledge) were forced to watch and stand upon their guard, considering the malice of their enemy, and the neighbourhood of his territories.

Pray, dear friend, said Pantagruel, if you find that by some honest means we may bring this war to an end, and reconcile them together, give me notice of it; I will use my endeavours in it, with all my heart, and spare nothing on my side to moderate and accommodate the points in dispute between both parties.

That is impossible at this time, answered Xenomanes. About four years ago, passing incognito by this country, I endeavoured to make a peace, or at least a long truce among them; and I certainly had brought them to be good friends and neighbours, if both one and the other parties would have yielded to one single article. Shrovetide would not include in the treaty of peace the wild puddings, nor the highland sausages, their ancient gossips and confederates. The Chitterlings demanded, that the fort of Cacques[3] might be under their government, as is the Castle of Sullouoir,[4] and that a parcel of I don't know what stinking villains,[5] murderers, robbers, that held it then, should be expelled. But they could not agree in this, and the terms that were offered seemed too hard to either party. So the treaty broke off, and nothing was done. Nevertheless, they became less severe, and gentler enemies than they were before; but since the denunciation of the national Council of Chesil, whereby they — the Chitterlings — were roughly handled,[6] hampered, and cited; whereby also Shrovetide was declared filthy, beshitten, and bewrayed,[7] in case he made any league, or agreement

---

[3] Cacque is what we call a cag, keg, or barrel, or other vessel, to keep salt fish in, and herrings, which two are Shrovetide's chief ammunition.

[4] In some editions, Sallouoir. Allusion between the castle of Souleurre, in Switzerland (*castrum Salodorense*), and *saloir*, a powdering tub: which is commonly shaped like an antique tower, and the Chitterlings for the most part keep garrison therein.

[5] Stinking herring, and putrefied stock-fish, which are in the cags, enough to poison such as come near them, or eat of them.

[6] Read, towzed, groped, grabbled, ruffled, tumbled, crumpled, and berumpled. *Farfouillées, godelurées, etc.* It means the council branded the Chitterlings with infamy, for suffering themselves and the entrails to be so handled.

[7] Add unfledged and stock-fishified: *hellebrené* and *stocfisé*. *Hallebrené*; incapable of supporting themselves, or flying, like unfledged wild ducklings, called *hallebrens*. *Stocfisé*, excommunicated, or headless like a dried cod, which the Germans call stoc-fisch, from a word which in their language signifies a fish without a head.

with them ; they are grown wonderfully inveterate, incensed, and obstinate against one another, and there is no way to remedy it. You might sooner reconcile cats and rats, or hounds and hares together.

CHAPTER XXXVI

HOW THE WILD CHITTERLINGS LAID AN AMBUSCADE FOR PANTAGRUEL

WHILE Xenomanes was saying this, Friar John spied twenty or thirty young slender-shaped Chitterlings, posting as fast as they could towards their town, citadel, castle, and fort of Chimney, and said to Pantagruel, I smell a rat : there will be here the devil upon two sticks,[1] or I am much out. These worshipful Chitterlings may chance to mistake you for Shrovetide, though you are not a bit like him. Let us once in our lives leave our junketing for a while, and put ourselves in a posture to give them a bellyful of fighting, if they would be at that sport. There can be no false Latin in this, said Xenomanes ; Chitterlings are still Chitterlings, always double-hearted,[2] and treacherous.

Pantagruel then arose from table, to visit and scour the thicket, and returned presently ; having

[1] Rabelais, 'Il y aura icy de l'asne, je le prevoy.' We shall have the braying scene here, or I am much out. That is, says M. Duchat, there will be a scene of errors, as between the two country-bumpkins, in Don Quixote, who, by their counterfeit brayings, always met each other, instead of meeting with the ass they were in quest of.
[2] He quibbles upon *andouilles* being (*doublées*) lined with small guts.

discovered, on the left, an ambuscade of squab Chitterlings; and on the right, about half a league from thence, a large body of huge giantlike armed Chitterlings, ranged in battalia along a little hill, and marching furiously towards us at the sound of bagpipes, sheep's paunches, and bladders, the merry fifes and drums, trumpets, and clarions, hoping to catch us as Moss caught his mare. By the conjecture of seventy-eight standards, which we told, we guessed their number to be two and forty thousand, at a modest computation.

Their order, proud gait, and resolute looks, made us judge that they were none of your raw, paltry links, but old warlike Chitterlings and Sausages. From the foremost ranks to the colours they were all armed cap-à-pié with small arms, as we reckoned them at a distance: yet, very sharp, and casehardened. Their right and left wings were lined with a great number of forest puddings, heavy pattipans, and horse sausages, all of them tall and proper islanders, banditti, and wild.

Pantagruel was very much daunted, and not without cause; though Epistemon told him that it might be the use and custom of the Chitterlingonians to welcome and receive thus in arms their foreign friends, as the noble kings of France are received and saluted at their first coming into the chief cities of the kingdom, after their advancement to the crown. Perhaps, said he, it may be the usual guard of the queen of the place; who, having notice given her, by the junior Chitterlings of the forlorn hope whom you saw on the tree, of the arrival of your fine and pompous fleet, hath judged that it was, without doubt, some rich and potent prince, and is come to visit you in person.

Pantagruel, little trusting to this, called a council,

to have their advice at large in this doubtful case. He briefly showed them how this way of reception, with arms, had often, under colour of compliment and friendship, been fatal. Thus, said he, the Emperor Antonius Caracalla, at one time, destroyed the citizens of Alexandria, and at another time, cut off the attendants of Artabanus, King of Persia, under colour of marrying his daughter: which, by the way, did not pass unpunished: for, a while after, this cost him his life.

Thus Jacob's children destroyed the Sichemites, to revenge the rape of their sister Dinah. By such another hypocritical trick, Gallienus, the Roman emperor, put to death the military men in Constantinople. Thus, under colour of friendship, Antonius enticed Artavasdes, King of Armenia; then, having caused him to be bound in heavy chains, and shackled, at last put him to death.

We find a thousand such instances in history; and King Charles VI. is justly commended for his prudence to this day, in that, coming back victorious over the Ghenters and other Flemings, to his good city of Paris, and when he came to Bourget, a league from thence, hearing that the citizens with their mallets—whence they got the name of Maillotins [3]—were marched out of town in battalia, twenty thousand strong, he would not go into the town, till they had laid down their arms, and retired to their respective homes; though they protested to him, that they had taken arms with no other design than to receive him with the greater demonstration of honour and respect.

[3] *Maillotins.*—The Parisians had taken these two-headed hammers *(maillets)* out of the town house, and this happened in 1413.

CHAPTER XXXVII

HOW PANTAGRUEL SENT FOR COLONEL MAUL-CHITTER-LING, AND COLONEL CUT-PUDDING; WITH A DISCOURSE WELL WORTH YOUR HEARING, ABOUT THE NAMES OF PLACES AND PERSONS

The resolution of the council was, that, let things be how they would, it behoved the Pantagruelists to stand upon their guard. Therefore Carpalim and Gymnast were ordered by Pantagruel to go for the soldiers that were on board the Cup galley, under the command of Colonel Maul-chitterling, and those on board the Vine-tub frigate, under the command of Colonel Cut-pudding the younger. I will ease Gymnast of that trouble, said Panurge, who wanted to be upon the run: you may have occasion for him here. By this worthy frock of mine, quoth Friar John, thou hast a mind to slip thy neck out of the collar, and absent thyself from the fight, thou white-livered son of a dunghill! upon my virginity thou wilt never come back. Well, there can be no great loss in thee; for thou wouldest do nothing here but howl, bray, weep, and dishearten the good soldiers. I will certainly come back, said Panurge, Friar John, my ghostly father, and speedily too: do but take care that these plaguey Chitterlings do not board our ships. All the while you will be a-fighting, I will pray heartily for your victory, after the example of the valiant captain and guide of the people of Israel, Moses. Having said this, he wheeled off.

Then said Epistemon to Pantagruel, the denomination of these two colonels of yours, Maul-chitterling and Cut-pudding, promiseth us assurance, success, and victory, if those Chitterlings should chance to set upon us. You take it rightly, said Pantagruel, and it pleaseth me to see you foresee and prognosticate our victory by the name of our Colonels.

This way of foretelling by names is not new; it was in old times celebrated, and religiously observed by the Pythagoreans. Several great princes and emperors have formerly made use of it. Octavianus Augustus, second emperor of the Romans, meeting on a day a country fellow named Eutychus,—that is, fortunate,—driving an ass named Nicon,—that is in Greek, victorious,—moved by the signification of the ass's and ass-driver's names, remained assured of all prosperity and victory.

The Emperor Vespasian, being once all alone at prayers in the temple of Serapis, at the sight and unexpected coming of a certain servant of his, named Basilides,—that is, royal,—whom he had left sick a great way behind, took hopes and assurance of obtaining the empire of the Romans. Regilian was chosen emperor, by the soldiers, for no other reason, but the signification of his name. See the Cratylus of the divine Plato. (By my thirst I will read him, said Rhizotomus; I hear you so often quote him.) See how the Pythagoreans, by reason of the names and numbers, conclude that Patroclus was to fall by the hand of Hector; Hector by Achilles; Achilles by Paris; Paris by Philoctetes. I am quite lost in my understanding, when I reflect upon the admirable invention of Pythagoras, who by the number, either even or odd, of the syllables of every name,[1] would tell you of what side a man was lame, hunch-backed, blind, gouty, troubled with the palsy, pleurisy, or any other distemper incident to human kind; allotting

[1] Read every person's proper name, *d'ung chascun nom propre*. *Nom propre* is one's surname; *nom de batême* one's Christian name, says Boyer.

even numbers to the left, and odd ones to the right side of the body.

Indeed, said Epistemon, I saw this way of syllabising tried at Xaintes, at a general procession, in the presence of that good, virtuous, learned, and just president, Brian Vallée,[2] Lord of Douhait. When there went by a man or woman that was either lame, blind of one eye, or hump-backed, he had an account brought him of his or her name; and if the syllables of the name were of an odd number, immediately, without seeing the persons, he declared them to be deformed, blind, lame, or crooked of the right side; and of the left, if they were even in number: and such indeed we ever found them.

By this syllabical invention, said Pantagruel, the learned have affirmed, that Achilles kneeling, was wounded by the arrow of Paris in the right heel; for his name is of odd syllables (here we ought to observe that the ancients used to kneel the right foot); and that Venus was also wounded before Troy in the left hand; for her name in Greek is Αφροδίτη, of four syllables; Vulcan lamed of his left foot for the same reason; Philip, King of Macedon, and Hannibal, blind of the right eye; not to speak of sciaticas, broken bellies, and hemicranias, which may be distinguished by this Pythagorean reason.

But returning to names: do but consider how Alexander the Great, son of King Philip, of whom we spoke just now, compassed his undertaking, merely by the interpretation of a name. He had besieged the strong city of Tyre, and for several weeks battered it with all his power: but all in vain. His engines and attempts were still baffled by the Tyrians, which

---

[2] It was he who saved Scaliger from the stake when accused of having feasted in Lent. It is not unlikely Rabelais lay under a similar obligation to him.

made him finally resolve to raise the siege, to his great grief; foreseeing the great stain which such a shameful retreat would be to his reputation. In this anxiety and agitation of mind he fell asleep, and dreamed that a satyr was come into his tent, capering, skipping, and tripping it up and down, with his goatish hoofs, and that he strove to lay hold on him. But the satyr still slipt from him, till at last, having penned him up into a corner, he took him. With this he awoke, and telling his dream to the philosophers and sages of his court, they let him know that it was a promise of victory from the gods, and that he should soon be master of Tyre; the word *satyros*, divided in two, being *sa Tyros*, and signifying Tyre is thine; and in truth, at the next onset, he took the town by storm, and, by a complete victory, reduced that stubborn people to subjection.

On the other hand, see how, by the signification of one word, Pompey fell into despair. Being overcome by Cæsar at the battle of Pharsalia, he had no other way left to escape but by flight; which, attempting by sea, he arrived near the island of Cyprus, and perceived on the shore, near the city of Paphos, a beautiful and stately palace: now asking the pilot what was the name of it, he told him, that it was called κακοβασιλέα,[3] that is, evil king; which struck such a dread and terror in him, that he fell into despair, as being assured of losing shortly his life; insomuch that his complaints, sighs, and groans were heard by the mariners and other passengers. And indeed, a while after, a certain strange peasant, called Achillas, cut off his head.

To all these examples might be added what happened to L. Paulus Emilius,[4] when the senate

[3] Read, κακοβασιλεῦς. See Val. Max. l. 1, c. 5.
[4] See Cicero *De Divinatione*, etc.

elected him imperator, that is, chief of the army which they sent against Perses, King of Macedon. That evening returning home to prepare for his expedition, and kissing a little daughter of his called Trasia, she seemed somewhat sad to him. What is the matter, said he, my chicken? Why is my Trasia[5] thus sad and melancholy? Daddy, replied the child, Persa[6] is dead. This was the name of a little bitch, which she loved mightily. Hearing this, Paulus took assurance of a victory over Perses.

If time would permit us to discourse of the sacred Hebrew writ, we might find a hundred noted passages, evidently showing how religiously they observed proper names and their significations.

He had hardly ended this discourse, when the two colonels arrived with their soldiers, all well armed and resolute. Pantagruel made them a short speech, entreating them to behave themselves bravely, in case they were attacked; for he could not yet believe that the Chitterlings were so treacherous: but he bade them by no means to give the first offence; giving them Carnival for the watchward.

[5] Rabelais has it Tratia. It should indeed be Tertia, which, being abbreviated into Tria, the printers, often none of the best guessers, made it Tratia instead of Tertia.

[6] Plutarch, in the life of Paulus Emilius, copied this passage from Cicero; but not being thoroughly versed in the Latin tongue, as he somewhere owns himself, he made of this bitch, a dog, which he calls Perseus.

CHAPTER XXXVIII

HOW CHITTERLINGS ARE NOT TO BE SLIGHTED BY MEN

You shake your empty noddles now, jolly topers, and do not believe what I tell you here, any more than if it were some tale of a tub. Well, well, I cannot help it. Believe it if you will; if you will not, let it alone. For my part, I very well know what I say. It was in the Wild Island, in our voyage to the Holy Bottle; I tell you the time and place; what would you have more ? I would have you call to mind the strength of the ancient giants, that undertook to lay the high mountain Pelion, on the top of Ossa, and set among those the shady Olympus, to dash out the gods' brains, unnestle them, and scour their heavenly lodgings. Theirs was no small strength, you may well think, and yet they were nothing but Chitterlings from the waist downwards, or, at least, serpents, not to tell a lie for the matter.

The serpent that tempted Eve, too, was of the Chitterling kind, and yet it is recorded of him, that he was more subtle than any beast of the field. Even so are Chitterlings. Nay, to this very hour they hold in some universities, that this same tempter was the Chitterling called Ithyphallus,[1] into which was transformed bawdy Priapus, arch-seducer of females in paradise, that is, a garden, in Greek.[2]

Pray now tell me, who can tell but that the Swiss, now so bold and warlike, were formerly Chitterlings ? For my part I would not take my oath to the contrary. The Himantopodes, a nation very famous

---

[1] See H. Cornelius Agrippa, in his treatise *De Origine Peccati*.
[2] Read, ' in paradise, as the Greeks call it, but garden in French.'

in Ethiopia, according to Pliny's description, are Chitterlings, and nothing else. If all this will not satisfy your worships, or remove your incredulity, I would have you forthwith (I mean drinking first, that nothing be done rashly) visit Lusignan, Parthenay, Vouant, Mervant, and Ponzauges in Poictou. There you will find a cloud of witnesses, not of your affidavit men of the right stamp, but credible, time out of mind, that will take their corporal oath, on Rigomé's knuckle-bone,[3] that Melusina, their founder, or foundress, which you please, was woman from the head to the prick-purse,[4] and thence downwards was a serpentine Chitterling, or if you will have it otherwise, a Chitterlingdized serpent. She nevertheless had a genteel and noble gait, imitated to this very day by your hop-merchants of Brittany, in their paspié and country dances.

What do you think was the cause of Erichthonius' being the first inventor of coaches, litters, and chariots? Nothing but because Vulcan had begot him with Chitterlingdized legs; which to hide, he chose to ride in a litter, rather than on horseback; for Chitterlings were not yet in esteem at that time.

The Scythian nymph, Ora,[5] was likewise half woman and half Chitterling; and yet seemed so beautiful to Jupiter, that nothing could serve him but he must give her a touch of his godship's kindness; and accordingly he had a brave boy by her, called Colaxes; and therefore I would have you

[3] Read, right arm.
[4] *Aux boursavits.* See the old romance of Melusina.
[5] Herodotus, in the beginning of his fourth book, speaks of one Colaxis, son of Jupiter, and immediately after tells a story of a Scythian nymph, half woman and half serpent, who lay with Hercules. Rabelais, writing by memory, has confounded and altered these two fables.

leave off shaking your empty noddles at this, as if it were a story, and firmly believe that nothing is truer than the gospel.

CHAPTER XXXIX

HOW FRIAR JOHN JOINED WITH THE COOKS TO FIGHT THE CHITTERLINGS

FRIAR JOHN, seeing these furious Chitterlings thus boldly march up, said to Pantagruel, Here will be a rare battle of hobby-horses, a pretty kind of puppet-show fight, for aught I see. Oh! what mighty honour and wonderful glory will attend our victory! I would have you only be a bare spectator of this fight, and for any thing else, leave me and my men to deal with them. What men? said Pantagruel. Matter of breviary, replied Friar John. How came Potiphar, who was head cook of Pharaoh's kitchens, he that bought Joseph, and whom the said Joseph might have made a cuckold, if he had not been a Joseph; how came he, I say, to be made general of all the horse in the kingdom of Egypt? Why was Nabuzardan, King Nebuchadnezzar's head cook, chosen, to the exclusion of all other captains, to besiege and destroy Jerusalem. I hear you, replied Pantagruel. By St Christopher's whiskers, said Friar John, I dare lay a wager that it was because they had formerly engaged Chitterlings, or men as little valued; whom to rout, conquer, and destroy, cooks are, without comparison, more fit, than cuirassiers and gens-d'armes armed at all points, or all the horse and foot in the world.

You put me in mind, said Pantagruel, of what is written amongst the facetious and merry sayings of Cicero. During the more than civil wars between Cæsar and Pompey, though he was much courted by the first, he naturally leaned more to the side of the latter. Now one day, hearing that the Pompeyians, in a certain rencontre, had lost a great many men, he took a fancy to visit their camp. There he perceived little strength, less courage, but much disorder. From that time, foreseeing that things would go ill with them, as it since happened, he began to banter now one and then another, and be very free of his cutting jests: so some of Pompey's captains, playing the good fellows, to show their assurance, told him, do you see how many eagles we have yet? (They were then the device of the Romans in war.) They might be of use to you, replied Cicero, if you had to do with magpies.

Thus seeing we are to fight Chitterlings, pursued Pantagruel, you infer thence that it is a culinary war, and have a mind to join with the cooks. Well, do as you please, I will stay here in the meantime, and wait for the event of the rumpus.

Friar John went that very moment among the sutlers, into the cooks' tents, and told them in a pleasing manner: I must see you crowned with honour and triumph this day, my lads; to your arms are reserved such achievements as never yet were performed within the memory of man. Odd's belly, do they make nothing of the valiant cooks? let us go fight yonder fornicating Chitterlings! I will be your captain. But first let us drink, boys,— come on—let us be of good cheer. Noble captain, returned the kitchen tribe, this was spoken like yourself; bravely offered: huzza! we are all at your excellency's command, and will live and die by you. Live, live, said Friar John, a God's name: but die by no means. That is the Chitterlings' lot; they shall have their bellyful of it: come on then, let us put ourselves in order; Nabuzardan's the word.

CHAPTER XL

HOW FRIAR JOHN FITTED UP THE SOW; AND OF THE VALIANT COOKS THAT WENT INTO IT

THEN, by Friar John's order, the engineers and their workmen fitted up the great sow that was in the ship Leathern-bottle. It was a wonderful machine, so contrived, that, by means of large engines that were round about in rows, it threw forked iron bars, and four-square steel-bolts; and in its hold two hundred men at least could easily fight, and be sheltered. It was made after the model of the sow of Riolle, by the means of which Bergerac was retaken from the English, in the reign of Charles the Sixth.[1]

Here are the names of the noble and valiant cooks who went into the sow, as the Greeks did into the Trojan horse.

Sour-sauce.	Crisp-pig.	Carbonadoe.
Sweet-meat.	Greasy-slouch.	Sop-in-pan.
Greedy-gut.	Fat-gut.	Pick-fowl.
Liquorice-chops.	Bray-mortar.	Mustard-pot.

[1] Rabelais mistakes. It was in Charles the Fifth's reign, in the year 1378, two years before that prince's death. Froissart, vol. ii., c. 2, on that year. They sent to Riolle for a huge machine called a sow, which was so contrived as to cast prodigious stones, and could easily shelter a hundred men-at-arms, in their approaches to attack the town.

Pantagruel

Soused-pork.	Lick-sauce.	Hog's-haslet.
Slap-sauce.	Hog's-foot.	Chopt-phiz.
Cock-broth.	Hodge-podge.	Gallimaufrey.
Slip-slop.		

All these noble cooks, in their coat of arms, did bear, in a field gules, a larding-pin vert, charged with a chevron argent.

Lard, hog's-lard.	Pinch-lard.	Snatch-lard.
Nibble-lard.	Top-lard.	Gnaw-lard.
Filch-lard.	Pick-lard.	Scrape-lard.
Fat-lard.	Save-lard.	Chew-lard.

Gaillardon (by syncope) born near Rambouillet. The culinary doctor's name was Gaillardlardon, in the same manner as you use to say idolatrous for idololatrous.

Stiff-lard.	Catch-lard.	Waste-lard.
Dainty-lard.	Cut-lard.	Ogle-lard.
Watch-lard.	Mince-lard.	Weigh-lard.
Sweet-lard.	Fresh-lard.	Gulch-lard.
Eat-lard.	Rusty-lard.	Eye-lard.
Snap-lard.		

Names unknown among the Marranes and Jews.[2]

Ballocky.	Monsieur-Ragout.	Mustard-sauce.
Pick-salad.	Snail-dresser.	Claret-sauce.
Broil-rasher.	Soup-monger.	Swill-broth.
Cony-skin.	Brewis-belly.	Thirsty.
Dainty-chops.	Chine-picker.	Kitchen-stuff.
Pie-wright.	Crack-pipkin.	Verjuice.
Pudding-pan.	Scrape-pot.	Salt-gullet.
Save-dripping.	Porridge-pot.	Suck-gravy.
Water-cress.	Lick-dish.	Macaroon.
Scrape-turnip.	Toss-pot.	Skewer-maker.
Trivet.		

[2] Who abominate bacon, and all sorts of lardings.

Rabelais' Works [Book iv.

Smell-smock; he was afterwards taken from the kitchen, and removed to chamber-practice, for the service of the noble Cardinal Hunt-venison.[3]

Rot-Roast.	Prick-madam.	Fox-tail.
Dish-clout.	Pricket.	Fly-flap.
Save-suet.	Flesh-smith.	Old-Grizzle.
Fire-fumbler.	Cram-gut.	Ruff-belly.
Pillicock.	Tuzzy-mussy.	Sirloin.
Long-tool.	Jacket-liner.	Spit-mutton.
Prick-pride.	Guzzle-drink.	Fritter-fryer.
Hog's-gullet.	Strutting-tom.	Smutty-face.
Saffron-sauce.	Slashed-snout.	

Mondam, that first invented madam's sauce, and for that discovery, was thus called in the Scotch-French dialect.[4]

Loblolly.	Goodman Goosecap.	Snap-gobbet.
Slabber-chops.	Munch-turnip.	Scurvy-phiz.
Scum-pot.	Sloven.	Trencher-man.
Gully-guts.	Swallow-pitcher.	Pudding-bag.
Rince-pot.	Wafer-monger.	Pig-sticker.
Drink-spiller.		

Robert: he invented Robert's sauce, so good and necessary for roasted conies, ducks, fresh pork, poached eggs, salt fish, and a thousand other such dishes.

Cold-eel.	Frying-pan.	Big-snout.
Thornback.	Man of dough.	Lick-finger.

[3] In Rabelais, Cardinal le Veneur. John le Veneur-Carrouges, Bishop of Lisieux, made Cardinal at Marseilles by Pope Clement VII. in 1533. He was such a lover of partridge, that he had them kept all the year round at his country house.

[4] Our author ridicules the Scotch pronunciatiou of the French tongue, which Brantôme likewise says, is perfect jargon in the mouth of a Scotchman, whose natural speech is in itself 'rurale, barbare, malsonnante, and malseante.' See Dam. illust. of Brantôme, disc. 3. Before in l. ii., c. 9. 'Saint Treignan foutys vous d'Escouss ou j'ay failly à entendre.'

Gurnard.	Sauce-doctor.	Tit-bit.
Grumbling-gut.	Waste-Butter	Sauce-box.
Alms-scrip.	Shitbreech.	All fours.
Taste-all.	Thick-brawn.	Whimwham
Scrap-merchant.	Tom T—d.	Baste-roast.
Belly-timberman.	Mouldy-crust.	Gaping-Hoyden.
Hashee.	Hasty.	Calf's pluck.
Frig-palate.	Red-herring.	Leather-breeches.
Powdering-tub.	Cheesecake.	

All these noble cooks went into the sow, merry, cheery, hale, brisk, old dogs at mischief, and ready to fight stoutly. Friar John, ever and anon waving his huge scimitar, brought up the rear, and double-locked the doors on the inside

CHAPTER XLI

HOW PANTAGRUEL BROKE THE CHITTERLINGS
AT THE KNEES

THE Chitterlings advanced so near, that Pantagruel perceived that they stretched their arms, and already began to charge their lances; which caused him to send Gymnast to know what they meant, and why they thus, without the least provocation, came to fall upon their old trusty friends, who had neither said nor done the least ill thing to them. Gymnast being advanced near their front, bowed very low, and said to them, as loud as ever he could: We are friends, we are friends; all, all of us your friends, yours, and at your command; we are for Carnival, your old confederate. Some have since told me, that he mistook, and said cavernal instead of carnival.[1]

Whatever it was, the word was no sooner out of his mouth, but a huge little squab Sausage, starting out of the front of their main body, would have gripped him by the collar. By the helmet of Mars, said Gymnast, I will swallow thee; but thou shalt only come in in chips and slices; for, big as thou art, thou couldest never come in whole. This spoke, he lugs out his trusty sword, kiss-mine-arse (so he called it), with both his fists, and cut the sausage in twain. Bless me, how fat the foul thief was? it puts me in mind of the huge bull of Berne, that was slain at Marignan, when the drunken Swiss were so mauled there. Believe me, it had little less than four inches lard on its paunch.

The Sausage's job being done, a crowd of others flew upon Gymnast, and had most scurvily dragged him down, when Pantagruel with his men came up to his relief. Then began the martial fray, higgledy piggledy. Maul-chitterling did maul Chitterlings; Cut-pudding did cut puddings; Pantagruel did break the Chitterlings at the knees;[2] Friar John played at least in sight within his sow, viewing and observ-

[1] Gymnast had said, after the manner of the Gascons, Gradimars, instead of Mardigras; which provoked the Chitterlings' wrath: for he imagined they did it on purpose to affront their good friend Mardigras (which here means our Shrove Tuesday, or rather all the whole Carnival).

[2] A proverbial expression for attempting impossibilities; as is that of breaking Chitterlings by mere strength of arm. Amadis, l. 8, c. 53. 'The gods have permitted the death of your brother. They have preserved my father; they are pleased to frustrate your designs, and favour his; and you are for breaking the eel at your knees.' Rabelais' early commentators will have this chapter to pourtray the Battle of Marignan. His modern editors regard it as a mock recital of the combats so frequently occurring in the romances of chivalry.

ing all things; when the pattipans, that lay in ambuscade, most furiously sallied out upon Pantagruel.

Friar John, who lay snug all this while, by that time perceiving the rout and hurly-burly, set open the doors of his sow, and sallied out with his merry Greeks, some of them armed with iron-spits, others with handirons, racks, fire-shovels, frying-pans, kettles, gridirons, oven forks, tongs, dripping-pans, brooms, iron pots, mortars, pestles, all in battle array, like so many housebreakers, hallooing and roaring out altogether most frightfully, Nabuzardan. Thus shouting and hooting, they fought like dragons, and charged through the pattipans and sausages. The Chitterlings perceiving this fresh reinforcement and that the others would be too hard for them, betook themselves to their heels, scampering off with full speed, as if the devil had come for them. Friar John, with an iron crow, knocked them down as fast as hops : his men too were not sparing on their side. O! what a woeful sight it was! the field was all over strewed with heaps of dead or wounded Chitterlings; and history relates, that had not heaven had a hand in it, the Chitterling tribe had been totally routed out of the world, by the culinary champions. But there happened a wonderful thing, you may believe as little or as much of it as you please.

From the north flew towards us a huge, fat, thick, grizzly swine, with long and large wings, like those of a wind-mill; its plumes red crimson,[3] like those of a phenicoptere (which in Languedoc they call *flaman*); its eyes were red, and flaming like a carbuncle; its ears green like a Prasin emerald; its teeth

[3] If, as some imagine, the Chitterlings in this chapter are the Swiss at the battle of Marignan, this phenicoptere may mean the Cardinal of Sion; and the mustard which he laid to their wounds, may be the gold with which he pacified them.

like a topaz; its tail long and black like jet; its feet white, diaphanous, and transparent like a diamond, somewhat broad, and of the splay kind, like those of geese, and as Queen Dick's[4] used to be at Thoulouse, in the days of yore. About its neck it wore a gold collar, round which were some Ionian characters, whereof I could pick out but two words, ΎΣ ΑΘΗΝΑΝ: hog-teaching Minerva.

The sky was clear before; but at that monster's appearance, it changed so mightily for the worse, that we were all amazed at it. As soon as the Chitterlings perceived the flying hog, down they all threw their weapons, and fell on their knees, lifting up their hands, joined together without speaking one word, in a posture of adoration. Friar John and his party kept on mincing, felling, braining, mangling, and spitting the Chitterlings like mad: but Pantagruel sounded a retreat, and all hostility ceased.

The monster having several times hovered backwards and forwards between the two armies, with a tail-shot voided above twenty-seven butts of mustard on the ground; then flew away through the air, crying all the while, Carnival, Carnival, Carnival.

ON CHAP. XXXV. AND THE SIX FOLLOWING.—Pantagruel lands in the Wild Island to refresh his men, whom the fish had disordered. He would not come where Shrovetide lived, but goes ashore at the dwelling of the Chitterlings, because he did not love Lent. There they pitched their tents, fixed their kitchen batteries; the cloth is immediately laid, supper brought in, and all eat cheerfully, as is usual after Lent. What happens in that island, and the fight in which the chitterlings, sausages, and pastry-pans, are mauled by Pantagruel and his men, and

---

[4] *La Royne Pedaucque. Pié d'oie:* Goose-foot. At Toulouse there is a bridge called Queen Pedauque's bridge. Ménage says, that the statue of that queen, with goose feet, is to be seen at Dijon, in the porch of St Benigne's church, and at Nevers, in the cathedral church there; and asserts, that she was called *Pedauque,* because of her splay-footedness.

Chap. xli.] *Pantagruel*

particularly by the friar at the head of the cooks, partly seems a comical allegory, which denotes the good cheer at Easter, after the Lent-keepers have mastered that time of mortification. Sausages, chitterlings, etc., which are preserved with salt, help them to appease hunger, at the same time that they create and heighten thirst.

It is obvious that the 37th chapter ridicules the method used by some of the ancients, and to this day, of foretelliug things by the names of persons. We find that the Chitterlingonians knowing at last that Pantagruel is Shrovetide's foe, and a friend to Carnival, their old confederate, pay him their homage, and send, under the conduct of young Niphleseth, seventy-eight thousand royal Chitterlings to Gargantua, who made a present of them to the great King of Paris: but most of them died, and were buried in heaps in a part of Paris, called to this day the street paved with Chitterlings; yet, at the request of the court ladies, young Niphleseth was preserved, honourably used, and since that married to heart's content. We need not understand Hebrew to find out what our joking author means by that young Chitterling (*mentula*) Niphleseth, of whom the charitable, or rather selfish ladies took such mighty care.

After all, the description of a misunderstanding between the French, and the Swiss and Germans that had reformed, may be couched under those notions of Chitterlings. In the 35th chapter we find a treaty on foot to reconcile them to Shrovetide: and as the council was then sitting, some concessions were made by the Pope's party in case of a likelihood of an accommodation. Besides, Rabelais mentions, that Shrovetide (by which may be meant here the Swiss, or Germans of the Roman Communion) was threatened with being declared bewrayed (*i.e.*, excommunicated) in case he made any league or agreement with the Chitterlings: since which they were grown wonderfully inveterate and obstinate against one another. He also tells us, that they desired the expulsion of I do not know what stinking villains, murderers and robbers, that held the castle of Salloir (which means a powdering-tub). These might be monks and friars. What's more, in the 37th chapter, Rabelais, enumerating the power and antiquity of Chitterling-like people, says, Who can tell but that the Swiss, now so bold and resolute, were formerly Chitterlings? For my part, I would not take my oath to the contrary. Some of the Swiss are now, and were then, a wild sort of people, as our author calls his Chitterlings, whom he brings in marching up boldly in battalia. By the queen may be meant the republic, which word is feminine in Latin and in French. The Chitterlings sent by the Queen, are the soldiers which Switzerland sent them, as it does still, to the French; many of which died by change of air, for want of mustard (*i.e.*, pay), and other accidents. And what Xenomanes said, that Chitterlings were double-hearted and treacherous, suits also very well with their taking side now with the Emperor, then with the French, *vice versa*, in that age. In the 41st chapter, Gymnast, having lugged out his sword with both his fists, cut a huge wild squab sausage in two. Bless me, says our historian, how fat the foul thief was! It puts me in mind of the huge bull of Berne, that was slain at Marignan, when the drunken Swiss were so mauled there: believe me, it had little less than four inches lard on its paunch. By this great bull of Berne is meant Pontiner, a famous gigantic fat captain of the Swiss, who being killed at the battle of Marignan, some of the Germans who sided with the French, to show they were fully revenged on the Swiss, who had been too hard for them in several other engagements, ran the points of their pikes and lances in that monstrous officer's fat paunch, as Paulus Jovius observes in the account he gives of that battle.

CHAPTER XLII

HOW PANTAGRUEL HELD A TREATY WITH NIPHLESETH, QUEEN OF THE CHITTERINGS.

THE monster being out of sight, and the two armies remaining silent, Pantagruel demanded a parley with the lady Niphleseth, Queen of the Chitterlings, who was in her chariot,[1] by the standards; and it was easily granted. The Queen

[1] In chap. 38. it is said, that Erichthonius first brought into use coaches and litters to hide the ugliness of his legs; which is taken from Servius, on these verses of the third book of the Georgics:

' Primus Erichthonius currus et quatuor ausus
    Jungere equos, rapidisque rotis insistere victor.'

It was with the same view that Niphleseth chose to appear in her chariot.

alighted, courteously received Pantagruel, and was glad to see him. Pantagruel complained to her of this breach of peace; but she civilly made her excuse, telling him that a false information had caused all this mischief; her spies having brought her word, that Shrovetide, their mortal foe, was landed, and spent his time in examining the urine of physeters.

She therefore entreated him to pardon them their offence; telling him that sir-reverence was sooner found in Chitterlings than gall; and offering, for herself and all her successors, to hold of him, and his, the whole island and country; to obey him in all his commands, be friends to his friends, and foes to his foes; and also to send every year, as an acknowledgment of their homage, a tribute of seventy-eight thousand Chitterlings, to serve him at his first course at table, six months in the year;[2] which was punctually performed. For the next day she sent the aforesaid quantity of royal Chitterlings to the good Gargantua, under the conduct of young Niphleseth, infanta of the island.

The good Gargantua made a present of them to the great King of Paris. But by change of air, and for want of mustard (the natural balsam and restorer of Chitterlings), most of them died. By the great king's particular grant, they were buried in heaps in a part of Paris, to this day called *La Rue pavée d'Andouilles;* the street paved with Chitterlings. At the request of the ladies at his court, young Niphleseth was preserved, honourably used, and since that married to her heart's content; and was the mother of many fine children, for which heaven be praised.

[2] Chitterlings are not eaten above six months in the year at most.

Pantagruel civilly thanked the Queen, forgave all offences, refused the offer she had made of her country, and gave her a pretty little knife.[3] After that he asked her several nice questions concerning the apparition of that flying hog. She answered, that it was the idea of Carnival, their tutelary god in time of war, first founder, and original of all the Chitterling race; for which reason he resembled a hog; for Chitterlings drew their extraction from hogs.

Pantagruel asking for what purpose, and curative indication, he had voided so much mustard on the earth, the Queen replied, that mustard [4] was their sanc-greal, and celestial balsam, of which, laying but a little in the wounds of the fallen Chitterlings, in a very short time the wounded were healed, and the dead restored to life. Pantagruel held no further discourse with the Queen, but retired on shipboard. The like did all the boon companions, with their implements of destruction, and their huge sow.

CHAPTER XLIII

HOW PANTAGRUEL WENT INTO THE ISLAND OF RUACH

Two days after, we arrived at the island of Ruach; and I swear to you, by the celestial hen and chickens, that I found the way of living of the

[3] As they do the savages of America. These knives are called *parguois*, corruptly for *pragois*, being made at Prague, in Bohemia.

[4] Henry V., King of England, was wont to say, in the same sense, that war without fire was not worth a rush, any more than sausages without mustard. See J. Juvenal des Ursins' Hist., ch. vi., on the year 1420.

Chap. xliii.]   *Pantagruel*

people so strange and wonderful, that I cannot, for the heart's blood of me, half tell it you. They live on nothing but wind, eat nothing but wind, and drink nothing but wind. They have no other houses but weathercocks. They sow no other seeds but the three sorts of wind-flowers, rue, and herbs that make one break wind to the purpose; these scour them off charmingly. The common sort of people, to feed themselves, make use of feather, paper, or linen fans, according to their abilities. As for the rich,[1] they live by the means of wind-mills.

When they would have some noble treat, the tables are spread under one or two wind-mills.[2] There they feast as merry as beggars, and during the meal, their whole talk is commonly of the goodness, excellency, salubrity, and rarity of winds; as you, jolly topers, in your cups, philosophise and argue upon wines. The one praises the south-east, the other the south-west, this the west and by south, and this the east and by north; another the west, and another the east; and so of the rest. As for lovers and amorous sparks, no gale for them like a smock-gale. For the sick they use bellows, as we use clysters among us.

Oh! (said to me a little diminutive swollen

[1] Rabelais introduces into the Isle of Winds, divers sorts of persons, and even more than one nation. By the common sort of people, who make use of fans of various kinds, we may understand, literally, the great number of male and female dealers in fans: who not only make fans for Paris, and all France, but also send them abroad to England and other countries. As for the rich, who feed on wind-mills, they are the proprietors of such sort of useful country houses (explained in the Trevoux Dictionary, under the word *usines*) which are very frequent about Paris, and bring in a considerable revenue to the owners.

[2] In Italy and South France they make use of large fans, which are hung to the ceiling, and are waved to and fro by a servant, to cool the rooms, particularly at meals.

bubble) that I had now but a bladderful of that same Languedoc wind which they call Cierce. The famous physician, Scurron,³ passing one day by this country, was telling us, that it is so strong, that it will make nothing of overturning a loaded waggon. Oh! what good would it not do my œdipodic leg.⁴ The biggest are not the best; but, said Panurge, rather would I had here a large butt of that same good Languedoc wine, that grows at Mirevaux, Canteperdrix, and Frontignan.

I saw a good likely sort of a man there, much resembling Ventrose, tearing and fuming in a grievous fret, with a tall, burly groom, and a pimping little page of his, laying them on, like the devil, with a buskin. Not knowing the cause of his anger, at first I thought that all this was by the doctor's advice, as being a thing very healthy to the master to be in a passion, and to his man to be banged for it. But as last I heard him taxing his man with stealing from him, like a rogue as he was, the better half of a large leathern bag of an excellent southerly wind, which he had carefully laid up, like a hidden reserve, against the cold weather.⁵

³ His name was Schyron; witness the inscription over the gate of the anatomy theatre at Montpellier, built by King Henry II. 'Curantibus Johanne Schyronio, Antonio Saporta, Gulielmo Rondeletio, et J. Boccatio, 1556.' Schyron was counsellor of the king, royal professor, and Chancellor of the University of Montpelier, and died very old, in the aforesaid year 1556, after he had made a figure among the learned from the year 1530.
⁴ Lame or gouty leg.
⁵ Read, against the sultry hot weather, not cold weather. *Arrière-saison* means autumn, vintage, or harvest-time. In Lower Languedoc they call *garbin* a certain cool breeze of wind, which freshens up in that country about noon in autumn. It comes very seasonably for the harvesters and vintagers, who, without it, would never be able to endure the excessive heats of

They neither exonerate, dung, piss, nor spit in that island; but, to make amends, they belch, fizzle, funk, and give tail shots in abundance. They are troubled with all manner of distempers; and, indeed, all distempers are engendered and proceed from ventosities, as Hippocrates demonstrates, lib. *De Flatibus.* But the most epidemical among them is the wind-cholic. The remedies which they use are large clysters, whereby they void store of windiness. They all die of dropsies and tympanies; the men farting, and the women fizzling; so that their soul takes her leave at the back-door.

Some time after, walking in the island, we met three hair-brained, airy fellows, who seemed mightily puffed up, and went to take their pastime, and view the plovers,[6] who live on the same diet as themselves, and abound in the island, I observed that as your true topers, when they travel, carry flasks, leathern bottles, and small runlets along with them, so each of them had at his girdle a pretty little pair of bellows. If they happened to want wind, by the help of those pretty bellows they immediately drew some, fresh and cool, by attraction and reciprocal expulsion; for, as you well know, wind essentially defined, is nothing but fluctuating and agitated air.

Awhile after, we were commanded, in the King's name, not to receive, for three hours, any man or woman of the country, on board our ships; some having stolen from him a rousing fart, of the very individual wind which old good-man Æolus, the snorer, gave Ulysses, to conduct his ship, whenever that season. Which makes the author say, that he had carefully laid it up *comme une viande rare*, as a tit-bit.

[6] The 23rd novel of the Heptameron: 'You live, then, upon faith and hope, as the plover does upon wind? you are very easy to maintain, and are subsisted at a cheap rate.'

it should happen to be becalmed. Which fart the King kept religiously, like another sanc-greal, and performed a world of wonderful cures with it, in many dangerous diseases, letting loose, and distributing to the patient, only as much of it as might frame a virginal fart; which is, if you must know, what our sanctimoniales, *alias* nuns, in their dialect, call ringing backwards.[7]

CHAPTER XLIV

HOW SMALL RAIN LAYS A HIGH WIND

PANTAGRUEL commended their government and way of living, and said to their hypenemian mayor: If you approve Epicurus' opinion, placing the *summum bonum* in pleasure (I mean pleasure that is easy and free from toil), I esteem you happy; for your food being wind, costs you little or nothing, since you need but blow. True, sir, returned the mayor, but, alas! nothing is perfect here below: for too often, when we are at table, feeding on some good blessed wind of God, as on celestial manna, merry as so many friars, down drops on a sudden some small rain, which lays our wind, and so robs us of it. Thus many a meal is lost for want of meat.

Just so, quoth Panurge, Jenin Toss-pot, of Quin-

[7] Rabelais says, 'les sanctimoniales appellant ung pet *sonnet*;' *i.e.*, the nuns call a fart *sonnet*. Sonnet I take to be a diminutive of the *son* (sound), and means a sort of a small, still, silent sound. It likewise signfies a song, or tune. Nuns are so very chaste, at least in speech, that they scruple to call a fart by its right name; and an escape of that nature is never mentioned by them any otherwise than by the term *sonnet*.

quenais, evacuating some wine of his own burning [urine] on his wife's posteriors, laid the ill-fumed wind that blowed out of their centre, as out of some magisterial æolipile. Here is a kind of a whim on that subject, which I made formerly:

> One evening when Toss-pot had been at his butts,
> And Joan, his fat spouse, crammed with turnips her guts,
> Together they pigg'd, nor did drink so besot him,
> But he did what was done when his daddy begot him.
> Now, when to recruit, he'd fain have been snoring,
> Joan's back-door was filthily puffing and roaring:
> So, for spite he bepiss'd her, and quickly did find,
> That a very small rain lays a very high wind.

We are also plagued yearly with a very great calamity, cried the mayor, for a giant, called Widenostrils, who lives in the island of Tohu, comes hither every spring to purge, by the advice of his physicians, and swallows us, like so many pills, a great number of wind-mills, and of bellows also, at which his mouth waters exceedingly.

Now this is a sad mortification to us here, who are fain to fast over three or four whole Lents every year for this, besides certain petty Lents, ember weeks, and other orison and starving tides. And have you no remedy for this? asked Pantagruel. By the advice of our Mezarims, replied the mayor, about the time that he uses to give us a visit, we garrison our wind-mills with good store of cocks and hens. The first time that the greedy thief swallowed them, they had like to have done his business at once: for they crowed and cackled in his maw, and fluttered up and down athwart and along in his stomach, which threw the glutton into a lipothymy cardiac passion, and dreadful and dangerous convulsions, as if some serpent, creeping in at his mouth, had been frisking in his stomach.

Here is a comparative, as altogether incongruous and impertinent, cried Friar John, interrupting them: for I have formerly heard, that if a serpent chance to get into a man's stomach, it will not do him the least hurt, but will immediately get out, if you do but hang the patient by the heels, and lay a pan full of warm milk near his mouth. You were told this, said Pantagruel, and so were those who gave you this account; but none ever saw or read of such a cure. On the contrary, Hippocrates, in his fifth book of *Epidem.* writes, that such a case happening in his time, the patient presently died of a spasm and convulsion.

Besides the cocks and hens, said the mayor, continuing his story, all the foxes in the country whipped into Widenostrils' mouth, posting after the poultry; which made such a stir with Reynard at their heels, that he grievously fell into fits each minute of an hour.

At last, by the advice of a Baden enchanter,[1] at the time of the paroxysm, he used to flay a fox,[2] by way of antidote and counter-poison. Since that he took better advice, and eases himself with taking a clyster made with a decoction of wheat and barley corns, and of livers of goslings; to the first of which the poultry run, and the foxes to the latter. Besides, he swallows some of your badger or fox-dogs,[3] by the way of pills and boluses. This is our misfortune.

Cease to fear, good people, cried Pantagruel: this

[1] *Ung enchanteur badin,* not *baden.* It only means a juggler, or mountebank quack, or tumbler.
[2] This proverbial expression for vomiting, does admirably well here in speaking of Widenostrils disemboguing the foxes that were got down to the bottom of his maw.
[3] Badger-dogs, or fox-hounds. The former are what the Germans call Dachshunden, little bandy-legged dogs, well-fitted by nature for entering a hole in the earth.

huge Widenostrils, this same swallower of wind-mills, is no more, I will assure you: he died, being stifled and choked with a lump of fresh butter at the mouth of a hot oven, by the advice of his physicians.

ON CHAPS. XLIII. AND XLIV.—The island of Ruach, where people live on nothing but wind, according to the sense of the Hebrew word, is the island of Wind, or the Vane island.

It is an emblem of the court, where men feed themselves, and are fed by others, with wind, compliments, flattery, promises, and empty vain hopes, more than anywhere else. The weathercocks, which are the only houses in that island, imply the uncertain and variable state of courtiers; first, because the court is still where the prince is: and as the weathercock is always in motion, now to the east, and then presently to the west, yet is still fixed in one place, and only moves round its centre: so the courtier is still at home when at court, yet the court is sometimes in one place, and sometimes another. Besides, as the warm south sometimes gently blows on a weathercock, and soon the cold north rudely whirls it about; so the courtier's house is either cherished, or roughly blown upon, according to the prince's breath.

The wind-flowers, rue, and such carminative herbs, which are the only things sowed there, which scour them off in that island, denote the attendance, craft, and pains, which are the seeds by which we hope to rise and reap favour at court; but when the time of harvest comes, we find ourselves only rid (by a thorough knowledge of the place, and chiefly by balks and disappointments) of a great deal of wind—vain, empty hopes, that swelled and puffed us up.

The common sort of people, who, to feed themselves, make use of feather, paper, or linen fans, according to their abilities, put me in mind of a poor fellow, who fed himself a long time with hopes of obtaining a place worth at least £50 a year, only because he knew Sir J. F——'s coachman, with whom he spent some £20 or £30 that were his all, in hopes of a recommendation to his master, which his patron even wanted for himself, while he fooled him out of his money. Thus the poor, as well as the rich, aim at something generally above their reach. The wind-mills, by the means of which the rich live, may be designed to denote the kings and princes of those days: mills with mighty sails, which gave that nourishing wind plentifully, according to the dispositions in which they were with respect to the courtiers that continually surrounded them. It also signifies that the latter sometimes get nothing but words or favours, merely honorary, and void of substance and solidity. Some of those royal windmills have been used to wheel round, with every wind, as readily as weathercocks; turning their backs, in an unaccountable manner, to those on whom they looked most favourably but a moment before.

The age during which our doctor flourished has given many instances of this sad truth; as Jacques de Baune, Lord of Semblançay, Admiral Chabot, and the Constable de Bourbon, who having all three possessed King Francis I.'s favour, became the objects and the victims of his hatred. The first, hanged at Montfaucon (the Tyburn of Paris), for a crime of which Louis de Savoy, the King's mother, alone was guilty. The second, condemned without reason, to lose his head on a scaffold, and then declared not guilty; the sense of which usage worked so strongly on his mind, that it effected what the executioner was to have done. And the third, a prince of the blood, and by his great merit high constable of France (a trust thought too great nowadays), first deprived of his government of the Milanese, his master being grown jealous of his glory; then of the profits and exercise of his great office; and, finally, of the vast estate of the house of Bourbon, which was his right of inheritance, as eldest of that branch of the royal family.—*M.*

CHAPTER XLV

HOW PANTAGRUEL WENT ASHORE IN THE ISLAND OF POPE-FIGLAND

THE next morning we arrived at the island of Popefigs; formerly a rich and free people, called the Gaillardets; but now, alas! miserably poor, and under the yoke of the Papimen.[1] The occasion of it was this.

[1] Read Papimanes, as in the original. It is a word composed of *papa*, Pope, and *mania*, madness (in Greek), and means such whose love and zeal for the Pope is so excessive, that it may be counted madness. Here M. Duchat observes, that Spain is a true Papimany country: therefore, adds he, it is not at all

On a certain yearly high holiday, the burgomaster, syndics, and topping rabbies of the Gaillardets, chanced to go into the neighbouring island Papimany to see the festival, and pass away the time. Now one of them having espied the Pope's picture (with the sight of which, according to a laudable custom, the people were blessed on high-offering holidays), made mouths at it, and cried, A fig for it! as a sign of manifest contempt and derision. To be revenged of this affront, the Papimen, some days after, without giving the others the least warning, took arms, and surprised, destroyed, and ruined the whole island of the Gaillardets; putting the men to the sword, and sparing none but the women and children; and those too only on condition to do what the inhabitants of Milan were condemned to, by the Emperor Frederic Barbarossa.

These had rebelled against him in his absence, and ignominiously turned the Empress out of the city, mounting her a-horseback[2] on a mule called Thacor,[3] with her breech foremost towards the old jaded mule's head, and her face turned towards the crupper. Now Frederick being returned, mastered them, and caused so careful a search to be made, that he found out and got the famous mule Thacor. Then the hangman, by his order, clapped a fig into

unlikely, that by the island of Pope-figland, subject to the Papimanes, Rabelais means Navarre, after that about the year 1512, Ferdinand, the Catholic, had seized that kingdom, by virtue of a certain pretended bull, which had put it under an interdict, for adhering, as was pretended, to the council, convened at Pisa, against Pope Julius II.

[2] This infamous punishment is still inflicted in Germany, on professed prostitutes.

[3] A scab or pile in the fundament, Cotgrave says; but, according to the Cambridge Dictionary, it means the fundament itself. See under the word *anus*. The Hebrew word is *tachor*, not *thacor*.

the mule's gimcrack, in the presence of the enslaved cits that were brought into the middle of the great market-place, and proclaimed, in the Emperor's name, with trumpets, that whosoever of them would save his own life, should publicly pull the fig out with his teeth, and after that, put it in again in the very individual cranny whence he had drawn it, without using his hands, and that whoever refused to do this, should presently swing for it, and die in his shoes. Some sturdy fools, standing upon their punctilio, chose honourably to be hanged, rather than submit to so shameful and abominable a disgrace; and others, less nice in point of ceremony, took heart of grace, and even resolved to have at the fig, and a fig for it, rather than make a worse figure with a hempen collar, and die in the air, at so short warning: accordingly when they had neatly picked out the fig with their teeth, from old Thacor's snatch-blatch, they plainly showed it the headsman, saying, *Ecco lo fico!* Behold the fig!

By the same ignominy the rest of these poor distressed Gaillardets saved their bacon, becoming tributaries and slaves, and the name of Pope-figs was given them, because they said, A fig for the Pope's image! Since this, the poor wretches never prospered, but every year the devil was at their doors, and they were plagued with hail, storms, famine, and all manner of woes, as an everlasting punishment for the sin of their ancestors and relations. Perceiving the misery and calamity of that generation, we did not care to go further up into the country; contenting ourselves with going into a little chapel near the haven, to take some holy water. It was dilapidated and ruined, wanting also a cover—like Saint Peter's at Rome. When we were in, as we dipped our fingers in the sanctified cistern,

Pantagruel

we spied, in the middle of that holy pickle, a fellow muffled up with stoles, all under water, like a diving duck, except the tip of his snout, to draw his breath. About him stood three priests, true shavelings, clean shorn and polled, who were muttering strange words to the devils out of a conjuring book.

Pantagruel was not a little amazed at this, and, inquiring what kind of sport these were at, was told, that, for three years last past, the plague had so dreadfully raged in the island, that the better half of it had been utterly depopulated, and the lands lay fallow and unoccupied. Now, the mortality being over, this same fellow, who had crept into the holy tub, having a large piece of ground, chanced to be sowing it with white winter wheat, at the very minute of an hour that a kind of a silly sucking devil, who could not yet write or read, or hail and thunder, unless it were on parsley or coleworts, had got leave of his master Lucifer to go into this island of Pope-figs, where the devils were very familiar with the men and women, and often went to take their pastime.

This same devil being got thither, directed his discourse to the husbandman, and asked him what he was doing. The poor man told him, that he was sowing the ground with corn, to help him to subsist the next year. Ay! but the ground is none of thine, Mr Plough-jobber, cried the devil, but mine; for since the time that you mocked the Pope, all this land has been proscribed, adjudged, and abandoned to us. However, to sow corn is not my province: therefore I will give thee leave to sow the field, that is to say, provided we share the profit. I will, replied the farmer. I mean, said the devil, that of what the land shall bear, two lots shall be made, one of what shall grow above ground, the other of what shall be covered with earth : the right of choosing belongs to me ; for I am a devil of noble and ancient race; thou art a base clown. I therefore choose what shall lie under ground, take thou what shall be above. When dost thou reckon to reap, hah ? About the middle of July, quoth the farmer. Well, said the devil, I'll not fail thee then : in the meantime, slave as thou oughtest. Work, clown, work : I am going to tempt to the pleasing sin of whoring, the nuns of Dryfart, the sham saints of the cowl, and the gluttonish crew : I am more than sure of these. They need but meet, and the job is done : true fire and tinder, touch and take : down falls nun and up gets friar.

ON CHAP. XLV.—By the island of the Pope-figs, is meant those who followed Luther or Calvin's reformation, and chiefly the Germans and the French. They were called the Gaillardes at first ; principally, because they were at first brisk and merry, or gaillard; as when the landsknechts, generally Protestants, plundered Rome in 1527, they led several bishops and cardinals, in their proper accoutrements, through the streets on mules and asses, with their faces turned towards the tail ; threw the host, relics, and images of saints about the streets, and forced the Pope to buy a peace with 400,000 ducats, and remain a prisoner till it was paid, after he had been almost starved in Castel St Angelo, where he invited the cardinals to a treat of ass's flesh, as if it had been one of the greatest dainties imaginable. This our author calls *faire la figue*, to revile and feague, or say, a fig for the Pope ; and he has ingeniously brought in the story of the citizens of Milan, who used an empress just as the landsknechts served the cardinals, which also is somewhat like the practice of the inquisition, who served Protestants so. Now when the Emperor, Charles V., had been too hard for the Protestants in Germany, and the Kings Francis I. and Henry II. had persecuted them in France, they were in a dismal condition, and under the yoke of the Papimanes, and got the name of Pope-figs, not only because they had reviled the Pope, but because they were forced to creep to him, and lay under his lash. The hail, storms, and famine, that plague them continually, mean the persecutions ; the hobgoblins and devils that haunt them, are the monks, as the author insinuates at the latter end of chapter 46.

By the country fellow, who runs into the holy-water-stock, and is immersed in that blessed pickle, all but the tip of the snout, for fear of being clawed off by the devil, we must understand the constraint in which the Protestants lived, while to deliver themselves from the persecutions of the Popish hobgoblins, they were forced to be plunged over head and ears in the superstitious worship of the Church of Rome; took holy water by handfuls, and hid themselves under stoles, which are the badge of priesthood: that is to say, they professed Popery, as they are now forced to do in France: and some even entered into orders, and were priests, monks, bishops, and even cardinals, though they were far from being Papists in their hearts.

Brissonet, Bishop of Meaux, was one of these; for having silenced the preaching Franciscans throughout his diocese, and appointed James Fabre, *alias* La Fevre of Estaple, Girard Ruffi, Michael Arande, and Martial, to preach against the errors of the Church of Rome, he recanted, through fear, as soon as he was called to an account about it. Ruffi himself did the same, and, from a Lutheran preacher, became a Roman bishop; and so did Martial, who being at first Brissonet's disciple, was afterwards penitentiary, or head-confessor at Paris. The Bishop of Valence, our Panurge, was one of those dissemblers; and even the great Admiral Chatillon's brother, Odet, the cardinal to whom this book is dedicated by Rabelais, who himself did like the rest.—*M.*

CHAPTER XLVI

HOW A JUNIOR DEVIL WAS FOOLED BY A HUSBANDMAN OF POPE-FIGLAND

In the middle of July, the devil came to the place aforesaid, with all his crew at his heels, a whole choir of the younger fry of hell; and having met the farmer, said to him, Well, clod-pate, how hast thou done, since I went? Thou and I must share the concern. Ay, master devil, quoth the clown, it is but reason we should. Then he and his men began to cut and reap the corn : and, on the other side, the devil's imps fell to work, grubbing up and pulling out the stubble by the root.

The countryman had his corn thrashed, winnowed it, put it into sacks, and went with it to market. The same did the devil's servants, and sat them down there by the man to sell their straw.[1] The countryman sold off his corn at a good rate, and with the money filled an old kind of a demi-buskin, which was fastened to his girdle. But the devil a sou the devils took : far from taking hansel, they were flouted and jeered by the country louts.

Market being over, quoth the devil to the farmer, Well, clown, thou hast choused me once, it is thy fault ; chouse me twice, it will be mine. Nay, good sir devil, replied the farmer, how can I be said to have choused you, since it was your worship that chose first ? The truth is, that, by this trick, you thought to cheat me, hoping that nothing would spring out of the earth for my share, and that you should find whole underground the corn which I had sowed, and with it tempt the poor and needy, the close hypocrite, or the covetous griper ; thus making them fall into your snares. But troth, you must even go to school yet : you are no conjurer, for aught I see : for the corn that was sown is dead and rotten, its corruption having caused the generation of that which you saw me sell : so you chose the worst, and therefore are cursed in the gospel.[2] Well, talk no more of it ! quoth the devil : what canst thou sow our field with for next year ? If a man

---

[1] Read stubble.
[2] An old proverb, which involves slanderers and devils in one and the same malediction ; for as much as the former choosing rather to speak evil than good of their neighbours, are like the devils, who, in the day of judgment, shall fall on the wicked, and let good men alone.

would make the best of it, answered the ploughman, it were fit he sow it with radishes. Now, cried the devil, thou talkest like an honest fellow, bumpkin: well, sow me good store of radishes, I will see and keep them safe from storms, and will not hail a bit on them. But hark ye me! this time I bespeak for my share what shall be above ground; what is under shall be thine. Drudge on, looby, drudge on! I am going to tempt heretics; their souls are dainty victuals,[3] when broiled in rashers, and well powdered. My Lord Lucifer has the griping in the guts; they will make a dainty warm dish for his honour's maw.

When the season of radishes was come, our devil failed not to meet in the field, with a train of rascally underlings, all waiting devils, and finding there the farmer and his men, he began to cut and gather the leaves of the radishes. After him the farmer with his spade dug up the radishes, and clapped them up into pouches. This done, the farmer, and their gangs, hied them to market, and there the farmer presently made good money of his radishes: but the poor devil took nothing; nay, what was worse, he was made a common laughing-stock by the gaping hoydens. I see thou hast played me a scurvy trick, thou villainous fellow! cried the angry devil: at last I am fully resolved even to make an end of the business betwixt thee and myself, about the ground, and these shall be the terms: we will clapperclaw each other, and whoever of us two shall first cry, Hold! shall quit his share of the field, which shall wholly belong to the conqueror. I fix the time for this trial of skill, on this day seven-night: assure thyself that I will claw thee off like a devil. I was

[3] Those whom the devil, in those days tempted to burn the Lutherans, did really believe his devilship's mouth watered at the souls of those supposed strayers from the fold of the church.

going to tempt your fornicators, bailiffs, perplexers of causes, scriveners, forgers of deeds, two-handed councillors, prevaricating solicitors, and other such vermin; but they were so civil as to send me word by an interpreter, that they are all mine already. Besides our master Lucifer is so cloyed with their souls, that he often sends them back to the smutty scullions, and slovenly devils of his kitchen, and they scarce go down with them, unless now and then, when they are high-seasoned.[4]

Some say there is no breakfast like a student's, no dinner like a lawyer's, no afternoon's nunchion like a vine-dresser's, no supper like a tradesman's, no second supper [5] like a serving-wench's, and none of these meals equal to a frockified hobgoblin's.[6] All this is true enough. Accordingly, at my Lord Lucifer's first course, hobgoblins, *alias* imps in cowls, are a standing dish. He willingly used to breakfast on students; but, alas, I do not know by what ill luck they have of late years joined the Holy Bible [7] to their studies: so the devil a one we can get down among us; and I verily believe that unless the hypocrites of the tribe of Levi help us in it, taking from the enlightened book-mongers their St Paul, either by threats, revilings, force, violence, fire, and faggot, we shall not be able to hook in any more of them, to nibble at below. He dines commonly on councillors, mischief-mongers, multipliers of law

---

[4] It is said, such sort of souls soon corrupt.

[5] *Reguoubillonner;* to steal an after supper : banquet late at nights ; as servants frequently do, when their masters and mistresses are in bed.

[6] *Il n'est vie que de coquin,* no life like a beggar's, says the old proverb.

[7] Here Rabelais smells of the fagot, says M. Duchat. [A French way of speaking, significative of the danger one runs of being burned for a heretic.]

suits, such as wrest and pervert right and law, and grind and fleece the poor: he never fears to want any of these. But who can endure to be wedded to a dish?

He said, the other day, at a full chapter, that he had a great mind to eat the soul of one of the fraternity of the cowl, that had forgot to speak for himself, in his sermon; and he promised double pay, and a large pension, to any one that should bring him such a tit-bit piping hot. We all went a hunting after such a rarity, but came home without the prey: for they all admonish the good women to remember their convent. As for afternoon nunchions, he has left them off, since he was so woefully griped with the cholic; his fosterers, sutlers, charcoal-men, and boiling cooks having been sadly mauled and peppered off in the northern countries.[8]

His high devilship sups very well on tradesmen, usurers, apothecaries, cheats, coiners, and adulterers of wares. Now and then, when he is on the merry pin, his second supper is of serving-wenches; who, after they have, by stealth, soaked their faces with their master's good liquor, fill up the vessel with it at second hand, or with other stinking water.

Well, drudge on, boor, drudge on: I am going to tempt the students of Trebisonde,[9] to leave father and mother, forego for ever the established and common rule of living, disclaim and free themselves from obeying their lawful sovereign's edicts,

[8] This seems to regard the expulsion of the monks out of England, under Henry VIII. and Edward VI.; and also that of the religious out of the two northern kingdoms.

[9] Read Trebizonde. The author seems here to derive the name of the imperial city of Trebizonde from the Greek $\tau\rho\alpha\pi\epsilon\zeta\alpha$, *mensa*, a table, for the opportunity of insinuating that none but gormandizers and idle bellies would take up with a cloistered life.

live in absolute liberty, proudly despise every one, laugh at all mankind, and taking the fine jovial little cap of poetic licence,[10] become so many pretty hobgoblins.[11]

ON CHAP. XLVI.—The stubble and the leaves of the radishes, which are all that falls to the young devil's share, while the countryman reaps the profit of the corn and fruit he had sowed in his field, show that the pretended Papists only gave the outside and insignificant forms to the Church of Rome, and that their hearts and minds were not inclinable to follow its doctrine. Our author's honest boldness is very remarkable, both in this chapter and many of the next.' He makes the young devil say, that at Lucifer's first course, hobgoblins (*alias* imps in cowls) are a standing dish. He willingly, says the imp, used to breakfast on students ; but alas, I do not know by what ill luck they have of late joined the Holy Bible to their studies ; so the devil a one can get down among us ; and I verily believe, that unless the cafards (*i.e.*, hypocrites of the tribe of Levi) help us in it, taking from the enlightened bookmongers their St Paul, either by threats, revilings, force, violence, or fire and faggot, we shall not be able to hook in any more of them to nibble at below.

---

[10] Rabelais says, And taking the fine jovial little *biggin* of poetic innocence. On which M. Duchat observes *beguin* is the capuche or monachal hood, invented to distinguish from seculars (or people of the world) such persons as make professions of a benignity and an innocence worthy of the golden age of the poets. In Flanders, they called *benings* and *beningues* (some years after the establishment of the two first orders of religious mendicants) certain men and certain women, who, without making vows, devoting themselves in an especial manner to works of charity and mercy, took, in imitation of the said religious, a sort of hood, as a badge, that should prevent people's looking upon them, to be entirely of the secular kind. From those words it is, that they have since corruptly been called *beguins*, and *beguines*, and at length their hood too was called *beguin*. Friar James de Guise, in his Chronicles of Hainault, vol. 3, ch. 133, says the Countess of Flanders began the *benignage*, and instituted the first *chapellany*.
[11] *Farfadets gentils*. Gentlemen hobgoblins, *i.e.*, gentlemen monks. The author ridicules the Benedictines and Bernardins, who assume the title of *dom* (from *dominus*) as if they were all gentlemen.

The fosterers, sutlers, charcoal-men, and boiling cooks of hell, that were mauled and peppered off in the northern countries, are the monks and priests who were routed there, particularly in England.

By the students of Trebisonde, he means those of the Popish universities, where, as he says, they are tempted by the devils (by which he means monks and priests, professors, and their tutors) to leave father and mother, forego forever the established and common rule of living, free themselves from obeying their lawful sovereign's edicts, live in absolute liberty, and taking the fine jovial little cap of poetic licence, become so many pretty hobgoblins. The cap of licence means their degrees, or the cowl ; and poetic is only added to blind the thing ; so the monks leave father and mother, and disclaim all authority but the Pope's.—*M.*

CHAPTER XLVII

HOW THE DEVIL WAS DECEIVED BY AN OLD WOMAN OF POPE-FIGLAND

The country lob trudged home very much concerned and thoughtful, you may swear; insomuch that his good woman, seeing him thus look moping, weened that something had been stolen from him at market: but when she had heard the cause of his affliction, and seen his budget well lined with coin, she bade him be of good cheer, assuring him that he would be never the worse for the scratching bout in question; wishing him only to leave her to manage that business, and not trouble his head about it; for she had already contrived how to bring him off cleverly. Let the worst come to the worst, said the husband-man, it will be but a scratch; for I'll yield at the first stroke, and quit the field. Quit a fart! replied the wife; he shall have none of the field: rely upon me, and be quiet; let me alone to deal with him. You say he is a pimping little devil, that is enough; I will soon make him give up the field, I will warrant you. Indeed, had he been a great devil, it had been somewhat.

The day that we landed in the island happened to be that which the devil had fixed for the combat. Now the countryman, having, like a good Catholic, very fairly confessed himself, and received,[1] betimes in the morning, by the advice of the vicar, had hid himself, all but the snout, in the holy water pot, in the posture in which we found him; and just as they were telling us the story, news came that the old woman had fooled the devil, and gained the field. You may not be sorry, perhaps, to hear how this happened.

The devil, you must know, came to the poor man's door, and rapping there, cried, So, ho! ho the house! ho, clodpate! where art thou? Come out with a vengeance! come out with a wannion! come out and be damned! now for clawing! Then briskly and resolutely entering the house, and not finding the countryman there, he spied his wife lying on the ground, piteously weeping and howling. What is the matter? asked the devil. Where is he? what does he? Oh! that I knew where he is, replied threescore and five, the wicked rogue! the butcherly dog! the murderer! He has spoiled me; I am undone; I die of what he has done to me. How! cried the devil, what is it? I will tickle him off for you by and by. Alas! cried the old dissembler, he told me, the butcher, the tyrant, the tearer of devils, told me, that he had made a match to scratch with you this day, and to try his claws, he

[1] *Avoit communié*, *i.e.*, had taken the sacrament.

did but just touch me with his little finger, here betwixt the legs, and has spoiled me for ever. Oh! I am a dead woman; I shall never be myself again: do but see! Nay, and besides, he talked of going to the smith's, to have his pounces sharpened and pointed. Alas! you are uudone, Mr Devil; good sir! scamper quickly, I am sure he won't stay; save yourself, I beseech you. While she said this, she uncovered herself up to the chin, after the manner in which the Persian women met their children who fled from the fight,[2] and plainly showed her what-do-ye-call-it. The frightened devil, seeing the enormous solution of the continuity in all its dimensions, blessed himself, and cried out, Mahon! Demiourgon! Megæra! Alecto! Persephone! Slife! catch me here when he comes! I am gone: Sdeath! what a gash! I resign him the field.

Having heard the catastrophe of the story, we retired a-shipboard, not being willing to stay there any longer. Pantagruel gave to the poor's box of the fabric of the church,[3] eighteen thousand good royals, in commiseration of the poverty of the people, and the calamity of the place.

ON CHAP. XLVII.—By the old woman of Pope-figland, who frights the devil and puts him to flight, the author means that the monks and priests of the Church of Rome were so ignorant, and their tenets so groundless, that the very women could make fools of them even at demonstrative arguments.—*M.*

---

[2] See Plutarch. These women, when their sons were flying from the enemy, pulled up their clothes, and in scorn bade them come and hide themselves once more in their mother's bellies.

[3] A good lesson for princes to be generous and liberal on occasion. Pantagruel went nowhere but he bestowed his favours liberally, and left all the marks of a princely munificence.

CHAPTER XLVIII

HOW PANTAGRUEL WENT ASHORE AT THE ISLAND OF PAPIMANY

HAVING left the desolate island of the Pope-figs, we sailed, for the space of a day, very fairly and merrily, and made the blessed island Papimany. As soon as we had dropped anchor in the road, before we had well moored our ship with ground-tackle, four persons, in different garbs, rowed towards us in a skiff. One of them was dressed like a monk in his frock, draggle-tailed, and booted: the other like a falconer, with a lure, and a long-winged hawk on his fist: the third like a solicitor, with a large bag, full of informations, subpœnas, breviates, bills, writs, cases, and other implements of pettifogging. The fourth looked like one of your vine barbers about Orleans, with a jantee pair of canvas trousers, a dosser, and a pruning-knife at his girdle.

As soon as the boat had clapped them on board, they all with one voice asked, Have you seen him, good passengers, have you seen him?—Who? asked Pantagruel. You know who, answered they. Who is it? asked Friar John. 'Sblood and 'ounds, I'll thrash him thick and threefold. This he said, thinking that they inquired after some robber, murderer, or church-breaker. Oh, wonderful! cried the four, do not you foreign people know the one? Sirs, replied Epistemon, we do not understand those terms: but if you will be pleased to let us know who you mean, we will tell you the truth of the matter, without any more ado. We mean, said they, He that' is. Did you ever see him? He that is, returned Pantagruel, according to our theological doctrine, is God, who said to Moses, I am that I am.[1] We never saw Him, nor can He be beheld by mortal eyes. We mean nothing less than that supreme God, who rules in heaven, replied they; we mean the god on earth. Did you ever see him? Upon my honour, replied Carpalim, they mean the Pope. Ay, ay! answered Panurge: yea verily, gentlemen, I have seen three of them, whose sight has not much bettered me. How! cried they, our sacred decretals inform us, that there never is more than one living. I mean successively, one after the other, returned Panurge: otherwise I never saw more than one at a time.

O thrice and four times happy people! cried they, you are welcome, and more than double welcome! They then kneeled down before us and would have kissed our feet, but we would not suffer it, telling them that, should the Pope come thither in his own person, it is all they could do to him. No, certainly, answered they, for we have already resolved upon the matter. We would kiss his bare arse without boggling at it, and eke his two-pounders: for he has a pair of them, the holy father, that he has; we find it so by our fine decretals, otherwise he could

---

[1] Instead of those words, Rabelais only says, 'Et en tel mot se declaira à Moses,' *i.e.*, and in that word He declared Himself to Moses. What word? *He that is*: not, I am that I am. God said not to Moses, I am that I am, but *I am He that is*. And therefore Rabelais makes him say so too. Our English Bibles indeed have it, I am that I am, and so has the Latin, *Ego sum qui sum*; but the former should be, as I said before, I am He that is, and the latter, *Ego sum qui est*. The Septuagint translation has it right, ἐγώ εἰμι ὁ ὤν, I am He that is. Accordingly Rabelais begins this period with *He that is*; for no being besides God truly is.

not be Pope. So that, according to our subtile decretaline philosophy, this is a necessary consequence: he is Pope; therefore, he has genitories, and should genitories no more be found in the world, the world could no more have a Pope.

While they were talking thus, Pantagruel inquired of one of the coxswain's crew, who those persons were? he answered, that they were the four estates of the realm; and added, that we should be made as welcome as princes, since we had seen the Pope. Panurge having been acquainted with this by Pantagruel, said to him in his ear, I swear and vow, sir, it is even so.; he that has patience may compass any thing. Our seeing the Pope hath [hitherto] done us no good: now, in the devil's name, it will do us a great deal. We then went ashore, and the whole country, men, women, and children, came to meet us as in a solemn procession. Our four estates cried out to them with a loud voice, 'They have seen him! they have seen him! they have seen him!' That proclamation being made, all the mob kneeled before us, lifting up their hands towards heaven, and crying, O happy men! O most happy! and this acclamation lasted about a quarter of an hour.

Then came the schoolmaster of the place, with all his ushers, and schoolboys, whom he magisterially flogged, as they used to whip children in our country formerly, when some criminal was hanged, that they might remember it. This displeased Pantagruel, who said to them, Gentlemen, if you do not leave off whipping these poor children, I am gone. The people were amazed, hearing his stentorian voice; and I saw a little hump with long fingers, say to the hypodidascal, What! in the name of wonder! do all those that see the Pope grow as tall as yon huge fellow that threatens us? Ah! how I shall think time long till I have seen him too, that I may grow and look as big. In short, the acclamations were so great, that Homenas² (so they called their bishop) hastened thither, on an unbridled mule, with green trappings, attended by his apposts (as they said) and his supposts, or officers, bearing crosses, banners, standards, canopies, torches, holy waterpots, etc. He too wanted to kiss our feet (as the good Christian, Valfinier, did to Pope Clement), saying, that one of their hypothetes, that is, one of the scavengers, scourers, and commentators of their holy decretals, had written that, in the same manner as the Messiah, so long and so much expected by the Jews, at last appeared among them; so, on some happy day of God, the Pope would come into that island; and that, while they waited for that blessed time, if any who had seen him at Rome, or elsewhere, chanced to come among them, they should be sure to make much of them, feast them plentifully, and treat them with a great deal of reverence. However, we civilly desired to be excused.

² This word is a production of that of *homme*. They use it in Languedoc, when they would say, a great loggerheaded booby, that has neither wit nor breeding.

CHAPTER XLIX

HOW HOMENAS, BISHOP OF PAPIMANY, SHOWED US THE URANOPET[1] DECRETALS

HOMENAS then said to us: It is enjoined us by our holy decretals to visit churches first, and taverns after. Therefore, not to decline that fine institution, let us go to church; we will afterwards go and feast ourselves. Man of God, quoth Friar John, do you go before, we will follow you; you spoke in the matter properly, and like a good Christian; it is long since we saw any such. For my part this rejoices my mind very much, and I verily believe that I shall have the better stomach after it. Well, it is a happy thing to meet with good men! Being come near the gate of the church, we spied a huge thick book, gilt, and covered all over with precious stones, as rubies, emeralds, diamonds, and pearls, more, or at least as valuable as those which Augustus consecrated to Jupiter Capitolinus. This book hung in the air, being fastened with two thick chains of gold to the zoophore[2] of the porch. We looked on it, and admired it. As for Pantagruel, he

---

[1] Descending from heaven, or ascending to heaven.
[2] Cotgrave defines it, A painted carved girdle, or border, about a porch or pillar. But he does not tell us whence it is derived. The Cambridge Dictionary, under the word zophorus (which certainly is misspelt for zoophorus), says, 'A frieze or border in pillars, or other works, set off with the shapes of several things (he should have said living creatures, Ζωα, and other things) graven upon it.' I shall only add, that the Greeks sometimes mean by it the oblique circle of the heavens, called the Zodiac, filled with the representations of animals, etc. Architects call it, as I said before, the frieze, which everybody knows is between the architrave and the cornice.

handled it, and dandled it, and turned it as he pleased, for he could reach it without straining; and he protested, that whenever he touched it, he was seized with a pleasant tickling at his finger's end, new life and activity in his arms, and a violent temptation in his mind to beat one or two serjeants, or such officers, provided they were not of the shaveling kind.³ Homenas then said to us, The law was formerly given to the Jews by Moses, written by God himself. At Delphos, before the portal of Apollo's temple, this sentence, ΓΝΩΘΙ ΣΕ ΑΥΤΟΝ, was found written with a divine hand. And some time after it, E I was also seen,⁴ and as divinely written and transmitted from heaven. Cybele's image was brought out of heaven, into a field called Pessinunt, in Phrygia; so was that of Diana to Tauris, if you will believe Euripides; the oriflamme, or holy standard, was transmitted out of heaven to the noble and most Christian kings of France, to fight against the unbelievers. In the reign of Numa Pompilius, second King of the Romans, the famous copper buckler called Ancile, was seen to descend from heaven. At Acropolis, near Athens, Minerva's statue formerly fell from the imperial heaven. In like manner

---

³ Because by the decretals it was forbid, under pain of excommunication, on any account whatever, to strike either clerics or laics that were tonsured. Now, before the year 1425, there were in France multitudes of serjeants clerical, and others laical, who had undergone tonsure, and who, under favour of that, committed several grievous offences in the execution of their offices, without being liable to any punishment; and though, in that year, and even in 1518, endeavours were used to redress those grievances, both by arrêt and edict, the disorder still continued in some when our author wrote this.

⁴ Plutarch has written a treatise, showing the signification of this mysterious E I; which two letters were also divinely written, and transmitted from heaven, says the Dutch scholiast.

the sacred decretals, which you see, were written with the hand of an angel,[5] of the cherubim kind. You outlandish people will hardly believe this, I fear. Little enough of conscience, said Panurge.— And then, continued Homenas, they were miraculously transmitted to us here from the very heaven of heavens; in the same manner as the river Nile is called Diipetes, by Homer, the father of all philosophy (the holy decretals always excepted). Now, because you have seen the Pope, their evangelist and everlasting protector, we will give you leave to see and kiss them on the inside, if you think meet. But then you must fast three days before, and canonically confess; nicely and strictly mustering up, and inventorising your sins, great and small, so thick that one single circumstance of them may not escape you; as our holy decretals, which you see, direct. This will take up some time. Man of God, answered Panurge, we have seen and descried decrees, and eke decretals enough of conscience; some on paper, others on parchment, fine and gay like any painted paper lantern,[6] some on vellum, some in manuscript, and others in print: so you need not take half these pains to show these. We will take the good-will for the deed, and thank you as much as if we had. Ay, marry! said Homenas, but you never saw these that are angelically written. Those in your country are only transcripts from ours; as we find it written by one of our old

---

[5] Erasmus, in his *Exequiæ Seraphicæ*. 'Christus legem evangelicam promulgavit: Franciscus legem suam, angeli manibus descriptam, tradidit seraphicis fratribus.' This tradition could not but be known to Homenas: but, as it would have derogated from the dignity of the decretals, he did not think himself obliged to take any notice of it, much less to lay any stress upon it.

[6] *Parchemin lanterné* means only transparent, as the horn of a lantern.

decretaline scholiasts. For me, do not spare me;
I do not value the labour, so I may serve you; do
but tell me whether you will be confessed, and fast
only three short little days of God? As for con-
fessing, answering Panurge, there can be no great
harm in it; but this same fasting, master of mine,
will hardly down with us at this time, for we have
so very much overfasted ourselves at sea, that the
spiders have spun their cobwebs over our grinders.
Do but look on this good Friar John des Entonneures
(Homenas then courteously demy-clipped him about
the neck), some moss is growing in his throat, for
want of bestirring and exercising his chaps. He
speaks the truth, vouched Friar John; I have so
much fasted that I am almost grown hump-
shouldered.[7] Come, then, let us go into the
church, said Homenas; and pray forgive us if, for
the present, we do not sing you a fine high mass.
The hour of mid-day is past, and after it our sacred
decretals forbid us to sing mass, I mean your high
and lawful mass. But I will say a low and dry one,[8]
for you. I had rather have one moistened with
some good Anjou wine, cried Panurge; fall to, fall
to your low mass, and dispatch. Odd's-boddikins!
quoth Friar John, it frets me to the guts that I must
have an empty stomach at this time of day. For,
had I eaten a good breakfast, and fed like a monk,
if he should chance to sing us the *Requiem æternam
dona eis, Domine*, I had then brought thither bread
and wine for the traits passez [9] (those that are gone

[7] It should be, grown quite hump-shouldered, or hump-backed.
Tout bossu, in French. This expression is taken from the corre-
spondency there is between a stomach that is empty, and a sack
that is so, which cannot stand on end, but falls together of a
heap.
[8] A little mass, or low mass: a mass without communion.
[9] Rabelais plays upon the word *trépasséz* (the dead). You

before). Well, patience; pull away, and save tide: short and sweet,[10] I pray you, and this for a cause.

CHAPTER L

HOW HOMENAS SHOWED US THE ARCH-TYPE, OR REPRESENTATION OF A POPE

MASS being mumbled over, Homenas took a huge bundle of keys out of a trunk near the head altar, and put thirty-two of them into so many keyholes; put back so many springs; then with fourteen more mastered so many padlocks, and at last opened an iron window strongly barred above the said altar. This being done, in token of great mystery, he covered himself with wet sackcloth, and drawing a curtain of crimson satin, showed us an image

must know that, to go to mass for the dead, is, say the Italians, 'andar alla messa doppo haver fatta collatione, perche vi si porta pane e vino,' *i.e.*, to go to mass after having taken a repast, because then you carry with you bread and wine (in your belly suppose). This is what Friar John merrily alludes to.

[10] Don't be long about your mass. Rabelais says, 'Troussez la court, de paour (peur) que ne se crotte.' Tuck it up short, for fear of its daggling. Thus in the play called the Passion of Jesus Christ, with four dramatis personæ, St John, to the headsman who was come to dispatch him:

'Amy, puis que finer me fault, Pour tenir justice et raison, Accorde que face oraison, A Dieu, per pensée devote.'	'Friend, since I must suffer death For having been sincere, Grant me to finish my last breath, To God in humble prayer.'
GRONGNART, *Bourreau*.	GRUMBLESBY, *the Headsman*.
'Fay le donc court, que ne se crotte, Je ne veuil plus attendre a l'huis.'	'Then make it short for fear of daggling; I cannot stand much longer haggling.'

Pantagruel

daubed over, coarsely enough, to my thinking: then he touched it with a pretty long stick, and made us all kiss the part of the stick that had touched the image. After this he said unto us, What think you of this image? It is the likeness of a Pope, answered Pantagruel: I know it by the triple crown, his furred amice, his rochet, and his slipper. You are in the right, said Homenas; it is the idea of that same good god on earth, whose coming we devoutly await, and whom we hope one day to see in this country. O happy, wished-for, and much-expected day! and happy, most happy you, whose propitious stars have so favoured you, as to let you see the living and real face of this good god on earth! by the single sight of whose picture we obtain full remission of all the sins which we remember that we have committed, as also a third part, and eighteen quarantaines of the sins which we have forgot:[1] and indeed we only see it on high annual holidays.

This caused Pantagruel to say, that it was a work like those which Dædalus used to make,[2] since, though it were deformed and ill-drawn, nevertheless some divine energy, in point of pardons, lay hid and concealed in it. Thus, said Friar John, at Sevillé, the rascally beggars being one evening on a solemn holiday at supper in the spital, one bragged of having got six blancs, or twopence halfpenny; another eight liards, or twopence; a third, seven caroluses, or sixpence; but an old mumper

[1] This is the style of the penitential canons.
[2] Wrong; it should have been translated, A work like that which once, upon a certain occasion, was made by Dædalus. For Dædalus was a most ingenious artificer, and this work here alluded to was as clumsily made as possibly he could make it, and that for a cause, which the reader will see in M. Duchat's note; a pleasant story enough about Juno's jealousy, but too long to be here inserted.

made his vaunts of having got three testons, or five shillings. Ah! but, cried his comrades, thou hast a leg of God;[3] as if, continued Friar John, some divine virtue could lie hid in a stenching ulcerated rotten shank. Pray, said Pantagruel, when you are for telling us some such nauseous tale, be so kind as not to forget to provide a basin, Friar John: I'll assure you, I had much ado to forbear bringing up my breakfast. Fie! I wonder a man of your coat is not ashamed to use thus the sacred name of God, in speaking of things so filthy and abominable! fie, I say. If among your monking tribes such an abuse of words is allowed, I beseech you leave it there, and do not let it come out of the cloisters. Physicians, said Epistemon, thus attribute a kind of divinity to some diseases: Nero also extolled mushrooms, and, in a Greek proverb, termed them divine food, because with them he had poisoned Claudius, his predecessor. But methinks, gentlemen, this same picture is not over-like our late Popes.[4] For I have seen them, not with their pallium, amice, or rochet on, but with helmets on their heads, more like the top of a Persian turban; and while the Christian commonwealth was in peace, they alone were most furiously and cruelly making war. This must have been then, returned Homenas, against the rebellious, heretical Protestants; reprobates, who are disobedient to the holiness of this good god on earth. It is not only lawful for him to do so, but it is enjoined him by the sacred decretals; and if any dare transgress one single iota against their commands, whether they be

[3] Both a Hebrew and Greek expression for a rotten ulcerated leg.
[4] Alexander VI. and Julius II. But chiefly the last, who in 1511, with a helmet on his head, and cuirass on his back and breast, appeared before Miranda, to hasten the siege of that place, which he thought his generals were slack in carrying on.

emperors, kings, dukes, princes, or commonwealths, he is immediately to pursue them with fire and sword, strip them of all their goods, take their kingdoms from them, proscribe them, anathematize them, and destroy not only their bodies, those of their children, relations, and others, but damn also their souls to the very bottom of the most hot and burning cauldron in hell. Here, in the devil's name! said Panurge, the people are no heretics; such as was our Raminagrobis, and as they are in Germany and England. You are Christians of the best edition, all picked and culled, for aught I see. Ay! marry are we, returned Homenas, and for that reason we shall all be saved. Now let us go and bless ourselves with holy-water, and then to dinner.

CHAPTER LI

TABLE-TALK IN PRAISE OF THE DECRETALS

Now, topers, pray observe that while Homenas was saying his dry mass, three collectors, or licensed beggars of the church, each of them with a large basin, went round among the people, with a loud voice: Pray remember the blessed men who have seen his face. As we came out of the temple, they brought their basins, brim-full of Papimany chink, to Homenas, who told us that it was plentifully to feast with; and that, of this contribution and voluntary tax, one part should be laid out in good drinking, another in good eating, and the remainder in both: according to an admirable exposition hidden in a corner of their holy decretals; which was performed to a T, and that at a noted tavern not much unlike that of Will's at Amiens.[1] Believe me, we tickled it off there with copious cramming, and numerous swilling.

I made two notable observations at that dinner: the one, that there was not one dish served up, whether of cabrittas, capons, hogs (of which latter there is great plenty in Papimany),[2] pigeons, conies, leverets, turkeys, or others, without abundance of magistral stuffing: the other, that every course, and the fruit also, were served up by unmarried females of the place, tight lasses, I will assure you, waggish, fair, good-conditioned, and comely, spruce and fit for business. They were all clad in fine long white albs, with two girdles; their hair interwoven with narrow tape and purple riband, stuck with roses, gilly-flowers, marjoram, daffidown-dillies, thyme, and other sweet flowers.

At every cadence, they invited us to drink and bang it about, dropping us neat and genteel courtesies: nor was the sight of them unwelcome to all the company: and as for Friar John, he leered on them sideways, like a cur that steals a capon. When the first course was taken off, the females melodiously sang us an epode in the praise of the sacrosanct decretals; and then, the second course being served up, Homenas, joyful and cheery, said to one of the she butlers, Light here, Clerica.[3]

[1] It has been already said, in a note on ch. xi. of this book, how it came about there were formerly so many cooks' shops at Amiens.

[2] The sneerers, among the Catholics, call their canons God Almighty's hogs.

[3] Rabelais' words are *Clerice, esclaire icy*. A sensible pun to such as speak French. Light here, clerk. Words properly of a curate ordering his young clerk to light him with his lantern, in administering the sacraments to a sick person. Homenas makes

Pantagruel

Immediately one of the girls brought him a tallboy brim-full of extravagant wine.[4] He took fast hold of it, and fetching a deep sigh,[5] said to Pantagruel, My lord, and you, my good friends, here's to ye, with all my heart ! you are all very welcome. When he had tipped that off, and given the tall-boy to the pretty creature, he lifted up his voice and said, O most holy Decretals, how good is good wine found through your means! This is the best jest we have had yet, observed Panurge. But it would still be a better, said Pantagruel, if they could turn bad wine into good.

O seraphic Sextum! continued Homenas, how necessary are you not to the salvation of poor mortals! O cherubic Clementinæ! how perfectly the perfect institution of a true Christian is contained and described in you! O angelical Extravagantés! how many poor souls that wander up and down in mortal bodies, through this vale of misery, would perish, were it not for you! When, ah! when shall this special gift of grace be bestowed on mankind, as to lay aside all other studies and concerns, to use you, to peruse you, to understand you, to know you by heart, to practise you, to incorporate you, to turn you into blood, and incentre you into the deepest ventricles of their brains, the inmost marrow of their bones, and most intricate labyrinth of their arteries?

use of it here, to let his servants know they should fill him nothing but bumpers (*lampées*, in French), which likewise alludes to lamp-light.

[4] Tythe wine, granted to Homenas' church by some *extravaganté*, *i.e.*, extraordinary constitution added to the body of the canon law.

[5] Much cause indeed to sigh, like the fat prior, in Marot, who cried :

'Qu'on ha de maulx pour servir saincte eglise !
O ! how much we go through who serve the church !'

Then, ah! then, and no sooner than then, nor otherwise than thus, shall the world be happy! While the old man was thus running on, Espistemon rose and softly said to Panurge, For want of a close stool, I must even leave you for a moment or two: this stuff has unbunged the orifice of my mustard-barrel: but I'll not tarry long.

Then, ah! then, continued Homenas, no hail, frost, ice, snow, overflowing, or *vis major:* then, plenty of all earthly goods here below. Then, uninterrupted and eternal peace through the universe, an end of all wars, plunderings, drudgeries, robbing, assassinates, unless it be to destroy these cursed rebels the heretics. Oh! then, rejoicing, cheerfulness, jollity, solace, sports, and delicious pleasures, over the face of the earth. Oh! what great learning, inestimable erudition, and god-like precepts, are knit, linked, riveted, and mortised in the divine chapters of these eternal Decretals!

Oh! how wonderfully, if you read but one demy-canon, short paragraph, or single observation of these sacrosanct decretals, how wonderfully, I say, do you not perceive to kindle in your hearts a furnace of divine love, charity towards your neighbour (provided he be no heretic), bold contempt of all casual and sublunary things, firm content in all your affections, and extatic elevation of soul even to the third heaven!

CHAPTER LII

A CONTINUATION OF THE MIRACLES CAUSED BY
THE DECRETALS

SPOKE like an organ,[1] quoth Panurge; but for my part, I believe as little of it as I can. For, one day by chance I happened to read a chapter of them at Poictiers, at the most decretalipotent Scotch doctor's, and old Nick turn me into bumfodder, if this did not make me so hide-bound and costive, that for four or five days I hardly scumbered one poor butt of sir-reverence; and that, too, was full as dry and hard, I protest, as Catullus tells us were those of his neighbour Furius:

> 'Nec toto decies cacas in anno,
> Atque id durius est fabâ, et lapillis:
> Quod tu si manibus teras, fricesque,
> Non unquam digitum inquinare posses.'

Oh, ho! cried Homenas, by our lady! it may be you were then in a state of mortal sin, my friend. Well turned, cried Panurge, this was a new strain, egad!

One day, said Friar John, at Sevillé I had applied to my posteriors, by way of hind-towel, a leaf of an old Clementinæ, which our rent-gatherer, John Guimard had thrown out into the green of our cloister; now the devil broil me like a black pudding, if I was not so abominably plagued with chaps, chawns, and

[1] *Voicy, dist Panurge, qui dict d'orgues.* *Orgues* meaning organs, Panurge does as much as say to Homenas, You have heard others talk thus, and upon that footing you affirm it; and so you do just like the organs, which yield a delightful sound, when well managed; but for my part, I will not believe you without good vouchers.

piles at the fundament, that the orifice of my poor nockandroe was in a most woeful pickle for I do not know how long. By our lady! cried Homenas, it was a plain punishment of God, for the sin that you had committed in bewraying that sacred book, which you ought rather to have kissed and adored; I say with an adoration of latria, or of hyperdulia at least: the Panormitan[2] never told a lie in the matter.

Saith Ponocrates: At Montpellier, John Choüart having bought of the monks of St Olary a delicate set of Decretals, written on fine large parchment of Lamballe,[3] to beat gold between the leaves, not so much as a piece that was beaten in them came to good, but all were dilacerated and spoiled. Mark this! cried Homenas; it was a divine punishment and vengeance.

At Mans, said Eudemon, Francis Cornu, apothecary, had turned an old set of Extravagantés into waste paper: may I never stir, if whatever was lapped up in them was not immediately corrupted, rotten, and spoiled; incense, pepper, cloves, cinnamon, saffron, wax, cassia, rhubarb, tamarinds, all drugs and spices, were lost without exception. Mark! mark! quoth Homenas, an effect of divine justice! This comes of putting the sacred Scriptures to such profane uses.

At Paris, said Carpalim, Snip Groignet the tailor had turned an old Clementinæ into patterns and measures, and all the clothes that were cut on them were utterly spoiled and lost; gowns, hoods, cloaks, cassocks, jerkins, jackets, waistcoats, capes, doublets,

[2] *Nicolas de Tudeschi*, a Sicilian, Archbishop of Palermo in 1425. His Commentary on the Clementinæ was printed in 8vo, at Paris, 1516.
[3] A town of Bretagne, famous for the manufactory of parchment.

petticoats, *corps de robes*, farthingales, and so forth. Snip, thinking to cut a hood, would cut you out a codpiece; instead of a cassock, he would make you a high-crowned hat; for a waistcoat, he would shape you out a rochet; on the pattern of a doublet, he would make you a thing like a frying-pan; then his journeymen having stitched it up, did jag it and pink it at the bottom, and so it looked like a pan to fry chestnuts. Instead of a cape, he made a buskin; for a farthingale, he shaped a montero cap; and thinking to make a cloak, he would cut out a pair of your big out-strouting Swiss breeches, with panes like the outside of a tabor. Insomuch that Snip was condemned to make good the stuffs to all his customers; and to this day poor cabbage's hair grows through his hood, and his arse through his pocket-holes. Mark! an effect of heavenly wrath and vengeance! cried Homenas.

At Cahusac, said Gymnast, a match being made by the lords of Estissac and Viscount Lausun to shoot at a mark, Perotou had taken to pieces a set of Decretals,[4] and set one of the leaves for the white to shoot at: now I sell, nay! I give and bequeath for ever and aye, the mould of my doublet to fifteen hundred hampers full of black devils, if ever any archer in the country (though they are singular marksmen in Guienne) could hit the white. Not the least bit of the holy scribble was contaminated or touched: nay! and Sansornin the elder, who held stakes, swore to us, *figues dioures!*[5] (his greatest oath), that he had openly, visibly, and manifestly seen the bolt of Carquelin moving right to the round circle in the middle of the white; and that just on the point when it was going to hit

[4] Add, printed on canonge paper. A beautiful large paper, called by Vives, 'Charta grandis, augustana, sive imperialis.'
[5] Hard figs.

and enter, it had gone aside above seven foot and four inches wide of it towards the bakehouse.

Miracle! cried Homenas, miracle! miracle! Clerica, come wench, light, light here. Here's to you all, gentleman; I vow you seem to me very sound Christians. While he said this, the maidens began to snicker at his elbow, grinning, giggling, and twittering among themselves. Friar John began to paw, neigh, and whinny at the snout's end, as one ready to leap, or at least to play the ass, and get up and ride tantivy to the devil, like a beggar on horseback.[6]

Methinks, said Pantagruel, a man might have been more out of danger near the white of which Gymnast spoke, than was formerly Diogenes near another. How is that? asked Homenas; what was it? Was he one of our decretalists? Rarely fallen in again, egad! said Epistemon, returning from stool; I see he will hook his Decretals in, though by the head and shoulders.

Diogenes, said Pantagruel, one day, for pastime, went to see some archers that shot at butts, one of whom was so unskilful, that, when it was his turn to shoot, all the bystanders went aside, lest he should mistake them for the mark; Diogenes had seen him shoot extremely wide of it: so when the other was taking aim a second time, and the people removed at a great distance to the right and left of the white, he placed himself close by the mark; holding that place to be the safest, and that so bad an archer would certainly rather hit any other.

[6] It is in the original, 'monter dessus, comme Herbault sus paovres gens.' Which has two meanings; one is, fall upon them, as your gentlemen's dogs fall upon beggars at the gates; the other is, ride them, worry them, and harass them, as some lords of manors do their poor tenants.

One of the Lord d'Estissac's pages at last found out the charm, pursued Gymnast, and by his advice Peroton put in another white made up of some papers of Pouillac's lawsuit, and then every one shot cleverly.

At Landerousse, said Rhizotomus, at John Delif's wedding were very great doings, as it was then the custom of the country. After supper, several farces, interludes, and comical scenes were acted: they had also several morris-dancers with bells and tabors; and divers sorts of masks and mummers were let in. My school-fellows and I, to grace the festival to the best of our power (for, fine white and purple liveries had been given to all of us in the morning), contrived a merry mask with store of cockle-shells, shells of snails, periwinkles, and such other. Then for want of cuckoo-pintle or priest-pintle, lousebur, cloth, and paper, we made ourselves false faces with the leaves of an old Sextum, that had been thrown by, and lay there for any one that would take it up: cutting out holes for the eyes, nose, and mouth. Now, did you ever hear the like since you were born? when we had played our little boyish antic tricks, and came to take off our sham faces, we appeared more hideous and ugly than the little devils that acted the 'Passion' at Douay:[7] for our faces were utterly spoiled at the places which had been touched by those leaves: one had there the small-pox; another, God's token, or the plague-spot; a third, the crinckums; a fourth, the measles; a fifth, botches, pushes, and carbuncles; in short, he came off the least hurt, who only lost his teeth by the bargain. Miracle! bawled out Homenas, miracle!

Hold, hold! cried Rhizotomus, it is not yet time

[7] Read Doué. One is in France, the other in Flanders.

to clap. My sister Kate, and my sister Ren, had put the crepines of their hoods, their ruffles, snuffekins, and neck-ruffs, new washed, starched, and ironed, into that very Book of Decretals; for, you must know, it was covered with thick boards, and had strong clasps. Now by the virtue of God!—Hold, interrupted Homenas, what God do you mean? There is but one, answered Rhizotomus. In heaven, I grant replied Homenas; but we have another here on earth, do you see. Ay, marry! have we, said Rhizotomus; but on my soul I protest I had quite forgot it. Well then, by the virtue of god-the-pope, their pinners, neck-ruffs, bibs, coifs, and other linen, turned as black as a charcoal-man's sack. Miracle! cried Homenas. Here, Clerica, light me here; and pr'ythee, girl, observe these rare stories. How comes it to pass then, asked Friar John, that people say:

> Ever since decrees had tails,[8]
> And gens-d'armes lugged heavy mails,[9]

---

[8] It should be ever since decrees had wings. On which M. Duchat has this long, but not tedious, note. The Decretals, says he, which are of so great weight and authority with the canonists, were not only added to the body of the ancient decrees, as wings (*ailes*) to the main pile of a building, but they are likewise the wings of the decrees in another sense; inasmuch as, by the means and help of these wings, the Popes, whom the ancient canons kept pretty low, have soared to their present height, and have assumed the power they now exercise over the Latin church. *Prendre des ailes*, or, as they speak in Languedoc, *prendre ales*, to take wing, is to forget one's self so far as to lose sight of the lowness of one's true condition; as some years ago was the case of a certain arrogant fop not far from Montpellier, according to the following tale, made upon occasion of his taking too much upon him.

> A certain upstart citizen of late,
> Would cut a figure, and would needs looks great:

> Since each monk would have a horse,
> All went here from bad to worse.

I understand you, answered Homenas: this is one of the quirks and little satires of the new-fangled heretics.[10]

> A knot of country gentlemen were met ;
> And, like a row of onions, all were set,
> And he amidst them.—Supper being served,
> To this and that and the other man he carved.
> Ducks, levrets, partridge, turkey-pout he cuts,
> And on their plates what part he pleases puts ;
> In dealing out their pittances, the elf
> Took special care not to forget himself.
> Well-stored his plate was with the choicest things ;
> But, above all, a pile of partridge wings.
> One, that loved partridge wings as well as cit,
> Whips from his plate the best—' Sir, is it fit,'
> Said he to monsieur carver, ' is it right,
> You should have all the wings, in our despite,
> You, who already take too high a flight ? '

[9] Beza, l. 4, of his Ecclesiastical History, says, this is an allusion to the proverb *muli mariani:* which see explained in Sartorius. But Beza's reasoning thereupon is so confused, and his application so inexact and incoherent, that there is no making head or tail of what he says. It is more likely that what made the *gens-d'armes* carrying port-mantles, or mails, so odious to the people, was, that, after they had submitted to carry that luggage, nothing escaped them wherever they quartered or marched, but they would pouch up a thousand things they took a fancy to at people's houses, or in the fields.

[10] Homenas is mistaken. Nothing was more common than that proverb, or had been so for a long time.

CHAPTER LIII

HOW BY THE VIRTUE OF THE DECRETALS, GOLD IS SUBTILELY DRAWN OUT OF FRANCE TO ROME

I WOULD, said Epistemon, it had cost me a pint of the best tripe that ever can enter into gut, so we had but compared with the original the dreadful chapters, *Execrabilis. De multa. Si plures. De annatis per totum. Nisi essent. Cum ad monasterium. Quod dilectio. Mandatum;* and certain others, that draw every year out of France to Rome, four hundred thousand ducats and more.

Do you make nothing of this? asked Homenas. Though, methinks, after all, it is but little, if we consider that France, the most Christian, is the only nurse the See of Rome has. However, find me in the whole world a book, whether of philosophy, physic, law, mathematics, or other human learning, nay, even, by my God, of the Holy Scripture itself, will draw as much money thence? None, none, pshaw, tush! blurt! pish! none can.[1] You may look till your eyes drop out of your head, nay, till doomsday in the afternoon, before you can find another of that energy; I will pass my word for that.

Yet these devilish heretics refuse to learn and know it. Burn them, tear them, nip them with hot pincers, drown them, hang them, spit them at the bunghole, pelt them, pawt them, bruise them, beat them, cripple them, dismember them, cut

[1] Nargues, nargues, in the original. A term of contempt. We say a fig for it. So here Homenas' nargues, *i.e.*, a fig for other books; or nazardes, a rap of the nose for such as say there is any book to compare with the Decretals.

them, gut them, bowel them, paunch them, thrash them, slash them, gash them, chop them, slice them, slit them, carve them, saw them, bethwack them, pare them, hack them, hew them, mince them, flay them, boil them,[2] broil them, roast them, toast them, bake them, fry them, crucify them, crush them, squeeze them, grind them, batter them, burst them, quarter them, unlimb them, behump them, bethump them, belump them, belabour them, pepper them, spitchcock them, and carbonade them on gridirons, these wicked heretics, decretalifuges, decretalicides, worse than homicides, worse than patricides, decretalictiones of the devil of hell!

As for you other good people, I must earnestly pray and beseech you to believe no other thing, to think on, say, undertake, or do no other thing, than what's contained in our sacred Decretals, and their corollaries, this fine Sextum, these fine Clementinæ, these fine Extravagantés. O deific books! So shall you enjoy glory, honour, exaltation, wealth, dignities, and preferments in this world; be revered, and dreaded by all, preferred, elected, and chosen, above all men.

For, there is not under the cope of heaven a condition of men, out of which you will find persons fitter to do and handle all things, than those who by divine prescience, eternal predestination, have applied themselves to the study of the holy Decretals.

Would you choose a worthy emperor, a good captain, a fit general in time of war, one that can

---

[2] Punishments then in fashion. Mat. Corderius, ch. 49, n. 28, of his *De Corr. Serm. Emendatione*: They are going to execute him, *i.e.*, to hang, or burn, or behead, or quarter, or boil him. 'Ad capitale supplicium perductus est.'

well foresee all inconveniences, avoid all dangers, briskly and bravely bring his men on to a breach or attack, still be on sure grounds, always overcome without loss of his men, and know how to make a good use of his victory? Take me a decretist.—No, no, I mean a decretalist. Ho, the foul blunder,[3] whispered Epistemon.

Would you, in time of peace, find a man capable of wisely governing the state of a commonwealth, of a kingdom, of an empire, of a monarchy; sufficient to maintain the clergy, nobility, senate, and commons in wealth, friendship, unity, obedience, virtue, and honesty? Take a decretalist.

Would you find a man, who, by his exemplary life, eloquence, and pious admonitions, may in a short time, without effusion of human blood, conquer the Holy Land, and bring over to the holy church the misbelieving Turks, Jews, Tartars, Muscovites, Mamelukes, and Sarrabonites? Take me a decretalist.

What makes, in many countries, the people rebellious and depraved, pages saucy and mischievous, students sottish and duncical? Nothing but that their governors and tutors were not decretalists.

But what, on your conscience, was it, do you think, that established, confirmed, and authorised those fine religious orders, with whom you see the Christian world everywhere adorned, graced, and illustrated, as the firmament is with its glorious stars? The holy Decretals.

[3] *O le gros rat!* O the huge rat! A Poictevine expression, to rally one that makes a slip with his tongue, speaks one word for another, as Homenas does here. In chap. xxvii. of lib. 5. *O les gros rats à la table,* O the bouncing table rats, means the fat monks (rats signified shavelings as well as rats) who eat up mankind. There Friar John means that they are never more like real rats well fed, than at table, when they lay about them emptying the plates.

Chap. liii.] *Pantagruel*

What was it that founded, underpropped, and fixed, and now maintains, nourishes, and feeds the devout monks and friars in convents, monasteries, and abbeys; so that did they not daily and mightily pray without ceasing, the world would be in evident danger of returning to its primitive chaos? The sacred Decretals.

What makes and daily increases the famous and celebrated patrimony of St Peter in plenty of all temporal, corporeal, and spiritual blessings? The holy Decretals.

What made the holy apostolic See and Pope of Rome, in all times, and at this present, so dreadful in the universe, that all kings, emperors, potentates, and lords, willing, nilling, must depend upon him, hold of him, be crowned, confirmed, and authorised by him, come thither to strike sail, buckle, and fall down before his holy slipper, whose picture you have seen? The mighty Decretals of God.

I will discover you a great secret. The universities of your world have commonly a book, either open or shut, in their arms and devices: what book do you think it is? Truly, I do not know, answered Pantagruel; I never read it. It is the Decretals, said Homenas, without which the privileges of all universities would soon be lost. You must own, that I have taught you this; ha, ha, ha, ha, ha!

Here Homenas began to belch, to fart, to funk, to laugh, to slaver, and to sweat; and then he gave his huge greasy four-cornered cap to one of the lasses, who clapped it on her pretty head with a great deal of joy, after she had lovingly bussed it, as a sure token that she should be first married. *Vivat*, cried Epistemon, *fifat, bibat, pipat.*[4]

[4] *Germanis vivere, bibere est*, is the saying in France, on

O apocalyptic secret! continued Homenas, light, light, Clerica, light here with double lanterns.[5] Now for the fruit, virgins.

I was saying then, that giving yourselves thus wholly to the study of the holy Decretals, you will gain wealth and honour in this world: I add, that in the next you will infallibly be saved in the blessed kingdom of heaven, whose keys are given to our good god and decretaliarch. O my good god, whom I adore and never saw, by thy special grace open unto us, at the point of death at least, this most sacred treasure of our holy mother church, whose protector, preserver, butler, chief larder, administrator, and disposer thou art; and take care, I beseech thee, O lord, that the precious works of supererogation, the goodly pardons, do not fail us in time of need: so that the devils may not find an opportunity to gripe our precious souls, and the dreadful jaws of hell may not swallow us. If we must pass through purgatory, thy will be done. It is in thy power to draw us out of it when thou pleasest. Here Homenas began to shed huge hot briny tears, to beat his breast, and kiss his thumbs in the shape of a cross.[6]

ON CHAP. XLVIII. AND FIVE FOLLOWING.—The island of Papimany, is those whose love and zeal for the Pope is so

---

occasion of this cry of the Germans, which Epistemon pronounces after the German fashion. See Misson, Lett. 9, of his Travels into Italy.

[5] Being a couple of bumpers (*lampées*, in French), which equivocates to lanterns in sense.

[6] Allusion to what is usually done by bigots, whose devotion consists so essentially in kissing the cross, that, in order to have a cross always at hand, they form a cross with their two thumbs, and in that shape are continually lifting them to their mouths. In Languedoc they say of a man that bestirs him vigorously in an affair, and seems to have it at heart, he kisses his thumbs across that it may succeed.

excessive, that it may be counted madness. The word is made of *papa*, Pope, and *mania*, madness, from μαίνομαι, *insanio*. Thus in Plutarch, the Andromanes were women, whose love for men was most blind and furious; that name being given to those Lacedæmonian women, who used to fight before the people with bare thighs, whence they were called Phenomerides. This blind zeal for Popery is drawn in most lively colours, by our satirical painter, in all those chapters; and particularly appears by the discourse of the four estates of the country, the gentleman, the lawyer, the monk, and the clown, who will all give the Pope those epithets which only belong to God, calling the bishop of Rome, He that is, and God on earth. All know that the Pope's flatterers have been very prodigal of such epithets, principally in Rabelais' time; as to Paul III., who, as Alstedius and others write, was styled *Optimus maximus in terris Deus*; and the following distich was also made to compliment a Pope, and prove that he was justly called, God on earth.

'Ense potens gemino, mundi moderaris habenas,
Et meritò in terris diceris esse Deus.'

The four estates are brought in to show that the Pope's missionaries are of all sorts of conditions. Their frantic zeal does not only make them adore the Pope, but prostrate themselves at the feet of those who have seen him. Says Panurge to them, when they asked him whether he had been blest with the sight of that God on earth, Yea, verily, gentlemen, I have seen three of them, whose sight has not much bettered me. O thrice and four times happy people! cried the Papimanes, you are welcome, and more than double welcome; and they would have kissed Panurge's feet; saying, they would even kiss the Pope's arse, if ever he came among them. As soon as our travellers are landed, the people throng to see those blessed men, who had seen his holiness' face. Homenas, bishop of the place, hastens to them in pontificalibus, with his train of church-players, bearing crosses, banners, standards, holy water-pots, and canopies, such as the Pope and the host used to be under, when they are carried in procession. The mob conducts and attends the strangers to the church, where there is not one word mentioned of God, nor Jesus Christ, or the Gospel; but much of the most holy decretals, or Pope's decrees written with the hand of an angel. Our author admirably ridicules the credulity of those bigoted Papists. Then Homenas mumbles over a mass; after which, from the church he leads them to the tavern, where he feasts the strangers with the money that was gathered during the mass; yet not till he had showed them the Pope's picture, which Epistemon said was not like the late Pope's; For, said he, I have seen them, not thus with their pallium, amice, and rochet on, but with helmets on their heads, more like the top of a Persian turban; and, while the Christian commonwealth was in peace, they alone were furiously and cruelly making war. Homenas zealously takes their part, and replies, that then it was against those who transgressed against their decretals, and that whether they were emperors, kings, or commonwealths, he was immediately to pursue them with fire and sword, strip them of their kingdoms, anathematize them, and not only destroy their bodies, those of their children and adherents, but also damn their souls to the pit of hell. Nothing can be finer than the feast, and the discourse of Homenas and his guests. Young buxom lasses wait on them, principally Homenas' favourite, whom our author calls Clerica. Friar John, who leered on them sideways, like a cur that steals a capon, liked them better than some of the bon Christian pears: so does Homenas, who is very lavish of that fruit, like Horace's Calaber:

'Hæc porcis hodiè comedenda relinques.'

But he will by no means be persuaded to part with one of the doxies. The most holy and heavenly decretals are celebrated with swingeing bumpers of good wine, just as Belshazzar extolled his gods of gold and silver. In short, this feast is a triumph, in which our author has described the voluptuous life of those effeminate Papimanes, their superstitions, which are the foundation of their idleness and luxury, and their impious doctrine, that encourages subjects to kill their lawful sovereign, and massacre all those who will not blindly submit to the Pope, and the blind idolatrous worship which he has invented: by means whereof, saith our author, gold is subtilely drawn out of France to Rome, above four hundred thousand ducats every year. England was much more fleeced, till it had shaken off the Papal yoke; and we must own, that as Doctor Rabelais was very well informed of all these abuses, no man ever described them more to the life; and the best Protestant writers have not equalled him in this, though they did it out of interest, and made it their particular business. Neither can I tell, whether Rabelais' boldness be more to be wondered at in publishing such a work while fires were kindled, in every part of France, to burn the Lutherans, than his good fortune in having escaped those flames to which many were condemned for less every day where he wrote.—*M.*

CHAPTER LIV

HOW HOMENAS GAVE PANTAGRUEL SOME BON-
CHRISTIAN PEARS

EPISTEMON, Friar John, and Panurge, seeing this doleful catastrophe, began, under the cover of their napkins, to cry, Meeow! meeow! meeow! feigning to wipe their eyes all the while as if they had wept. The wenches were doubly diligent, and brought brimmers of Clementine wine[1] to every one, besides store of sweetmeats; and thus the feasting was revived.

Before we arose from table, Homenas gave us a great quantity of fair large pears; saying, Here, my good friends, these are singular good pears; you will find none such anywhere else, I dare warrant. Every soil bears not every thing, you know; India alone boasts black ebony; the best incense is produced in Sabæa; the sphragitid earth at Lemnos: so this island is the only place where such fine pears grow. You may, if you please, make nurseries with their kernels in your country.

I like their taste extremely, said Pantagruel. If they were sliced, and put into a pan on the fire with wine and sugar, I fancy they would be very whole-

---

[1] Clement the Fifth, who was of Bordeaux, and under whose name the Clementines were compiled, had planted in the territory of Pessac, a village within a league of Bordeaux, a vineyard, which still bears the name of that Pope. See Du Chesne's Antiquities of the Cities, etc., l. 3, c. 2. But this is not what Rabelais has his eye to here. There is a great deal more likelihood that he means wine of a certain growth, the tythe whereof had been granted to Homenas' church by some Clementine.

some meat for the sick, as well as for the healthy.[2] Pray what do you call them ? No otherwise than you have heard, replied Homenas. We are a plain downright sort of people, as God would have it, and call figs, figs; plums, plums; and pears, pears. Truly, said Pantagruel, if I live to go home,—which I hope will be speedily, God willing,—I'll set off and graff some in my garden in Touraine, by the banks of the Loire, and will call them bon-Christian or good-Christian pears : for I never saw better Christians than are these good Papimanes. I would like him two to one better yet, said Friar John, would he but give us two or three cart-loads of yon buxom lasses. Why, what would you do with them ? cried Homenas. Quoth Friar John, No harm, only bleed the kind-hearted souls straight between the two great toes, with certain clever lancets of the right stamp : by which operation good Christian children would be inoculated upon them, and the breed be multiplied in our country, in which there are not many over good, the móre's the pity.

Nay verily, replied Homenas, we cannot do this ; for you would make them tread their shoes awry, crack their pipkins, and spoil their shapes : you love mutton, I see, you will run at sheep ; I know you by that same nose and hair of yours, though I never saw your face before. Alas ! alas ! how kind you are ! And would you indeed damn your precious soul ? Our Decretals forbid this. Ah ! I wish you had them at your finger-end. Patience, said Friar John ; but, *si tu non vis dare, præsta, quæsumus*.[3]

[2] Pliny says, all pears are heavy and hard of digestion, especially to unhealthy people ; but in the same chapter he excepts baked pears.

[3] These words are in the style of the oremus, in the breviary and prayer books.

Matter of breviary. As for that, I defy all the world, and I fear no man that wears a head and a hood, though he were a chrystallin, I mean a decretalin doctor.

Dinner being over, we took our leave of the right reverend Homenas, and of all the good people, humbly giving thanks; and, to make them amends for their kind entertainment, promised them that, at our coming to Rome, we would make our applications so effectually to the Pope, that he would speedily be sure to come to visit them in person. After this we went on board.

Pantagruel, by an act of generosity, and as an acknowledgment of the sight of the Pope's picture, gave Homenas nine pieces of double-frized cloth of gold, to be set before the grates of the window. He also caused the church box, for its repairs and fabric, to be quite filled with double crowns of gold; and ordered nine hundred and fourteen angels to be delivered to each of the lasses, who had waited at table, to buy them husbands when they could get them.

CHAPTER LV

HOW PANTAGRUEL, BEING AT SEA, HEARD VARIOUS UNFROZEN WORDS[1]

WHEN we were at sea, junketing, tippling, discoursing, and telling stories, Pantagruel rose and stood up to look out: then asked us, Do you hear nothing,

[1] Rabelais has borrowed these from the *Courtisan* of Balthasar de Castillon, of which a French translation was printed in 1539, and from the Apologues of Cælius Calcagninus of Ferrara, published in 1544.

gentlemen? Methink I hear some people talking in
the air, yet I can see nobody. Hark! According
to his command we listened, and with full ears
sucked in the air, as some of you suck oysters, to find
if we could hear some sound scattered through the
sky; and to lose none of it, like the Emperor
Antoninus, some of us laid their hands hollow next
to their ears; but all this would not do, nor could
we hear any voice. Yet Pantagruel continued to
assure us he heard various voices in the air, some of
men, and some of women.

At last we began to fancy that we also heard
something, or at least that our ears tingled; and the
more we listened, the plainer we discerned the
voices, so as to distinguish articulate sounds. This
mightily frightened us, and not without cause; since
we could see nothing, yet heard such various sounds
and voices of men, women, children, horses, etc., insomuch that Panurge cried out, Cods belly! there is
no fooling with the devil; we are all beshit, let us
fly. There is some ambuscade hereabouts. Friar
John, art thou here, my love? I pray thee, stay by
me, old boy. Hast thou got thy swinging tool?
See that it do not stick in thy scabbard; thou never
scourest it half as it should be. We are undone.
Hark! They are guns, gad judge me! let us fly, I
do not say with hands and feet, as Brutus said at the
Battle of Pharsalia; I say, with sails and oars: let us
whip it away: I never find myself to have a bit of
courage at sea: in cellars, and elsewhere, I have
more than enough. Let us fly and save our bacon.
I do not say this for any fear that I have; for I dread
nothing but danger, that I do not; I always say it,
that should not. The free archer of Baignolet said
as much. Let us hazard nothing therefore, I say,
lest we come off bluely. Tack about, helm a-lee,

thou son of a bachelor! Would I were now well in Quinquenois,² though I were never to marry. Haste away, let us make all the sail we can; they will be too hard for us; we are not able to cope with them; they are ten to our one, I will warrant you; nay, and they are on their dunghill, while we do not know the country. They will be the death of us. We will lose no honour by flying: Demosthenes saith,³ that the man that runs away, may fight another day. At least, let us retreat to the leeward. Helm a-lee; bring the main tack aboard, hawl the bowlins, hoist the topgallants; we are all dead men; get off, in the devil's name, get off.

Pantagruel, hearing the sad outcry which Panurge made, said, Who talks of flying? Let us first see who they are; perhaps they may be friends: I can discover nobody yet, though I can see a hundred miles round me. But let us consider a little: I have read that a philosopher, named Petron, was of opinion, that there were several worlds, that touched each other in an equilateral triangle; in whose centre, he said, was the dwelling of truth: and that the words, ideas, copies, and images of all things past, and to come, resided there; round which was the age; and that with success of time part of them used to fall on mankind, like rheums and mildews; just as the dew fell on Gideon's fleece, till the age was fulfilled.

I also remember, continued he, that Aristotle affirms Homer's words to be flying, moving, and consequently animated. Besides, Antiphanes said,

² Before, in ch. 13, the good wine of that place is mentioned with great praise.
³ See Aulus Gellius, lib. 17, cap. 21. [Thus Hudibras:—
'For he that flies may fight again,
Which he can never do that's slain.']

that Plato's philosophy was like words, which, being spoken in some country during a hard winter are immediately congealed, frozen up, and not heard: for what Plato taught young lads, could hardly be understood by them when |they were grown old. Now, continued he, we should philosophise and search whether this be not the place where those words are thawed.

You would wonder very much, should this be the head and lyre of Orpheus. When the Thracian women had torn him to pieces, they threw his head and lyre into the river Hebrus; down which they floated to the Euxine Sea, as far as the island of Lesbos; the head continually uttering a doleful song, as it were, lamenting the death of Orpheus, and the lyre, with the wind's impulse, moving its strings, and harmoniously accompanying the voice. Let us see if we cannot discover them hereabouts.

CHAPTER LVI

HOW AMONG THE FROZEN WORDS PANTAGRUEL FOUND SOME ODD ONES

THE skipper made answer: Be not afraid, my lord, we are on the confines of the Frozen Sea, on which, about the beginning of last winter, happened a great and bloody fight between the Arimaspians and the Nephelibates.[1] Then the words and cries of men and women, the hacking, slashing, and hewing of battle-axes, the shocking, knocking, and jolting of armours and harnesses, the neighing of horses, and

[1] Græcè, those who dwell in the snows. An allusion to the battle of Marignan, between the French and the Swiss.

all other martial din and noise, froze in the air; and now, the rigour of the winter being over, by the succeeding serenity and warmth of the weather, they melt and are heard.

By jingo! quoth Panurge, the man talks somewhat like; I believe him: but could not we see some of them? I think I have read, that, on the edge of the mountain on which Moses received the Judaic law, the people saw the voices sensibly.—Here, here, said Pantagruel, here are some that are not yet thawed. He then threw us on the deck whole handfuls of frozen words, which seemed to us like your rough sugar-plums, of many colours, like those used in heraldry; some words *gules* (this means also jests and merry sayings), some *vert*, some *azure*, some *black*, some *or* (this means fair words); and when we had somewhat warmed them between our hands, they melted like snow, and we really heard them, but could not understand them, for it was a barbarous gibberish. One of them, only, that was pretty big, having been warmed between Friar John's hands, gave a sound much like that of chestnuts when they are thrown into the fire, without being first cut, which made us all start. This was the report of a fieldpiece in its time, cried Friar John.

Panurge prayed Pantagruel to give him some more; but Pantagruel told him, that to give words was the part of a lover.[2] Sell me some then, I pray you, cried Panurge. That is the part of a lawyer, returned Pantagruel. I would sooner sell you silence, though at a dearer rate; as Demosthenes formerly sold it by the means of his *argentangina*,[3] or silver quinsey.

[2] *Verba dat omnis amans,* says Ovid.
[3] Demosthenes being bought off by the Milesian ambassadors,

However, he threw three or four handfuls of them on the deck ; amongst which I perceived some very sharp words, and some bloody words, which, the pilot said, used sometimes to go back, and recoil to the place whence they came, but it was with a slit weasand : we also saw some terrible words, and some others not very pleasant to the eye.

When they had been all melted together, we heard a strange noise, hin, hin, hin, hin, his, tick, tock, taack, bredelinbrededack, frr, frr, frr, bou, bou, bou, bou, bou, bou, bou, bou, track, track, trr, trr, trr, trrr, trrrrrr ; on, on, on, on, on, on, ououououon, gog, magog, and I do not know what other barbarous words ; which, the pilot said, were the noise made by the charging squadrons, the shock and neighing of horses.

Then we heard some large ones go off like drums and fifes, and others like clarions and trumpets. Believe me, we had very good sport with them. I would fain have saved some merry odd words, and have preserved them in oil, as ice and snow are kept, and between clean straw. But Pantagruel would not let me, saying, that it is a folly to hoard up what we are never like to want, or have always at hand ; odd, quaint, merry, and fat words of *gules*, never being scarce among all good and jovial Pantagruelists.

Panurge somewhat vexed Friar John, and put him in the pouts ; for he took him at his word, while he dreamed of nothing less. This caused the friar to threaten him with such a piece of revenge

who had given him twenty talents, that is, twelve thousand crowns, for only one day's silence, the orator came next day into the senate-house, his neck muffled about with rollers, and his chin bolstered up with wool, as if he had a sore throat : but one of the assembly smelt a rat, and cried out, Demosthenes has not got a cold, but gold.

as was put upon G. Jousseaume, who having taken the merry Patelin at his word, when he had overbid himself in some cloth, was afterwards fairly taken by the horns like a bullock, by his jovial chapman, whom he took at his word like a man. Panurge, well knowing that threatened folks live long, bobbed, and made mouths at him, in token of derision, then cried, Would I had here the Word of the Holy Bottle, without being thus obliged to go further in pilgrimage to her.

ON CHAPS. LV. AND LVI.—By the unfrozen or thawed words, which Pantagruel and his company heard at sea in open air, just after they had left the Papimanes, our author ingeniously describes the freedom which our navigators took to speak their true sentiments of the gross ignorance, blind zeal, loose lives, and worse principles of those superstitious Papists, as soon as they were out of their reach. For among them the Pantagruelists did not dare discover their minds; so that their words were in a manner frozen within their mouths, which fear and interest kept shut. But when they were out of danger they could no longer thus contain their words, and then every one distinctly heard them; murmuring words against those bigots, very sharp words, bloody words, terrible words, angry words, occasioned by reflections made on those idolatrous persecutors; and to those words our jolly company add some words of *gules*, that is, merry words, jests, pleasant talk, probably about the young wenches so ready to wait on the strangers at table, and on the good bishop a-bed.

These frozen words that thawed, and then were heard, may also mean the books published at that time at Geneva, and elsewhere, against Popery and the persecution. Those who fled from it to places of safety, with a great deal of freedom, filled their writings with such truths as were not to be spoken among the bigoted Romanists: and many of those unfortunate men, having been used very cruelly in their slavery, and having nothing to defend their cause but their pens, while their adversaries were armed with fire and sword, their words could not but be very sharp. The words which Rabelais says were mere gibberish, which they could not understand, may be the books that were dark, ill-written, and without judgment: and the words of *gules*, or jests, may be pleasant books, such as were some of Marot's epigrams, and other pieces of that nature.—*M*.

… Rabelais' Works [Book iv.

CHAPTER LVII

HOW PANTAGRUEL WENT ASHORE AT THE DWELLING OF GASTER, THE FIRST MASTER OF ARTS IN THE WORLD [1]

THAT day Pantagruel went ashore in an island, which, for situation and governor, may be said not to have its fellow. When you just come into it, you find it rugged, craggy, and barren, unpleasant to the eye, painful to the feet, and almost as inaccessible as the mountain of Dauphiné,[2] which is somewhat like a toad-stool, and was never climbed, as any can remember, by any but Doyac, who had the charge of King Charles the Eighth's train of artillery.[3]

This same Doyac, with strange tools and engines, gained that mountain's top, and there he found an old ram. It puzzled many a wise head to guess

---

[1] Alluding to the *magister artis, ingeniique largitor venter*, of the poet Persius.

[2] This mountain is one of the four wonders which Louis XI. took notice of in Dauphiné. It is within three leagues of Grenoble, going towards Embrun, near the Grande Chartreuse; and being shaped like a pyramid reversed, it has got the name of inaccessible.

[3] The continuation of Monstrelet, folio 209, calls him Doyac, and fol. 229, de Doyac; but Seyssel calls him plain Oyac, which seems to suit best with the first condition of that man, who, from a hosier, as he was in Auvergne at Montferrant, the place of his birth, rose to be the chief favourite of Louis XI. See more of him, and of his fate, in Duchat. But this was not the person that formed and executed the bold design of climbing the mountain in question; it was one Damp Julian, a Lorrainer, a captain of Montelimar, who, by means of engines he had contrived himself, climbed to the top of it, the 26th of June 1492. We are told this in the Chevalier Bayard's life, written by Symphorian Champier.

how it got thither. Some said that some eagle, or great horn-coot,[4] having carried it thither while it was yet a lambkin, it had got away, and saved itself among the bushes.

As for us, having with much toil and sweat overcome the difficult ways at the entrance, we found the top of the mountain so fertile, healthful, and pleasant, that I thought I was then in the true garden of Eden, or earthly paradise, about whose situation our good theologues are in such a quandary, and keep such a pother.

As for Pantagruel, he said, that here was the seat of Areté—that is as much as to say, Virtue—described by Hesiod. This, however, with submission to better judgments. The ruler of this place was one Master Gaster, the first master of arts in the world. For, if you believe that fire is the great master of arts,[5] as Tully writes, you very much wrong him and yourself: alas, Tully never believed this.[6] On the other side, if you fancy Mercury to be the first inventor of arts, as our ancient Druids believed of old, you are mightily beside the mark. The satirist's sentence, that affirms Master Gaster to be the master of all arts, is true. With him peacefully resided old goody Penia, *alias* Poverty, the mother of the ninety-nine Muses, on whom Porus,[7] the lord of Plenty, formerly begot Love, that noble child, the mediator of heaven and earth, as Plato affirms *in Symposio*.

We were all obliged to pay our homage, and

[4] Owl.
[5] Opinion of Heraclitus, etc. See Plutarch.
[6] Indeed he confutes this opinion in his *De Natura Deorum*, l. 3.
[7] See Plato's Banquet, and Plutarch in his Discourse of Isis and Osiris.

swear allegiance to that mighty sovereign; for he is imperious, severe, blunt, hard, uneasy, inflexible: you cannot make him believe, represent to him, or persuade him anything.

He does not hear: and, as the Egyptians said that Harpocrates, the god of silence, named Sigalion [8] in Greek, was *astomé*, that is, without a mouth; so Gaster was created without ears,[9] even like the image of Jupiter in Candia.

He only speaks by signs: but those signs are more readily obeyed by every one, than the statutes of senates, or commands of monarchs: neither will he admit the least let or delay in his summons. You say, that when a lion roars, all the beasts at a considerable distance round about, as far as his roar can be heard, are seized with a shivering. This is written, it is true; I have seen it. I assure you, that at Master Gaster's command, the very heavens tremble, and all the earth shakes: his command is called, Do this or die! Needs must when the devil drives; there's no gainsaying of it.

The pilot was telling us how, on a certain time, after the manner of the members that mutinied against the belly, as Æsop describes it, the whole kingdom of the Somates [10] went off into a direct faction against Gaster, resolving to throw off his yoke: but they soon found their mistake, and most humbly submitted; for otherwise they had all been famished.

What company soever he is in, none dispute with

---

[8] Auson, Ep. 25, v. 27.
 'Aut tua Sigalion Ægyptius oscula signet.'
[9] See Plutarch in the same discourse.
[10] From σῶμα, the body. Now the author makes a kingdom of it, where lives Messer Gaster (a Greek word likewise, signifying the belly, stomach, or paunch).

him for precedence or superiority; he still goes first,[11] though kings, emperors, or even the Pope, were there. So he held the first place at the Council of Basle; though some will tell you that the council was tumultuous, by the contention and ambition of many for priority.

Every one is busied, and labours to serve him; and, indeed, to make amends for this, he does this good to mankind, as to invent for them all arts, machines, trades, engines, and crafts: he even instructs brutes in arts which are against their nature, making poets of ravens, jackdaws, chattering jays, parrots, and starlings, and poetesses of magpies, teaching them to utter human language, speak and sing; and all for the gut. He reclaims and tames eagles, gerfalcons, falcons gentle, sakers, lanners, goshawks, sparrow-hawks, merlins, haggards, passengers, wild rapacious birds; so that setting them free in the air, whenever he thinks fit, as high and as long as he pleases, he keeps them suspended, straying, flying, hovering, and courting him above the clouds: then on a sudden he makes them stoop, and come down amain from heaven next to the ground; and all for the gut.

Elephants, lions, rhinoceroses, bears, horses, mares, and dogs, he teaches to dance, prance, vault, fight, swim, hide themselves, fetch and carry what he pleases; and all for the gut.

Salt and fresh-water fish, whales, and the monsters of the main, he brings them up from the bottom of the deep; wolves he forces out of the woods, bears out of the rocks, foxes out of their holes, and serpents out of the ground; and all for the gut.

In short, he is so unruly, that in his rage he

[11] The belly will be foremost, especially if it is more than ordinary large and prominent.

devours all men and beasts: as was seen among the Vascons,[12] when Q. Metellus besieged them in |the Sertorian wars; among the Saguntines besieged by Hannibal; among the Jews besieged by the Romans, and six hundred more; and all for the gut. When his regent Penia takes a progress, wherever she moves, all senates are shut up, all statutes repealed, all orders and proclamations vain;[13] she neither knows, nor obeys, and has no law. All shun her, in every place choosing rather to expose themselves to shipwreck at sea, and venture through fire, rocks, caves, and precipices, than be seized by that most dreadful tormentor.

CHAPTER LVIII

HOW, AT THE COURT OF THE MASTER OF INGENUITY, PANTAGRUEL DETESTED THE ENGASTRIMYTHES AND THE GASTROLATERS

At the court of that great master of ingenuity, Pantagruel observed two sorts of troublesome and too officious apparitors,[1] whom he very much detested. The first were called Engastrimythes; the others Gastrolaters.

[12] 'Sed qui mordere cadaver
Sustinuit
Vascones, ut fama est, alimentis talibus usi
Produxere animas,'
Says Juvenal, Sat. 15. See Florus, l. 3, c. 22, and Val. Max., l. 7, c. 6.
[13] Necessity has no law, as the proverb says.
[1] Servants, incommodious to Gaster, their master, by preventing him in all his appetites. See Cæl. Rhodig., l. 9, c. 13, of his Ancient Readings.

Pantagruel

The first pretended to be descended of the ancient race of Eurycles;[2] and for this brought the authority of Aristophanes, in his comedy called The Wasps: whence of old they were called Euryclians, as Plato[3] writes, and Plutarch in his book of the Cessation of Oracles. In the holy decrees, 26, qu. 3, they are styled Ventriloqui: and the same name is given them in Ionian by Hippocrates, in his fifth book of Epid., as men who speak from the belly. Sophocles calls them Sternomantes. These were soothsayers, enchanters, cheats, who gulled the mob, and seemed not to speak and give answers from the mouth, but from the belly.

Such a one, about the year of our Lord 1513, was Jacoba Rodogina,[4] an Italian woman of mean extract: from whose belly, we, as well as an infinite number of others at Ferrara, and elsewhere, have often heard the voice of the evil spirit speak; low, feeble, and small, indeed; but yet very distinct, articulate, and intelligible, when she was sent for, out of curiosity, by the lords and princes of the Cisalpine Gaul.[5] To remove all manner of doubt, and be assured that this was not a trick, they used to have her stripped stark naked, and caused her mouth and nose to be stopped. This evil spirit would be called Curled-pate, or Cincinnatulo, seeming pleased when any called

[2] The name of an Engastrimuthe in Aristophanes' comedy of the Wasps.
[3] In his dialogue entitled the Sophist.
[4] Or of the Rouigue, a town of Italy, of which likewise was Cælius Rhodiginus, who, l. 5, c. 10, Of his Ancient Readings, had related this story, but without specifying the year.
[5] Beyond the Alps in respect of France, and the contrary with respect to Rome : it is an ancient part of Gaul, between Mount Cenis and the river Rubicon, near Rimini, comprehending Piedmont, Montferrat, Milan, Mantua, and Ferrara. (Dutch scholiast.)

him by that name; at which, he was always ready to answer. If any spoke to him of things past or present, he gave pertinent answers, sometimes to the amazement of the hearers; but if of things to come, then the devil was gravelled, and used to tell lies as fast as a dog can trot. Nay, sometimes he seemed to own his ignorance; instead of an answer, letting out a rousing fart, or muttering some words with barbarous and uncouth inflexions, and not to be understood.

As for the Gastrolaters,[6] they stuck close to one another in knots and gangs. Some of them merry, wanton, and soft as so many milksops;[7] others louring, grim, dogged, demure, and crabbed; all idle, mortal foes to business, spending half their time in sleeping, and the rest in doing nothing, a rent-charge and dead unnecessary weight on the earth, as Hesiod saith; afraid, as we judged, of offending or lessening their paunch. Others were masked, disguised, and so oddly dressed, that it would have done you good to have seen them.

There's a saying, and several ancient sages[8] write, that the skill of nature appears wonderful in the pleasure which she seems to have taken in the configuration of sea-shells, so great is their variety in figures, colours, streaks, and inimitable shapes. I protest the variety we perceived in the dresses of the gastrolatrous coquillons was not less. They all owned Gaster for their supreme god, adored him as a god, offered him sacrifices as to their omnipotent

---

[6] The same who are afterwards called by Rabelais, coquillons or cucullated gentry, are properly the monks, to whom he bore an old grudge.

[7] According to their natural disposition, and in proportion to their income.

[8] See Pliny, l. 9, c. 33.

deity, owned no other god, served, loved, and honoured him above all things.

You would have thought that the holy apostle spoke of those, when he said, Phil., chap. 3, 'Many walk, of whom I have told you often, and now tell you even weeping, that they are enemies of the cross of Christ: whose end is destruction, whose god is their belly.' Pantagruel compared them to the cyclops Polyphemus, whom Euripides[9] brings in speaking thus: I only sacrifice to myself (not to the gods) and to this belly of mine, the greatest of all gods.

CHAPTER LIX

OF THE RIDICULOUS STATUE MANDUCE; AND HOW, AND WHAT THE GASTROLATERS SACRIFICE TO THEIR VENTRIPOTENT GOD

WHILE we fed our eyes with the sight of the phizzes and actions of these lounging gulligutted Gastrolaters, we on a sudden heard the sound of a musical instrument called a bell; at which all of them placed themselves in rank and file, as for some mighty battle, every one according to his office, degree, and seniority.

In this order, they moved towards Master Gaster, after a plump, young, lusty, gorbellied fellow, who, on a long staff, fairly gilt, carried a wooden statue, grossly carved, and as scurvily daubed over with paint; such a one as Plautus,[1] Juvenal, and Pomp.

[9] In his tragedy of The Cyclops. See Plutarch in Cessation of Oracles.

[1] Plautus in his comedy of The Cable; Juvenal, Sat. iii., and Pompon. Festus, l. xi.

Festus describe it. At Lyons, during the Carnival, it is called Maschecroûte, or Gnaw-crust;[2] they call this Manduce.

It was a monstrous, ridiculous, hideous figure, fit to fright little children; its eyes were bigger than its belly, and its head larger than all the rest of its body: well mouth-cloven however, having a goodly pair of wide, broad jaws, lined with two rows of teeth, upper tier and under tier, which, by the magic of a small twine hid in the hollow part of the golden staff, were made to clash, clatter, and rattle dreadfully one against another; as they do at Metz with St Clement's dragon.[3]

Coming near the Gastrolaters, I saw they were followed by a great number of fat waiters and tenders, laden with baskets, dossers, hampers, dishes, wallets, pots, and kettles. Then under the conduct of Manduce, and singing I do not know what dithyrambics, crepalocomes, and epenons, opening their baskets and pots, they offered their god,

White hippo-cras, with dry toasts.	Fricassees, nine sorts.	Cold loins of veal, with spice.
White bread.	Monastical brewis.	Zinziberine. Beatille pies.

[2] They do not now carry it about at Lyons, though they still talk of it there, and frighten their children with threatening to throw them to Maschecroute, to be devoured by him.

[3] The people call it *graulli*, either from the German word *gæruliche*, horrible, terrible, or rather corruptly for *gargouille* (which see explained elsewhere). The image is carried in procession on St Mark's day, and during the Rogation week; but this not being the same figure Rabelais saw, the jaws of the graulli have now no motion. Only, on the end of his tongue, which is of iron, is fixed a small white loaf, which, together with as many more as each baker furnishes, before whose stall the procession passes, makes up the stipend or salary of the poor man who carries the graulli.

Pantagruel

Brown bread.	Gravy soup.	Brewis.
Carbonadoes, six sorts.	Hotch-pots. Soft bread.	Marrow - bones, toast, and cab-
Brawn.	Household bread.	bage.
Sweet-breads.	Capirotades.	Hashes.

Eternal drink intermixed. Brisk delicate white wine led the van; claret and champagne followed, cool, nay, as cold as the very ice, I say; filled and offered in large silver cups. Then they offered,

Chitterlings garnished with mustard.	Neat's tongues. Scotch collops. Puddings.	Hog's haslets. Brawn heads. Powdered venison,
Hams.	Carvelats.	with turnips.
Hung beef.	Bolognia sausages.	Pickled olives.
Sausages.	Chines and peas.	

All this associated with sempiternal liquor. Then they housed within his muzzle

Legs of mutton with shalots.	Ribs of pork with onion sauce.	Caponets. Caviare and toast.
Olias.	Roast capons, basted with their own dripping.	Fawns, deer.
Lumber pies with hot sauce.		Hares, leverets. Cygnets. A reinforcement of
Partridges and young partridges.	Pigeons, squabs, and squeakers. Herons, and young herons.	vinegar intermixed. Venison pasties. Lark-pies.
Plovers.		
Dwarf-herons.	Fieldfares.	Dormice-pies.
Teals.	Olives.	Cabretto pasties.
Duckers.	Thrushes.	Roe-buck pies.
Bitterns.	Young sea-ravens.	Pigeon pies.
Shovelers.		Kid pasties.
Curlews.	Geese, goslings.	Capon-pies.
Wood-hens.	Queests.	Bacon pies.
Coots, with leeks.	Widgeons.	Hedgehogs.

Fat kids.
Shoulders of mutton, with capers.
Sirloins of beef.
Breasts of veal.
Pheasants and pheasant poults.
Fried pasty-crust.
Forced capons.
Parmesan cheese.
Red and pale hippocras.
Gold-peaches.
Artichokes.
Dry and wet sweetmeats, seventy-eight sorts.
Boiled hens, and fat capons, marinated.
Pullets with eggs.
Chickens.
Rabbits, and sucking rabbits.
Quails, and young quails.

Souced hogs' feet.
Mavises.
Grouse.
Turtles.
Doe-conies.
Peacocks.
Storks.
Woodcocks.
Snipes.
Ortolans.
Turkey cocks, hen turkeys and turkey poults.
Stock-doves and woodculvers.
Pigs, with wine sauce.
Blackbirds, ousels, and rayles.
Moor-hens.
Bustards, and bustard poults.
Fig-peckers.
Young Guinea hens.

Flamingoes.
Snites.
Then large puffs.
Thistle-finches.
Whore's farts.
Fritters.
Cakes, sixteen sorts.
Crisp wafers.
Quince tarts.
Curds and cream.
Whipped cream.
Preserved myrabolans.
Jellies.
Welsh barrapyclids.
Macaroons.
Tarts, twenty sorts.
Lemon-cream, raspberry cream, etc.
Comfits, one hundred colours.
Cream wafers.
Cream cheese.

Vinegar brought up the rear to wash the mouth, and for fear of the squinsy: also toasts to scour the grinders.

CHAPTER LX

WHAT THE GASTROLATERS SACRIFICED TO THEIR GOD
ON INTERLARDED FISH-DAYS

PANTAGRUEL did not like this pack of rascally scoundrels, with their manifold kitchen sacrifices, and would have been gone, had not Epistemon prevailed with him to stay and see the end of the farce. He then asked the skipper, what the idle lobcocks used to sacrifice to their gorbellied god on interlarded fish-days? For his first course, said the skipper, they give him:

Caviare.	tops, bishop's-	Red herrings.
Botargoes.	cods, cellery,	Pilchards.
Fresh butter.	chives, rampions,	Anchovies.
Pease soup.	jew's-ears (a sort	Fry of tunny.
Spinage.	of mushrooms	Cauliflowers.[1]
Fresh herrings, full roed.	that sprout out of old elders) as-	Beans.[2] Salt salmon.
Salads, a hundred varieties, of cresses sodden hop-	paragus, woodbine, and a world of others.	Pickled griggs. Oysters in the shell.

Then he must drink, or the devil would gripe him at the throat: this, therefore, they take care to prevent, and nothing is wanting. Which being done, they give him lampreys with hippocras sauce:

Gurnards.	Smelts.	Dried melwels.
Salmon-trouts.	Rock-fish.	Flounders.

[1] Not mere cauliflowers, but *emb' olif*, *i.e.*, with oil. See this explained before in ch. 32.
[2] It is not plain beans in Rabelais, but *saulgrenées de febues*, which Cotgrave says is a porridge, or mess of beans, salad, oil, and some verjuice or vinegar.

Rabelais' Works [Book iv.

Barbels, great and small.
Roaches.
Cockerels.
Minnows.
Thornbacks.
Sleeves.
Sturgeons.
Sheath-fish.
Mackerels.
Maids.
Plaice.
Fried oysters.
Cockles.
Prawns.
Shrimps.
Congers.
Porpoises.
Basses.
Shads.
Murenes, a sort of lampreys.
Craylings.
Smys.
Turbots.
Trout, not above a foot long.
Salmon.
Meagers.

Gracious lords.
Sword-fish.
Skate-fish
Lamprels.
Jegs.
Pickerels.
Golden carps.
Burbotes.
Salmons.
Salmon-peels.
Dolphins
Barn-trouts.
Millers'-thumbs.
Precks.
Bret fish.
Sea breams.
Halibuts.
Soles.
Dog's tongue, or kind fool.
Mussels.
Lobsters.
Great prawns.
Dace.
Bleaks.
Tenches.
Ombres (grey-ling).
Fresh cods.

Sea-nettles.
Mullets.
Gudgeons.
Dabs and sandings.
Haddocks.
Carps.
Pikes.
Bottitoes.
Rochets.
Sea-bears.
Sharplings.
Tunnies.
Silver-eels.
Chevins.
Cray-fish.
Pallours.
Darefish.
Fausens, and grigs.
Eelpouts.
Tortoises.
Serpents, *i.e.*, wood-eels.
Dorees.
Moor-game.
Perches.
Loaches.
Crab-fish.
Snails and whelks.
Frogs.

If, when he had crammed all this down his guttural trap-door, he did not immediately make the fish swim again in his paunch, death would pack him off in a trice. Special care is taken to antidote his godship with vine-tree syrup. Then is sacrificed to him, haberdines, poor-jack, minglemangled mismashed, etc.

Pantagruel

Eggs fried, beaten, buttered, poached, hardened, boiled, broiled,	stewed, sliced, roasted in the embers, tossed in the chimney, etc.	Stock-fish. Green-fish. Sea-batts. Cods sounds. Sea-pikes.

Which to concoct and digest the more easily, vinegar is multiplied. For the latter part of their sacrifices they offer,

Rice, milk, and hasty pudding. Buttered wheat, and flummery. Water-gruel and milk porridge. Frumenty and bonny clabber.	Stewed prunes, and baked bullace. Pistachios, or fistic nuts. Figs. Almond-butter. Skirret-root.	White-pot. Raisins. Dates. Chestnuts and walnuts. Filberts. Parsnips. Artichokes.

Perpetuity of soaking with the whole.

It was none of their fault, I will assure you, if this same god of theirs was not publicly, preciously, and plentifully served in the sacrifices, better yet than Heliogabalus' idol; nay, more than Bel and the Dragon in Babylon, under King Belshazzar. Yet Gaster had the manners to own that he was no god, but a poor, vile, wretched creature. And as King Antigonus,[3] first of the name, when one Hermodotus (as poets will flatter, especially princes) in some of his fustian dubbed him a god, and made the sun adopt him for his son, said to him: My lasanophore (or in plain English, my groom of the close-stool) can give thee the lie; so Master Gaster very civilly used to send back his bigoted worshippers to his close-stool, to see, smell, taste, philosophise, and

[3] See Plutarch in his Apophthegms, and in his treatise of Isis and Osiris.

examine what kind of divinity they could pick out of his sir-reverence.

CHAPTER LXI

HOW GASTER INVENTED MEANS TO GET AND PRESERVE CORN

THOSE gastrolatrous hobgoblins being withdrawn, Pantagruel carefully minded the famous master of arts, Gaster. You know that, by the institution of nature, bread has been assigned him for provision and food; and that, as an addition to this blessing, he should never want the means to get bread.

Accordingly, from the beginning he invented the smith's art, and husbandry to manure the ground, that it might yield him corn; he invented arms, and the art of war, to defend corn; physic and astronomy, with other parts of mathematics, which might be useful to keep corn a great number of years in safety from the injuries of the air, beasts, robbers, and purloiners: he invented water, wind, and hand-mills, and a thousand other engines to grind corn, and to turn it into meal; leaven to make the dough ferment, and the use of salt to give it a savour; for he knew that nothing bred more diseases than heavy, unleavened, unsavoury bread.

He found a way to get fire to bake it; hourglasses, dials, and clocks to mark the time of its baking; and as some countries wanted corn, he contrived means to convey it out of one country into another.

He had the wit to pimp for asses and mares, animals of different species, that they might copulate for the generation of a third, which we call mules, more strong and fit for hard service than the other two. He invented carts and waggons, to draw him along with greater ease: and as seas and rivers hindered his progress, he devised boats, galleys, and ships (to the astonishment of the elements) to waft him over to barbarous, unknown, and far distant nations, thence to bring, or thither to carry corn.

Besides, seeing that, when he had tilled the ground, some years the corn perished in it for want of rain in due season, in others rotted, or was drowned by its excess, sometimes spoiled by hail, shook out by the wind, or beaten down by storms, and so his stock was destroyed on the ground; we are told that ever since the days of yore, he has found out a way to conjure the rain down from heaven only with cutting certain grass, common enough in the field, yet known to very few, some of which was then shown us. I took it to be the same as the plant, one of whose boughs being dipped by Jove's priest in the Agrian fountain,[1] on the Lycian mountain in Arcadia, in time of drought, raised vapours which gathered into clouds, and then dissolved into rain, that kindly moistened the whole country.

Our master of arts was also said to have found a way to keep the rain up in the air, and make it to fall into the sea; also to annihilate the hail, suppress the winds, and remove storms as the Methanensians[2] of Trœzene used to do. And as in the fields

[1] Read the fountain Agria. See Nicolas Leonicus, l. 1, c. 67, Of his Various Histories. In Pausanias' Arcadics, this fountain is called 'Αγνω, and Rhodiginus, l. 13, c. 17, likewise has called it Agnò.
[2] This is taken from the same work of Nicolas Leonicus, l. 2, c. 38. See Pausanias' Corinthiacs.

thieves and plunderers sometimes stole, and took by force the corn and bread which others had toiled to get, he invented the art of building towns, forts, and castles, to hoard and secure that staff of life. On the other hand, finding none in the fields, and hearing that it was hoarded up and secured in towns, forts, and castles, and watched with more care than ever were the golden pippins of the Hesperides, he turned engineer, and found ways to beat, storm, and demolish forts and castles, with machines and warlike thunderbolts, battering-rams, ballistas, and catapults, whose shapes were shown us, not over-well understood by our engineers, architects, and other disciples of Vitruvius; as Master Philebert de l'Orme, King Megistus' principal architect, has owned to us.[3]

And seeing that sometimes all these tools of destruction were baffled by the cunning subtility or the subtle cunning (which you please) of fortifiers, he lately invented cannons, field-pieces, culverins, mortar-pieces, basilisks, murdering instruments that dart iron, leaden, and brazen balls, some of them outweighing huge anvils. This by the means of a most dreadful powder, whose hellish compound and effect has even amazed Nature, and made her own herself outdone by art; the Oxydracian thunders,[4] hails, and storms, by which the people of that name immediately destroyed their enemies in the field, being but mere popguns to these. For, one of our great guns, when used, is more dreadful,[5] more

[3] Henry II. in whose reign Philebert de l'Orme was architect and intendant of the buildings, as he continued to be under the Kings Francis II. and Charles IX.

[4] See Apollonius' life by Philostratus, l. 2, c. 14.

[5] Polydore Virgil had before expressed himself much after the same manner in his treatise 'De Rerum inventoribus.'

terrible, more diabolical, and maims, tears, breaks, slays, mows down, and sweeps away more men, and causes a greater consternation and destruction, than a hundred thunderbolts.

CHAPTER LXII

HOW GASTER INVENTED AN ART TO AVOID BEING HURT OR TOUCHED BY CANNON-BALLS

GASTER having secured himself with his corn within strongholds, has sometimes been attacked by enemies; his fortresses, by that thrice three-fold cursed instrument, levelled and destroyed: his dearly beloved corn and bread snatched out of his mouth, and sacked by a tyrannic force; therefore he then sought means to preserve his walls, bastions, rampiers, and sconces from cannon-shot, and to hinder the bullets from hitting him, stopping them in their flight, or at least from doing him or the besieged walls any damage. He showed us a trial of this, which has been since used by Fronton, and is now common among the pastimes and harmless recreations of the Thelemites. I will tell you how he went to work, and pray for the future be a little more ready to believe what Plutarch affirms to have tried. Suppose a herd of goats were all scampering as if the devil drove them, do but put a bit of eringo into the mouth of the hindmost nanny, and they will all stop stock-still, in the time you can tell three.

Thus Gaster, having caused a brass falcon to be charged with a sufficient quantity of gunpowder, well purged from all sulphur, and curiously made up with fine camphor; he then had a suitable ball put into the piece, with twenty-four little pellets like hail-shot, some round, some pearl fashion: then taking his aim, and levelling it at a page of his, as if he would have hit him on the breast; about sixty strides off the piece, half-way between it and the page in a right line, he hanged on a gibbet by a rope a very large siderite, or iron-like stone, otherwise called herculean, formerly found on Ida in Phrygia by one Magnes, as Nicander [1] writes, and commonly called load-stone; then he gave fire to the prime on the piece's touch-hole, which in an instant consuming the powder, the ball and hail-shot were with incredible violence and swiftness hurried out of the gun at its muzzle, that the air might penetrate to its chamber, where otherwise would have been a vacuum; which nature abhors so much, that this universal machine, heaven, air, land, and sea would sooner return to the primitive chaos, than admit the least void anywhere. Now the ball and small shot, which threatened the page with no less than quick destruction, lost their impetuosity, and remained suspended and hovering round the stone: nor did any of them, notwithstanding the fury with which they rushed, reach the page.

Master Gaster could do more than all this yet, if you will believe me: for he invented a way how to cause bullets to fly backwards, and recoil on those that sent them, with as great a force, and in the very numerical parallel for which the guns were planted. And indeed, why should he have thought this difficult, seeing the herb *ethiopis* opens all locks whatsoever [2]; and an *echinus* or *remora*, a silly weakly

[1] See Pliny, l. 36, c. 16.
[2] See Pliny, l. 24, c. 17. etc.

fish, in spite of all the winds that blow from the thirty-two points of the compass, will in the midst of a hurricane make you the biggest first-rate remain stock-still, as if she were becalmed, or the blustering tribe had blown their last: nay, and with the flesh of that fish, preserved with salt, you may fish gold [3] out of the deepest well that was ever sounded with a plummet; for it will certainly draw up the precious metal. Since, as Democritus affirmed,[4] and Theophrastus believed and experienced, that there was an herb at whose single touch an iron wedge, though never so far driven into a huge log of the hardest wood that is, would presently come out, and it is this same herb your hickways, *alias* wood-peckers, use, when with some mighty axe any one stops up the whole of their nests, which they industriously dig and make in the trunk of some sturdy tree. Since stags and hinds, when deeply wounded with darts, arrows, and bolts, if they do but meet the herb called dittany, which is common in Candia, and eat a little of it, presently the shafts came out, and all is well again; even as kind Venus cured her beloved by-blow Æneas, when he was wounded on the right thigh with an arrow by Juturna, Turnus' sister. Since the very wind of laurels, fig-trees, or sea-calves, makes the thunder sheer off insomuch that it never strikes them. Since at the sight of a ram, mad elephants recover their former senses. Since mad bulls coming near wild fig-trees, called *caprifici*, grow tame, and will not budge a foot, as if they had the cramp. Since the

---

[3] See Pliny, l. 9, c. 25.
[4] Though Democritus was reckoned by Pliny to be a great liar, yet in the point before us, Theophrastus, who is one of Pliny's heroes, gives full credit to Democritus' assertion. See Pliny for all or most of these particulars.

venomous rage of vipers is assuaged if you but touch them with a beechen bough. Since also Euphorion [5] writes, that in the Isle of Samos, before Juno's temple was built there, he has seen some beasts called *neades*, whose voice made the neighbouring places gape and sink into a chasm and abyss. In short, since elders grow of a more pleasing sound and fitter to make flutes, in such places where the crowing of cocks is not heard, as the ancient sages have writ, and Theophrastus relates: as if the crowing of a cock dulled, flattened, and perverted the wood of the elder, as it is said to astonish and stupefy with fear that strong and resolute animal, a lion. I know that some have understood this of wild elder, that grows so far from towns or villages, that the crowing of cocks cannot reach near it; and doubtless that sort ought to be preferred to the stenching common elder, that grows about decayed and ruined places; but others have understood this in a higher sense, not literal, but allegorical, according to the method of the Pythagoreans:[6] as when it was said that Mercury's statue could not be made of every sort of wood; to which sentence they gave this sense; that God is not to be worshipped in a vulgar form, but in a chosen and religious manner. In the same manner by this elder, which grows far from places where cocks are heard, the ancients meant, that the wise and studious ought not to give their minds to trivial or vulgar music, but to that which is celestial, divine, angelical, more abstracted, and brought from remoter parts, that is, from a

[5] See Ælian, l. 17, c. 28.
[6] Pythagoras used to say, allegorically, that all sorts of wood ought not to be employed indifferently in making Mercury's statue; which has been explained by Alex. ab Alex., l. 4, c. 12, Of his genial Days; and by Erasmus, in his Adages.

region where the crowing of cocks is not heard: for, to denote a solitary and unfrequented place, we say, cocks are never heard to crow there.

ON CHAP. LVII. AND THE FIVE FOLLOWING.—The dwelling of Master Gaster, whose entrance is rugged, craggy, barren, and unpleasant to the eye, is found at last to be very fertile, healthful, and delightful, when with much toil the difficult ways on its borders have been passed. This Gaster, the first master of arts in the world, is the belly in Greek.
'Magister artis, ingenîque largitor,
    Venter'——————   *Persius.*
Yet our author tells us that the muses are the offspring of Penia, that is to say, Poverty. I will not pretend to contradict him; neither will any contradict me, if I say, that at least poverty is the most common reward which their unhappy favourites reap for all their toilsome study. The description of the empire of Gaster is very curious: and the author displays there at once much learning, fancy, and wit. The Gastrolaters are those whose god is their belly; the Engastrimythes are parasites, and all those whom their hungry bellies cause to say many things against their consciences; so that they may be said to speak from the belly; the word *engastrimythe* also means one who by use and practice can speak as it were out of his belly, not moving his lips; and finally, one who has an evil spirit speaking out of his belly.

The Idol Manduce is the figure of gluttony, whose eyes are bigger than its belly, and its wide jaws armed with dreadful teeth: it is an imitation of the Manducus of the ancients.

The great number of· dishes of all sorts, that are sacrificed to Gaster, show that gluttony reigns among all sorts of people, the poor offering their gross food, as well as the rich their dainties; and that coarse fare will go down with belly gods, and with all men in general, for want of better. What is offered him on interlarded fish-days, shows that this noble Messer Gaster, as he is called in the French, is a true Papimane, and agrees pretty well with the *mass, messe* in French, which wants but an *r* of the word *messer*, used in those times for monsieur.—*M.*

CHAPTER LXIII

HOW PANTAGRUEL FELL ASLEEP NEAR THE ISLAND OF CHANEPH, AND OF THE PROBLEMS PROPOSED TO BE SOLVED WHEN HE WAKED

THE next day, merrily pursuing our voyage, we came in sight of the island of Chaneph,[1] where Pantagruel's ship could not arrive, the wind chopping about, and then failing us so that we were becalmed, and could hardly get ahead, tacking about from starboard to larboard, and larboard to starboard, though to our sails we added drabblers.

With this accident we were all out of sorts, moping, drooping, metagrabolized, as dull as dun in the mire, in C sol fa ut flat, out of tune, off the hinges, and I-don't-know-howish, without caring to speak one single syllable to each other.

Pantagruel was taking a nap, slumbering and nodding on the quarter-deck, by the cuddy, with an Heliodorus in his hand; for still it was his custom to sleep better by book than by heart.[2]

Epistemon was conjuring, with his astrolabe, to know what latitude we were in.

Friar John was got into the cook-room, examining, by the ascendant of the spits, and the horoscope of ragouts and fricassees, what time of day it might then be.

Panurge (sweet baby!) held a stalk of Panta-

---

[1] It means hypocrisy, in the Hebrew language. In this island, Rabelais places a sort of pretended saints, who under a mortified exterior, concealed, according to him, morals full of cynical indiscretions.

[2] He chose rather to sleep over a book than absolutely to do nothing.

gruelions, *alias* hemp, next his tongue, and with it made pretty bubbles and bladders.

Gymnast was making tooth-pickers with lentisk.

Ponocrates, dozing, dozed, and dreaming, dreamed; tickled himself to make himself laugh, and with one finger scratched his noddle where it did not itch.

Carpalim, with a nut-shell, and a trencher of verne (that's a card in Gascony), was making a pretty little merry wind-mill, cutting the card longways into four slips, and fastening them with a pin to the convex of the nut, and its concave to the tarred side of the gunnel of the ship.

Eusthenes, bestriding one of the guns, was playing on it with his fingers, as if it had been a trump-marine.

Rhizotomus, with the soft coat of a field tortoise, *alias* ycleped a mole, was making himself a velvet purse.

Xenomanes was patching up an old weather-beaten lantern, with a hawk's jesses.

Our pilot (good man!) was pulling maggots out of the seamen's noses.

At last Friar John, returning from the forecastle, perceived that Pantagruel was awake. Then breaking this obstinate silence, he briskly and cheerfully asked him how a man should kill time, and raise good weather, during a calm at sea?

Panurge, whose belly thought his throat cut, backed the motion presently, and asked for a pill to purge melancholy.

Epistemon also came on, and asked how a man might be ready to bepiss himself with laughing, when he has no heart to be merry?

Gymnast, arising, demanded a remedy for a dimness of eyes?

Ponocrates, after he had a while rubbed his

noddle, and shaken his ears, asked, how one might avoid dog-sleep? Hold, cried Pantagruel, the Peripatetics have wisely made a rule, that all problems, questions, and doubts, which are offered to be solved, ought to be certain, clear, and intelligible. What do you mean by dog's-sleep? I mean, answered Ponocrates, to sleep fasting in the sun at noon-day, as the dogs do.

Rhizotomus, who lay stooping on the pump, raised his drowsy head, and lazily yawning, by natural sympathy, set almost every one in the ship a-yawning too: then he asked for a remedy against oscitations and gapings.

Xenomanes, half puzzled, and tired out with new vamping his antiquated lantern, asked, how the hold of the stomach might be so well ballasted and freighted from the keel to the main hatch, with stores well stowed, that our human vessels might not heel, or be walt, but well trimmed and stiff?

Carpalim, twirling his diminutive wind-mill, asked how many motions are to be felt in nature, before a gentleman may be said to be hungry?

Eusthenes, hearing them talk, came from between decks, and from the capstern called out to know why a man that is fasting bit by a serpent also fasting, is in greater danger of death, than when man and serpent have eat their breakfasts? Why a man's fasting-spittle [3] is poisonous to serpents and venomous creatures?

One single solution may serve for all your problems, gentlemen, answered Pantagruel, and one single medicine for all such symptoms and accidents. My answer shall be short, not to tire you with a long needless train of pedantic cant. The belly [4]

[3] See Aristotle, of Animals, l. 8, c. 29, and Pliny, l. 7, c. 2.
[4] *L'estomac affamé.* A hungry stomach has no ears, said Cato

has no ears, nor is it to be filled with fair words: you shall be answered to content by signs and gestures. As formerly at Rome, Tarquin the proud, its last king, sent an answer by signs to his son Sextus, who was among the Gabii, at Gabii. (Saying this, he pulled the string of a little bell, and Friar John hurried away to the cook-room.) The son having sent his father a messenger, to know how he might bring the Gabii (Gabini) under a close subjection; the King, mistrusting the messenger, made him no answer, and only took him into his privy garden, and, in his presence, with his sword, lopped off the heads of the tall poppies that were there. The express returned without any other dispatch: yet having related to the prince what he had seen his father do, he easily understood that by those signs he advised him to cut off the heads of the chief men in the town, the better to keep under the rest of the people.

CHAPTER LXIV

HOW PANTAGRUEL GAVE NO ANSWER TO THE PROBLEMS

PANTAGRUEL then asked what sort of people dwelt in that damned island?[1] They are, answered Xenomanes, all hypocrites,[2] holy mountebanks, tumblers

the censor, in one of his speeches to the Roman people. See his life in Plutarch.

[1] *Isle de chien*, in Rabelais. On which M. Duchat says, *Chienne d'Isle* (Bitchington Island, if you will), island of people who bark at and bite all the world, as cursed curs do.

[2] Add hydropics, puffed up with a false opinion of their own sanctity.

of Ave Marias, spiritual comedians, sham saints, hermits, all of them poor rogues, who, like the hermit of Lormont between Blaye and Bordeaux, live wholly on alms given them by passengers. Catch me there if you can, cried Panurge! may the devil's head cook conjure my bum-gut into a pair of bellows, if ever you find me among them. Hermits, sham saints, living forms of mortification, holy mountebanks, avaunt! in the name of your father Satan, get out of my sight! when the devil's a hog, you shall eat bacon. I shall not forget yet awhile our fat Concilipetes of Chesil.[3] O that Beelzebub and Astaroth had counselled them to hang themselves out of the way, and they had done it! we had not then suffered so much by devilish storms as we did for having seen them. Hark ye me, dear rogue, Xenomanes, my friend, I prithee are these hermits, hypocrites, and eavesdroppers, maids or married? Is there anything of the feminine gender among them? Could a body hypocritically take there a small hypocritical touch? Will they lie backwards, and let out their fore-rooms? There's a fine question to be asked, cried Pantagruel. Yes, yes, answered Xenomanes; you may find there many goodly hypocritesses, jolly spiritual actresses, kind hermitesses, women that have a plaguey deal of religion: then there's the copies of them, little hypocritillons, sham sanctitos, and hermetillons. Foh! away with them, cried Friar John; a young saint, an old devil! (Mark this, an old saying, and as true a one as a young whore an old saint.) Were there not such, continued Xenomanes, the isle of Chaneph, for want of a multiplication of progeny, had long ere this been desert and desolate.

Pantagruel sent them by Gymnast, in the pinnace,

[3] Fathers of the Council of Trent. See before, ch. 18.

seventy-eight thousand fine pretty little gold half-crowns,[4] of those that are marked with a lantern. After this he asked, What's o'clock? Past nine, answered Epistemon. It is then the best time to go to dinner, said Pantagruel: for the sacred line, so celebrated by Aristophanes in his play called Concionatores, is at hand, never failing when the shadow is decempedal.

Formerly, among the Persians, dinner time was at a set hour only for kings: as for all others, their appetite and their belly was their clock; when that chimed, they thought it time to go to dinner. So we find in Plautus a certain parasite making a heavy do, and sadly railing at the inventors of hour-glasses and dials, as being unnecessary things, there being no clock more regular than the belly.

Diogenes, being asked at what times a man ought to eat, answered, The rich when he is hungry, the poor when he has anything to eat. Physicians more properly say, that the canonical hours are,

> To rise at five, to dine at nine,
> To sup at five, to sleep at nine.

The famous king Petosiris'[5] magic was different.

[4] Cyrus, being reduced to beggary in the other world, begged Epictetus to bestow a penny upon him in charity. I give no pennies, said that philosopher, who was become a great lord ı that country; here, sirrah, here's a crown for you. (Rab., l. 2, c 30.) The reason of this proceeding of Epictetus is, that when great men bestow their favours, they ought to have more regard to their own grandeur than to the meanness and indispensable occasions of the necessitous.

[5] Juvenal, Sat. 6.
    ' Ægra licet jaceat, capiendo nulla videtur
    Aptior hora cibo, nisi quam dederit Petosiris.'
The pretended magic of Petosiris, as also that of the physician Cnidias in Pliny, l. 29, c. 1, was properly not more than an inordinate fondness for the mathematics, which persuaded those

—Here the officers for the gut came in, and got ready the tables and cupboards; laid the cloth, whose sight and pleasant smell were very comfortable; and brought plates, napkins, salts, tankards, flagons, tall-boys, ewers, tumblers, cups, goblets, basins, and cisterns.

Friar John, at the head of the stewards, sewers, yeomen of the pantry and of the mouth, tasters, carvers, cup-bearers, and cupboard-keepers, brought four stately pasties, so huge, that they put me in mind of the four bastions at Turin. Odsfish, how manfully did they storm them! What havoc did they make with the long train of dishes that came after them! How bravely did they stand to their pan-puddings, and paid off their dust! How merrily did they soak their noses!

The fruit was not yet brought in, when a fresh gale at west and by north began to fill the main-course, mizzen-sail, fore-sail, tops, and top-gallants: for which blessing they also sung divers hymns of thanks and praise.

When the fruit was on the table, Pantagruel asked: Now tell me, gentlemen, are your doubts fully resolved or no? I gape and yawn no more, answered Rhizotomus. I sleep no longer like a dog, said Ponocrates. I have cleared my eyesight, said Gymnast. I have broke my fast, said Eusthenes: so that for this whole day I shall be secure from the danger of my spittle, of

| Asps.[6] | Alhatrabans. | Attelabes. |
| Amphisbenes. | Aractes. | Ascalabotes. |

two men that the knowledge of the stars was so extensive, that therein might be discovered whether a sick person had best take a new-laid egg or broth.

[6] A great part of these different names of serpents and other venomous creatures, disposed by Rabelais in alphabetical order, is to be found in Pliny.

Amerudutes.
Abedissimons.
Alhartafs.
Ammobates.
Apimaos.
Black wag-leg flies.
Spanish flies.
Catoblepes.
Horned snakes.
Caterpillars.
Crocodiles.
Toads.
Night-mares.
Mad dogs.
Colotes.
Cychriodes.
Cafezates.
Cauhares.
Snakes.
Cuhersks, two-tongued adders.
Amphibious serpents.
Cenchres.
Cockatrices.
Dipsades.
Domeses.
Dryinades.
Dragons.
Elopes.
Enhydrides.

Asterions.
Alcharates.
Arges.
Spiders.
Starry Lizards.
Falvises.
Galeotes.
Harmenes.
Handons.
Icles.
Jarraries.
Ilicines.
Pharaoh's mice.
Kesudures.
Sea-hares.
Chalcidic newts.
Footed serpents.
Manticores.
Molures.
Mouse-serpents.
Shrew-mice.
Miliares.
Megalaunes.
Spitting-asps.
Porphyri.
Pareades.
Phalanges.
Penphredons.
Pine-tree-worms.
Rutulæ.
Worms.

Hæmorrhoids.
Basilisks.
Fitches.
Sucking water-snakes.
Rhagious.
Rhaganes.
Salamanders.
Slow-worms.
Stellions.
Scorpenes.
Scorpions.
Horn-worms.
Scalavotins.
Solofuidars.
Deaf-asps.
Horse-leeches.
Salt-haters.
Rot-serpents.
Stink-fish.
Stuphes.
Sabrins.
Blood-sucking flies.
Hornfretters.
Scolopendras.
Tarantulas.
Blind worms.
Tetragnathias.
Teristales.
Vipers, etc.

ON CHAPS. LXIII. AND LXIV.—Chaneph is hypocrisy in Hebrew; so the island of Chaneph is the island of the hypocrites. Accordingly our author says it was wholly inhabited by sham saints, spiritual comedians, forms of holiness, tumblers of beads, dissembling mumblers of ave-marias, and so forth; poor sorry rogues, who wholly lived on the alms that were given them by passengers, like the hermit of Lormont, between Blaye and Bordeaux. Thus he chiefly places the orders of mendicant friars among the hypocrites, because their convents have no revenue but mumping ; and so they are obliged to affect a greater devotion than those religious orders who do not make a vow of poverty, as these do.

Our author tells us, that the Pantagruelian fleet was becalmed when it came in sight of that island, and was forced to tack from larboard to starboard, and from starboard to larboard ; yet could not get a-head, though they had added drabblers to their sails. By this he insinuates, that this inferior crew of hypocrites did put a stop to the progress of the reformation, and the discovery of truth in general; as when he himself was misused by some of them in the convent of Cordeliers at Fontenay-la-Comte, merely because he studied Greek. These beggarly tribes had not the power to raise a storm, like the nine sail of fathers who were going to the Council of Chesil ; they could do little more than hinder the advancement of those who searched after truth. Thus we find, not only that the fleet could not proceed, but that every ship's company in a manner fell asleep, dozed, and were out of sorts, and off the hinges. At last this is remedied by sending to those poor hypocrites seventy-eight thousand little half-crowns, and by eating and drinking : which perhaps may mean, that provided those poor hungry curs have meat and drink, or money to get food, which is all they beg, they cease to bark, and will suffer you to go on without any further impediment. This has been, and is still observable in France, and other parts, among some of those begging friars ; whereas your Jesuits, Dominicans, Austins, Bernardins, Celestins, Theatins, and others, such as were in the nine sail, are not to be bribed or pacified so easily. One of these, whose poetry and criticisms are deservedly esteemed among us, has reflected on our author's admirable satire too severely for a man of his sense, though not for one of his order ; I mean Father Rapin: but who could expect less from a Jesuit, and a Jesuit too, whose sodality it satirised in this work ? Yet, after all, that able critic durst not but own that it is a most ingenious satire.[1]

Panurge asks whether there be not something of the feminine gender among them, and whether they would not take a small hypocritical touch by the bye ? To which answer is made by Xenomanes, that were there not some pretty, kind-hearted hypocritesses, hermitesses, and spiritual actresses, who beget a race of

---

[1] Rapin's ' Reflect. on Poetry.'

young hypocritillons and sham sanctitoes, the island of Chaneph had long since been without inhabitants.

This is true in more than one sense ; for did not hypocrites beget others, some parts of the world would be very thin of people; then those sham sanctitoes and hermitillons, whom our author means, are chiefly the young bastardly monastic fry, the only fruit many nuns bear, by the means of the father confessor's kind applications : for such of those by-blows as escape abortion, or an untimely death, are reared up for a while as the pious father's or sister's poor relations; and then caged with father or mother to sing matins and vespers, and increase the larger tribe of hypocrites world without end.—*M.*

CHAPTER LXV

HOW PANTAGRUEL PASSED THE TIME WITH HIS SERVANTS

IN what hierarchy of such venomous creatures do you place Panurge's future spouse ? asked Friar John. Art thou speaking ill of women, cried Panurge, thou mangy scoundrel, thou sorry, noddy-peaked shaveling monk ? By the cenomanic paunch and gixie, said Epistemon, Euripides has written, and makes Andromache say it, that by industry, and the help of the gods, men had found remedies against all poisonous creatures ; but none was yet found against a bad wife.

This flaunting Euripides, cried Panurge, was gabbling against women every foot, and therefore was devoured by dogs, as a judgment from above ; as Aristophanes observes.—Let us go on. Let him speak that is next. I can leak now like any stone-horse, said then Epistemon. I am, said Xenomanes, full as an egg and round as a hoop; my ship's hold can hold no more, and will now make shift to bear a steady sail. Said Carpalim, a truce with thirst, a truce with hunger; they are strong, but wine and meat are stronger. I am no more in the dumps, cried Panurge; my heart is a pound lighter. I am in the right cue now, as brisk as a body-louse, and as merry as a beggar. For my part, I know what I do when I drink; and it is a true thing (though it is in your Euripides) that is said by that jolly toper Silenus of blessed memory, that

> The man's emphatically mad,
> Who drinks the best, yet can be sad.

We must not fail to return our humble and hearty thanks to the Being, who, with this good bread, this cool delicious wine, these good meats and rare dainties, removes from our bodies and minds these pains and perturbations, and at the same time, fills us with pleasure and with food.

But methinks, Sir, you did not give an answer to Friar John's question; which, as I take it, was how to raise good weather? Since you ask no more than this easy question, answered Pantagruel, I will strive to give you satisfaction; some other time we will talk of the rest of the problems if you will.

Well then, Friar John asked how good weather might be raised. Have we not raised it? Look up and see our full top-sails: Hark! how the wind whistles through the shrouds, what a stiff gale it blows; observe the rattling of the tacklings, and see the sheets, that fasten the main-sail behind; the force of the wind puts them upon the stretch. While we passed our time merrily, the dull weather also passed away; and while we raised the glasses to our mouths, we also raised the wind by a secret sympathy in nature.

Thus Atlas and Hercules clubbed to raise and underprop the falling sky,[1] if you will believe the wise mythologists; but they raised it half an inch too high; Atlas, to entertain his guest Hercules more pleasantly, and Hercules to make himself amends for the thirst which sometimes before had tormented him in the deserts of Africa.—Your good father, said Friar John, interrupting him, takes care to free many people from such an inconveniency; for I have been told by many venerable doctors, that his chief butler, Turelupin, saves about eighteen hundred pipes of wine yearly, to make servants, and all comers and goers, drink before they are a-dry.—As the camels and dromedaries of a caravan, continued Pantagruel, used to drink for the thirst that is past, for the present, and for that to come, so did Hercules: and being thus excessively raised, this gave new motion to the sky, which is that of *titubation and trepidation*, about which our crackbrained astrologers make such a pother.—This, said Panurge, makes the saying good,

> While jolly companions carouse it together
> A fig for the storm, it gives way to good weather.[2]

Nay, continued Pantagruel, some will tell you, that we have not only shortened the time of the calm,

[1] The poets feigned that Atlas supported the heavens on his shoulders, but that, in order to ease him, Hercules, who was not to be conquered by labour, one day lent him his back. See Lucian in his dialogue entitled Caron, or the Contemplators, and Seneca's tragedy of Hercules Furens.

[2] Read these two lines thus:
> While round a fat ham we carouse it together,
> The storm spends itself, and gives way to fair weather.

'Le mal temps passe, et retourne le bon,
Pendant qu'on trinque autour de gras jambon.'

but also much disburthened the ship; not like Æsop's basket, by easing it of the provisions, but by breaking our fasts; and that a man is more terrestrial and heavy when fasting, than when he has eaten and drank, even as they pretend that he weighs more dead than living. However it is, you will grant they are in the right, who take their morning's draught, and breakfast before a long journey; then say that the horses will perform the better, and that a spur in the head is worth two in the flank; or, in the same horse dialect,

> That a cup in the pate
> Is a mile in the gate.

Don't you know that formerly the Amycleans worshipped the noble Bacchus above all other gods, and gave him the name of Psila,[3] which in the Doric dialect signifies wings: for, as the birds raise themselves by a towering flight with their wings above the clouds; so, with the help of soaring Bacchus, the powerful juice of the grape, our spirits are exalted to a pitch above themselves, our bodies are more sprightly, and their earthly parts become soft and pliant.

CHAPTER LXVI

HOW, BY PANTAGRUEL'S ORDER, THE MUSES WERE SALUTED NEAR THE ISLAND OF GANABIM

THIS fair wind and as fine talk brought us in the sight of a high land, which Pantagruel discovering afar off, showed it Xenomanes, and asked him, Do

[3] See Pausanias' Laconics.

you see yonder to the leeward a high rock, with two tops much like Mount Parnassus in Phocis? I do plainly, answered Xenomanes; it is the isle of Ganabim.[1] Have you a mind to go ashore there? No, returned Pantagruel. You do well indeed, said Xenomanes; for there is nothing worth seeing in the place. The people are all thieves: yet there is the finest fountain in the world, and a very large forest towards the right top of the mountain. Your fleet may take in wood and water there.

He that spoke last spoke well, quoth Panurge; let us not by any means be so mad as to go among a parcel of thieves and sharpers. You may take my word for it, this place is just such another as, to my knowledge, formerly were the islands of Sark and Herm,[2] between the smaller and the greater Britain; such as was the Poneropolis of Philip in Thrace;[3] islands of thieves, banditti, picaroons, robbers, ruffians, and murderers, worse than raw-head and bloody-bones, and full as honest as the senior fellows of the college of iniquity, the very outcasts of the county gaol's common-side. As you love yourself, do not go among them: if you go, you will come off but bluely, if you come off at all. If you will not believe me, at least believe what the good and wise Xenomanes tells you: for may I never stir if they are not worse than the very cannibals: they would certainly eat us

[1] A Hebrew word for thieves, for *ganabim* is the plural of *ganab*, a thief.
[2] These are two small islands, or rather two whitish rocks, between Guernsey and Jersey, anciently dependent on Normandy, but united to England by William the Conqueror. As, in all probability, it was customary, in Rabelais' time, for such of his nation as were forced to quit their country for any crime, to retire to those two places, our author for that reason makes these two small islands a receptacle of thieves and sharpers.
[3] See Plutarch, in his Treatise of Curiosity.

alive. Do not go among them, I pray you; it were safer to take a journey to hell. Hark, by cod's body! I hear them ringing the alarum bell most dreadfully, as the Gascons about Bordeaux used formerly to do against the commissaries and officers for the tax on salt, or my ears tingle. Let's sheer off.

Believe me, Sir, said Friar John, let's rather land; we will rid the world of that vermin, and inn (lodge) there for nothing. Old Nick go with thee for me, quoth Panurge. This rash hair-brained devil of a friar fears nothing, but ventures and runs on like a mad devil as he is, and cares not a rush what becomes of others; as if every one was a monk, like his friarship. A pox on grinning honour, say I! Go to, returned the friar, thou mangy noddy-peak![4] thou forlorn druggle-headed sneaksby! and may a million of black devils anatomise thy cockle brain. The hen-hearted rascal is so cowardly, that he bewrays himself for fear every day. If thou art so afraid, dunghill, do not go, stay here and be hanged, or go and hide thy loggerhead under Madame Proserpine's petticoat.[5]

Panurge hearing this, his breech began to make buttons: so he slunk in in an instant, and went to hide his head down in the bread-room among the musty biscuits, and the orts and scraps of broken bread.

Pantagruel in the meantime said to the rest, I feel a pressing retraction in my soul, which like a voice admonishes me not to land there. Whenever I have felt such a motion within me, I have found myself

---

[4] In the original, *Ladre-verd*; which M. Duchat interprets, A man without courage, insensible to the spurrings of honour. The like says Cotgrave : A coward; one that's insensible and cannot, or fearful and will not, feel the wrongs done to him.

[5] *Cottardi*, an old word for a petticoat : used here, because it equivocates to *couhardie* (the cowardice of Panurge.)

happy in avoiding what it directed me to shun, or in undertaking what it prompted me to do; and never had occasion to repent following its dictates.[6]

As much, said Epistemon, is related of the dæmon of Socrates, so celebrated among the Academics. Well then, Sir, said Friar John, while the ship's crew water, have you a mind to have good sport? Panurge is got down somewhere in the hold, where he is crept into some corner, and lurks like a mouse in a cranny: let them give the word for the gunner to fire yon gun over the round-house on the poop: this will serve to salute the Muses of this Anti-Parnassus: besides, the powder doth but decay in it. You are in the right, said Pantagruel: here, give the word for the gunner.

The gunner immediately came, and was ordered by Pantagruel to fire that gun, and then charge it with fresh powder; which was soon done. The gunners of the other ships, frigates, galleons, and galleys of the fleet, hearing us fire, gave every one a gun to the island: which made such a horrid noise, that you would have sworn heaven had been tumbling about our ears.

ON CHAP. LXVI.—The island of Ganabim is the island of Thieves, from ganab, a thief, in Hebrew. Xenomanes says, that the people of that island are all such, and commends Pantagruel for not going ashore there. Friar John advises Pantagruel to cause a gun to be fired, as it were to salute the Muses of that Anti-Parnassus. By this, perhaps, our author may have a mind to reflect on most of the authors of that age, who, as well as some of this, were very great plagiaries. The fair fountain on that hill may mean the great number of subjects, which might employ their pens more to the purpose than in translating many foolish romances, as the best hands of France did at that time. That spring may also signify the French tongue,

---

[6] The Queen of Navarre, in her Memoirs, says much the same of herself, and of Catherine de Medicis, her mother.

which our author commends so much in the prologue to the fifth book, and inveighs against such sorts of plagiaries, whom he calls brokers and retailers of ancient rhapsodies, and such mouldy trash ; botchers of old threadbare stuff, a hundred and a hundred times clouted up and pieced together; wretched bunglers, that can do nothing but new-vamp old rusty saws; beggarly scavengers, that rake the muddiest canals of antiquity, etc. By which he would encourage his countrymen to follow his example, study it, and write something that might chiefly spring from their fancies,[1] without being wholly indebted to foreign nations for what they published : yet not disdaining to make improvements from the thoughts of the Greek and Latin authors, as he himself has done, and enrich the moderns with translations of the best works of the ancients.

The large forest, that is round the fountain, may mean the wild, dark, entangled, voluminous writings of some of that age. The mountain is called Anti-Parnassus, in opposition to that where the true Muses were said to dwell ; and is placed in the island of Thieves properly enough, because poets, as well as they, are the children of Penia, or poverty, according to our author.—*M.*

CHAPTER LXVII

HOW PANURGE BEWRAYED HIMSELF FOR FEAR; AND OF THE HUGE CAT RODILARDUS, WHICH HE TOOK FOR A PUNY DEVIL

PANURGE, like a wild, addle-pated, giddy goat, sallies out of the bread-room in his shirt, with nothing else about him but one of his stockings, half on half off, about his heel, like a rough-footed pigeon; his hair and beard all be-powdered with crumbs of bread, in which he had been over head and ears, and a huge and mighty puss partly wrapped up in his other stocking. In this equipage, his chops moving like a monkey's who is a louse-hunting, his eyes staring like a dead pig's, his teeth chattering, and his bum quivering, the poor dog fled to Friar John, who was then sitting by the chain-wales of the starboard side of the ship, and prayed him heartily to take pity on him, and keep him in the safeguard of his trusty bilbo; swearing, by his share of Papimany, that he had seen all hell broke loose.

Woe is me, my Jacky, cried he, my dear Johnny, my old crony, my brother, my ghostly father! all the devils keep holiday, all the devils keep their feast to-day, man: pork and peas choke me, if ever thou sawest such preparations in thy life for an infernal feast. Dost thou see the smoke of hell's kitchens? (This he said, showing him the smoke of the gunpowder above the ships.) Thou never sawest so many damned souls since thou wast born; and so fair, so bewitching they seem, that one would swear they are Stygian ambrosia. I thought at first, God forgive me, that they had been English souls; and I don't know, but that this morning the Isle of Horses, near Scotland, was sacked, with all the English who had surprised it, by the lords of Termes and Essay.[1]

[1] This happened about the month of July 1548. Henry II., King of France, had sent six thousand men to the assistance of the Scots, who, for some years, had been at war with England. The English having by surprise taken from the Scots the Isle of Keith (otherwise called the Isle of Horses), Andrew de Montalambert Sieur de Dessé, who commanded the body of French auxiliaries, so rightly took his measures for re-entering the island, that, making a descent on it not above three weeks after the English had possessed themselves of it, he made himself master of the island, after an engagement wherein the English lost 400 men, and all their baggage. See Thuanus, l. 5, in the year 1548. It was the souls of these English which Panurge thought he perceived in hell, though he had only a glimpse of them, his fear hindering him from seeing them perfectly : and they appeared to him *tant douillettes, tant blondelettes, tant delicates*, so soft, so fair, so nice and tender, that one would have taken them for *Stygian ambrosia*, as he tells Friar John : and indeed the English are naturally fairer and more tender than any other nation of the North.

Friar John, at the approach of Panurge, was entertained with a kind of smell that was not like that of gunpowder, nor altogether so sweet as musk; which made him turn Panurge about, and then he saw that his shirt was dismally bepawed, and bewrayed with fresh sir-reverence. The retentive faculty of the nerve which restrains the muscle called *sphincter* (it is the arse-hole, an it please you), was relaxed by the violence of the fear which he had been in during his fantastic visions.[2] Add to this, the thundering noise of the shooting, which seems more dreadful between decks than above. Nor ought you to wonder at such a mishap; for one of the symptoms and accidents of fear is, that it often opens the wicket of the cupboard wherein second-hand meat is kept for a time. Let us illustrate this noble theme with some examples.

Messer Pantolfe de la Cassina, of Sienna, riding post from Rome, came to Chamberry, and alighting at honest Vinet's, took one of the pitchforks in the stable; then turning to the innkeeper, said to him, '*Da Roma in qua, io non son andato del corpo. Di gratia piglia in mano questa forcha, et fa mi paura.*' I have not had a stool since I left Rome. I pray thee take this pitchfork, and fright me. Vinet took it, and made several offers, as if he would in good earnest have hit the signore, but did not: so the Sienese said to him, '*Si tu non fai altramente, tu non fai nulla: pero sforzati di adoperadi più guagliardamente.*' If thou dost not go another way to work, thou hadst as good do nothing: therefore try to bestir thyself more briskly. With this, Vinet lent him such a swingeing stoater with the pitchfork souce between

---

[2] Macrobius, l. 7, c. 11, of his Saturnalia.

the neck and the collar of his jerkin, that down fell signore on the ground arsyversy, with his spindle shanks wide straggling over his pole. Then mine host sputtering, with a full-mouthed laugh, said to his guest, By Beelzebub's bum gut, much good may it do you, Signore Italiano. Take notice this is *datum Camberiaci*, given at Chamberry. It was well the Sienese had untrussed his points, and let down his drawers: for this physic worked with him as soon as he took it; and as copious was the evacuation, as that of nine buffaloes and fourteen missificating arch-lubbers.[3] Which operation being over, the mannerly Sienese courteously gave mine host a whole bushel of thanks, saying to him, '*Io ti ringratio, bel messere; cosi facendo tu mhai esparmiata la speza d'un servitiale.*' I thank thee, good landlord; by this thou hast even saved me the expense of a clyster.

I will give you another example of Edward V., King of England. Master Francis Villon, being banished France, fled to him,[4] and got so far into his favour, as to be privy to all his household affairs. One day the King, being on his close-stool, showed Villon the arms of France, and said to him, Dost thou see what respect I have for thy French kings?

[3] *Archiprebstres de Hostie,* says Rabelais, arch-priests of Hostia. The buffalo, or buffle, is a kind of wild ox, common in Italy, and probably more so at Ostia than in any other parts of that country. Which, belike, gave occasion to Rabelais, always an enemy to ecclesiastics, to couple together the buffaloes and arch-priests of Ostia, as supposed to be greater eaters than your ordinary oxen and plain priests.

[4] Francis Corbueil, surnamed Villon, had committed several villainies, for which, in 1461, he was condemned by the Chatelet to be hanged. But the Parliament having changed the punishment of death into that of banishment, Villon, who at first retired to St Maixant in Poictou, went from thence into England, being then but thirty years old as he says himself, in the beginning of his (larger) will and testament.

I have none of their arms anywhere but in this
backside, near my close-stool. Odd's life, said the
buffoon, how wise, prudent, and careful of your
health, your highness is! How carefully your
learned doctor, Thomas Linacer,[5] looks after you!
He saw that, now you grow old, you are inclined
to be somewhat costive, and every day were fain to
have an apothecary; I mean, a suppository or clyster
thrust into your royal nockandroe; so he has, much
to the purpose, induced you to place here the arms
of France; for the very sight of them puts you into
such a dreadful fright, that you immediatety let fly,
as much as would come from eighteen squattering
bonasi of Pæonia.[6] And if they were painted in
other parts of your house,[7] by jingo, you would
presently conskite yourself wherever you saw them.
Nay, had you but here a picture of the great
oriflamme of France, odds bodikins! your tripes
and bowels would be in no small danger of drop-

[5] He died in 1524, aged three-score and four; and if we may
believe Konigius in his Bibliotheca, he was physician only to
Henry VII. and Henry VIII. Besides, Edward V. began his
reign but in 1483, full eighteen years after Villon's banishment.
Thus, as it is not at all likely that this banishment lasted so
long, so it is more than probable, that what is here said by
Rabelais concerning Edward V. and the poet Villon, is a mere
fable from one end to the other.

[6] Βονασος, Cambridge Dictionary, quoting Pliny, 8, 15. A
wild beast like a bull, only hath the mane of a horse : when he
is hunted, he saves himself by his ordure, which he throws out
in that abundance, and is so noisome, that the hunters are fain to
leave the pursuit. The remarks, said to be made by Rabelais
himself on the fourth book, say, that when the bonasus finds
himself pressed by the dogs, he squirts his dung at them almost
five paces off; and that it is so hot, it fetches off not only the
hair, but the very skin.

[7] The original says, painted in your bed-chamber, in your
guard-room, in your hall, in your chapel, in your galleries, or in
any other parts of your house.

ping out at the orifice of your posteriors. But henh, henh! *atque iterum* henh!

> A silly cockney am I not,
> As ever did from Paris come?
> And with a rope and sliding knot
> My neck shall know what weighs my bum.

A cockney of short reach, I say, shallow of judgment, and judging shallowly, to wonder, that you should cause your points to be untrussed in your chamber before you come into this closet. By our lady! at first I thought your close-stool had stood behind the hangings of your bed; otherwise it seemed very odd to me you should untruss so far from the place of evacuation. But now I find I was a gull, a wittol, a woodcock, a mere ninny, a dolt-head, a noddy, a changeling, a calf-lolly, a doddipole. You do wisely, by the mass, you do wisely; for had you not been ready to clap your hind face on the mustard-pot as soon as you came within sight of these arms, mark ye me, cop's body! the bottom of your breeches had supplied the office of a close-stool.

Friar John, stopping the handle of his face with his left hand, did, with the fore-finger of the right, point out Panurge's shirt to Pantagruel, who, seeing him in this pickle, scared, appalled, shivering, raving, staring, bewrayed, and torn with the claws of the famous cat Rodilardus,[8] could not choose but laugh, and said to him, Prythee what wouldst thou do with this cat? With this cat! quoth Panurge; the devil scratch me! if I did not think it had been a young

---

[8] Latin for bacon-gnawer. *Rodere* and *lardum*. The inventor of this name was Eliseus Calentius, one of Paul Jovius' eminent men.

soft-chinned devil, which, with this same stocking instead of mitten, I had snatched up in the great hutch of hell, as thievishly as any sizar of Montague College could have done. The devil take Tybert: I feel it has all bepinked my poor hide, and drawn on it to the life I do not know how many lobsters' whiskers. With this he threw his boar-cat down.

Go, go, said Pantagruel, be bathed and cleaned, calm your fears, put on a clean shift, and then your clothes. What! do you think I am afraid, cried Panurge? Not I, I protest by the testicles of Hercules! I am more hearty, bold, and stout,[9] though I say it that should not, than if I had swallowed as many flies as are put into plum-cakes, and other paste at Paris, from Midsummer to Christmas.[10] But what is this? hah? oh, ho! how the devil came I by this? Do you call this what the cat left in the malt, filth, dirt, dung, dejection, fœcal matter, excrement, stercoration,[11] sir-reverence, ordure,[12] second-hand meats, fumets, stronts, scybal,[13] or spyrathe?[14] 'Tis Hibernian saffron,[15] I protest. Hah, hah, hah! it is Irish saffron, by Shaint Pautrick, and so much for this time. Sela. Let us drink.[16]

[9] The fly is a symbol of temerity, inasmuch as that insect falls upon anything, to the hazard of its life. Thence the proverb.
[10] Read All Saints Day, or All Hallows Tide : *toussaint*, in the original.
[11] *Laisse*, in the original. *Lesses*, *i.e.*, wolf's or wild boar's dung.
[12] *Repaire*, in French : *i.e.*, *crotels*, or hare's dung.
[13] *Scybal*. The Dutch scholiast says, is *un estron endurcy*, a hard turd. M. Duchat says nothing of it.
[14] It means the dung of sheep or goats. Σπύραθος, *caprarum stercus*.
[15] Hibernian partly equivocates to *bren*, a twid.
[16] *Sela*, is as much as to say, most certainly. It is certainly

ON CHAP. LXVII.—Panurge's fear, increased by the noise of the guns, makes him run mad for a while, and lay hold of the huge cat Rodilardus, by which he was scratched. He saith, he took it to be a young soft-chinned devil, and thought he had snatched it up in the great hutch of hell, as thievishly as any sizar of Montague College could have done. Rodilardus stands for Croquelardon, lick-sauce, a parasitical smell-feast. This passage, doubtless, refers to some of Montluc's adventures, hardly to be discovered in our age; yet known in that during which he lived. Panurge's cowardice and impudence suit pretty well with that Bishop of Valence's character; as appears by what I said of his daring to preach before Queen Catherine of Medicis with a hat and cloak on, like a Geneva divine, and then not having the courage to go on, but leaving off in the midst of his sermon (though the Queen abetted him, and her presence secured him) as soon as the Constable of Montmorency spoke two words against his way of preaching.

Here Rabelais takes an opportunity to bring in a story, which, as well as some other things of as odious a nature, I would have omitted, did not many learned men despise a maimed or imperfect book, as much as some selfish women hate a male in those circumstances. That story is what is said of Edward V., King of England, and Francis Villon, the witty rogue of whom I have already spoken. But, with our author's good leave, this story is as false as it is filthy and improbable; though we should suppose there is a mistake in the printing (as there are thousands even in the best editions of this work I have seen yet). For none can imagine that Rabelais was so little versed in history, as not to know that Edward V. died a child, and can neither have been costive in his old age, nor familiar with Villon; who, according to Pasquier, must have been hanged before the reign of that unfortunate prince, and, perhaps, before his birth. And should any say that Rabelais means Edward the Fourth; I answer, that he neither died old, nor could be drolled upon at that rate, by a buffooning inmate; since, though he was not one of the wisest heads, yet he was one of the bravest warriors of his time, having fought nine pitched battles, generally on foot, and at last gloriously overcome all his enemies: so that the witty jester would hardly have offered to have told him, that the sight of Lewis the

---

saffron. The new editions have it *cela*; but Rabelais writ it *sela*, a Hebrew word denoting a serious and vehement affirmation. Here it alludes to the *sela* which concludes several lessons of the choir, after which every one betakes himself to drinking.

Eleventh's oriflamme, or royal standard, would have scared him into a looseness. The verses which Rabelais makes Villon speak, are mentioned as his by Pasquier, somewhat otherwise than in this chapter :

> ' Je suis François, dont ce me poise,
> Né de Paris, prez de Pontoise ;
> Où d'une corde d'une toise,
> Saura mon col, que mon cul poise.'—*M*.

END OF BOOK IV.

www.ingramcontent.com/pod-product-compliance
Lightning Source LLC
Chambersburg PA
CBHW031904220426
43663CB00006B/765